Mike & Eileen,

With very best wishes,

Roger.

SHIPSHAPE AND BRISTOL FASHION

THE STORY OF A WARTIME FRIGATE & HER MEN

ROGER SMITH

Published by

MELROSE BOOKS

An Imprint of Melrose Press Limited
St Thomas Place, Ely
Cambridgeshire
CB7 4GG, UK
www.melrosebooks.com

FIRST EDITION

Copyright © Roger Smith 2007

The Author asserts his moral right to
be identified as the author of this work

Cover designed by David Tupper

ISBN 978 1 906050 20 7

All rights reserved. No part of this publication may be reproduced,
stored in a retrieval system, or transmitted, in any form or by any means
electronic, mechanical, photocopying, recording or otherwise,
without the prior permission of the publishers.

This book is sold subject to the condition that it shall not,
by way of trade or otherwise, be lent, re-sold, hired out or
otherwise circulated without the publisher's prior consent
in any form of binding or cover other than that in which
it is published and without a similar condition including this
condition being imposed on the subsequent purchaser.

Printed and bound in Great Britain by:
CPI Antony Rowe, Bumpers Farm, Chippenham,
Wiltshire, SN14 6LH, UK

CONTENTS

Preface v

Introduction ix

1	First Sight of HMS *Porlock Bay*	1
2	The Gunnery Course	5
3	On Draft to *Porlock Bay*	15
4	Joining Ship	21
5	Bermuda Here We Come	31
6	Paradise Island, Bermuda	46
7	First Cruise – Newfoundland & Canada	68
8	Christmas in Bermuda	88
9	The Spring Cruise	100
10	Bermuda in the Spring	127
11	Recreation in Bermuda	149
12	Summer Cruise	156
13	Homecoming	175
14	Becoming Civilians Once More	187
15	Settling Down As Civilians	195
16	The Handover: *Porlock Bay* Becomes *Matti Kurki* ...	199
17	The HMS *Porlock Bay* Association	209
18	Return to Bermuda	231
19	Liaison With the Finnish Veterans	240
20	Epilogue	272

CONTENTS (cont.)

Appendix 1   The Badges of HMS *Porlock Bay* 275
Appendix 2   Vital Statistics of Our Ship 277
Appendix 3   Glossary of Naval Terms 279
Appendix 4   Letters to The Association 284
Appendix 5   Routes Taken by FNS *Matti Kurki* 288

About the Author 289

PREFACE

*Nihil tam absurde dici potest,
quod non dicatur ab aliquo philosophorum*
Cicero

This book is dedicated to all those who served in HMS *Porlock Bay/ Matti Kurki* during the thirty-one years of her existence. A finer band of brothers could surely not be found anywhere in the world. As for the quotation from Cicero which, being translated, means 'Nothing so absurd can be said, that some philosopher has not said it', the book will certainly not go down in history as an important work but the intention is to record for history the life of a unique ship, hopefully in a way that is not too absurd.

I would like to thank most sincerely all those who have helped in the compilation of the book, including in particular Humphrey D. Ixer and members of both the HMS *Porlock Bay* Association and the K.L. *Matti Kurki* Association of Finland. My wife, Barbara Mary Smith, has also given me considerable support and has been most long suffering. Of the Finnish veterans, I must mention Ilkka Ignatius, Ralph Suöström and Martti Leino and their wives for their friendship and for supplying some of the photographs. I would also like to thank Robert Davenport for sending his father's photograph album and John Kessel for reproducing some of the prints. Also John Stoker for the line drawing he commissioned.

With regard to the title of this book, it has always been my intention to use the well-known expression that was often used by our second captain, and this resolve was strengthened when, in May 2005, a group of do-gooders told Bristol Councillors that it should not be used because it is deemed not to be politically correct. They claimed that the phrase originated from the days of the slave trade and described black people being ready for sale.

However, one historian asserted that 'Shipshape and Bristol Fashion' originated from the good reputation that Bristol had for constructing ships. Additionally, *Brewers' Dictionary of Phrase and Fable* states that the derivation of the expression is the Port's reputation for efficiency in the days of sail. Furthermore, a correspondent writing to the *Daily Telegraph* has given the most credible reason which relates to the very high rise and fall of the tide in Bristol harbour, the second highest in Europe, resulting in a rapid tidal flow. The flow caused a scouring of the riverbed into a v-shaped section and much deeper in the centre. Ships trying to deliver or take cargo, prior to the building of the present floating harbour, had to ensure that any loose item would not slide off into the mud.

Whatever the reason, and the tidal explanation seems the most plausible, the title will remain as originally intended – *Shipshape and Bristol Fashion*. Political correctness is perhaps the most annoying aspect of life in the twenty-first century and no apology is given for using the expression as the title of my book.

At no time during the long history of the Royal Navy had there previously been an HMS *Porlock Bay* until 'Yard No. 302' was laid down at the Albion Dockyard, Bristol – Charles Hill's yard. She was to be the final warship built at that yard and she had been launched with due ceremony by Mrs Rayne. It was, however, fate that decreed that she carried the name '*Porlock Bay*' because she was originally intended to be a 'Loch' class frigate named HMS *Loch Seaforth* and this name was changed to 'Loch Muick' before final completion as '*Porlock Bay*'.

The reason for introducing a new 'Bay' class was that, with the European war coming to a close, the new requirement was not so much for an anti-submarine frigate but for a ship whose essential purpose was to provide heavier anti-aircraft fire to serve in the Far East. A total of twenty-six of the new 'Bays' were completed, including three by Charles Hill & Sons of which *Porlock Bay* was the last. The intention of sending these ships to the Far East was subsequently changed after the surrender of the Japanese and we were instead sent out west to join the American and West Indies Squadron on a two-and-a-half-year Commission.

The builder's plaque presented to the ship by Messrs Charles Hill

INTRODUCTION

It is perhaps difficult to understand what makes a 'Happy Ship' for that indeed was *Porlock Bay*. She had just missed becoming involved in the Second World War and was the first Royal Naval Ship to take up duties abroad on a peacetime two-and-a-half-year Commission. Lieutenant Dudley Davenport, R.N., an officer who had seen much service at sea during the war, commissioned her at Charles Hill's yard in Bristol, complete with builder's plaque, which adorned a bulkhead in the wardroom on which the words 'Shipshape and Bristol Fashion' appeared.

Model of FNS Matti Kurki *(ex HMS* Porlock Bay*).*
Model owned by Mr Ilkka Ignatius

The commissioning party were a mixed bunch consisting mainly of 'hostilities-only' ratings awaiting demobilisation, together with several old salts serving twelve years or 'seven-and-five' year periods in the regular Navy. Among the hostilities-only ratings were a number of Royal Navy

Commandos who wore a mixture of uniforms and who were not well disposed to the more restrictive discipline of life on board a peacetime ship. After such aggressive service careers they were generally 'bomb-happy', particularly during runs ashore when they called in to the nearest pub to swill unbelievable quantities of beer. Although they were mostly in their twenties, they had become old for their years and it would be a long time before they settled down to live a normal existence.

Gradually, the ship's permanent company was assembled, replacing those leaving as their demob groups were called for discharge from their service life. In small groups or singly, we were detailed by the drafting office in barracks to report for duty in our new ship, a frigate which began life as a 'Loch' class frigate, designed for anti-U-boat duties but which had been modified to assume a greater anti-aircraft role in view of the new requirements in the Far East. We became an even more mixed bunch than the original crew, a heterogeneous mob from a variety of backgrounds who had to be shaken down to work together in order to be an efficient unit. It took a long time for us to fully convert our training in the 'dry land dreadnoughts' to become useful crew members of a ship which could not afford to have any passengers.

When the time came eventually for us to be demobbed, the end came so suddenly that there was only time to exchange addresses with our closest friends before we were thrust upon an unsuspecting country to continue, or in many cases start, our civilian careers. We all said that we must meet up again each year, little knowing that studies, courting, getting married and having children would disrupt the best of intentions to such an extent that it would be forty-five years before we had our first reunion. In this respect we were similar to many other ships' companies that have formed associations during the last decade, to meet our old comrades often without recognising them at first sight but, after only a short time, becoming firm friends once more.

It was never my intention to write a book about the ship but two events in 1996 influenced me to set about the task, only to be interrupted by a spell in hospital followed by convalescence. The first reason for wanting to put on record the history of the ship occurred when Mary and I took a holiday in Bermuda, just over fifty years after my first landfall there. One of our first visits was to the old dockyard and to the former HMS *Malabar*, the shore base on Ireland Island North. Here we presented a wall plaque to the curator of the new dockyard museum, who said that they already had many

Introduction

HMS Porlock Bay *alongside Messrs Charles Hill & Sons Shipyard, Albion Dockyard, Bristol on Commissioning Day*

such ships' badges to commemorate the various commissions in the America and West Indies Squadron. On walking round the various old buildings forming the museum, it became obvious that there was a lamentable gap in their records because no mention was made of the immediate post-war period. Furthermore, I bought a book written by a former dockyard superintendent entitled *The Andrew and the Onions*, which allegedly covered the Royal Navy's presence in Bermuda from 1809 to 1975 but which contained no reference to any of our ships with the exception of the Flagship, HMS *Sheffield*, the 'Shiny Sheff', which had such a remarkable war record. How such an omission occurred remains a mystery but I became determined to put the record straight.

The second reason for wanting to set down on paper our experience in the America and West Indies Squadron came about when I ordered a book written by our second Captain, Commander Frank Twiss, D.S.C., R.N., later to become Admiral Sir Frank Twiss, who had such a profound effect on the social life in the Royal Navy during his term as Second Sea Lord. In his book, Admiral Twiss explains the need for the radical reforms in the Royal Navy occasioned by the greater technical requirements in the present day ships and the professionalism necessary for all members of a ship's company. He was, however, writing his book as an Officer and Captain of several warships, apart from many shore establishments, and my aim is now to represent the views of the 'Lower Deck' on the social changes which have taken place since the Second World War. In many aspects, fundamental change was essential if the Navy was to continue to operate and many of the pettyfogging regulations had to be altered in order to retain personnel. King's Regulations and Admiralty Instructions which had remained largely unchanged for generations, screamed out for amendments; not only by changing the word 'King's' for 'Queen's' on the death of His Majesty King George VI but also to have regard to the fact that service in the Royal Navy should no longer be subject to often harsh disciplinary punishments, which sometimes gave the impression that sailors were all criminals serving terms of penal servitude. 'Chokey', 'Two-and-Two' and 'Jankers' are so out of place in modern times, even if they were once justified, but their replacement by fining ratings could not have been implemented during our time in the service. Three shillings per day as an ordinary seaman was 'bread-line' pay, every penny of which was necessary to retain any sense of independence.

In 2003 yet another reason for writing a book came to light when we received a letter from Finland. Our old ship had become the K.L. *Matti Kurki*, the Training Ship in the Finnish Navy and they, too, had formed an association whose members wished to meet us. This resulted in reciprocal visits, and excellent friendships arose from these meetings, arrangements which are apparently unknown in other ships. *Porlock Bay/Matti Kurki* was indeed a unique ship, despite being just one of the many Loch and Bay Class Ships.

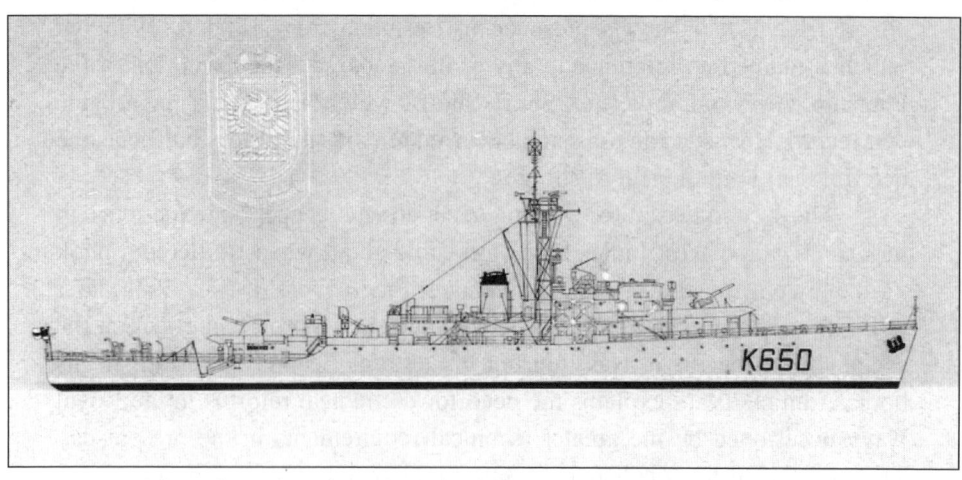

A line drawing of HMS Porlock Bay *prepared for John Stoker, a fellow Radar Control Rating*

1
FIRST SIGHT OF HMS *PORLOCK BAY*

*Take therefore no thought for the morrow:
for the morrow shall take thought for the things of itself.
Sufficient unto the day* is *the evil thereof.*
Matthew 6.34

The journey from HMS *Valkyrie*, the shore training establishment of Douglas, Isle of Man to Plymouth had been exhausting to say the least. We had received our basic radar training there and had been drafted to HMS *Drake*, our Port Division for the gunnery training which would qualify us for a badge on the right arm consisting of a single gun, a star above and the letter 'R' below. This then was our immediate aim, to become Radar Control, Third Class Ratings.

The train taking us to Plymouth eventually pulled in at North Road station, where we disembarked on that bitterly cold January morning at 0400 hours. Several hundred other ratings were also sleepily getting out of the compartments, which were warm by virtue of the mass of bodies in them, causing an unhealthy fug compounded by the smoke from the incessant cigarettes. As a non-smoker it seemed ridiculous to me that otherwise sensible people could puff away, cigarette after cigarette, spending a considerable proportion of their pay on polluting the atmosphere. Perhaps the reason was that cigarette tobacco was so cheap in the Navy that the chaps wanted to get all their rations and, at one shilling and nine pence per half-pound tin of 'Tickler', rolling their own fags was not considered an expensive way of smoking. Anyway, for the majority it was the thing to do, to give the impression that you were a hardened 'Salt' whereas you were in fact the

Pay book photograph of Ordinary Seaman Smith

lowest form of animal life, an Ordinary Seaman with no sea experience other than the return crossing to the Isle of Man.

Having emerged from Plymouth North Road station, we noticed an old caravan from which members of the WVS were serving tea in one-pound jam jars. At 0400 hours in the morning the tea, however it was served, tasted wonderful but, before we could enjoy a full jam jar of it, a gunnery Petty Officer had arrived on the scene shouting for the nasty little would-be radar ratings. With the greatest reluctance we handed back our half-full jam jars and were 'fell-in' by the PO and marched away to a naval bus for the trip to barracks. It was obvious that the Petty Officer did not like getting up at that time of the morning, possibly after a night on the beer, to escort a party of young ratings on their way to the depot and, in his choice use of expletives, he made it plain that we were in for a hard time at Gunnery School.

It was still dark when we went through the gate at HMS *Drake* and reveille would not be sounded for at least an hour. We therefore had to sit around with our kit in the Drill Shed waiting for the next orders, wrapped up in our overcoats and feeling pretty miserable. Hammocks had been issued to us on the second day after joining HMS *Royal Arthur*, otherwise known as Butlin's Holiday Camp at Skegness, but, so far, there had been no occasion to use them. They lay there in the Drill Shed in almost pristine condition after being carted around without having been usefully employed. The large, orange kit bags were also dumped nearby with hardly a mark on them, indicating to all that their owners were a bunch of rookies. Another issue item was a small, brown, attaché case carrying personal and essential things such as one's tooth kit, soap and a 'housewife', pronounced 'hussif'. The attaché case was issued to all ratings in place of the 'ditty box' which all entrants received on joining up during the First World War and my uncle's box still serves very well to house shoe cleaning kits.

After what seemed an age, an announcement was made over the SRE, or loudspeaker, to the effect that we were to report forthwith to the DFDO, where we would get orders regarding accommodation and future training programme. "Where was this mysterious DFDO?" was the question, but other ratings were too busy to even explain its location and it took a few minutes until we eventually arrived there and knocked on the window. A PO writer slid back the window, guessed that we were the young sprogs who were starting their gunnery training, and told us our home for the next six weeks – Trevol Rifle Range, Torpoint, Cornwall. We thought that this new place must be miles away but the PO told us to fetch a handcart from the store, load it up with our kit and proceed to the gate leading to the dockyard. Here we would be directed to a jetty where a motor cutter would be waiting to take us to Torpoint.

The handcart was duly collected, kit loaded and, in accordance with naval practice, the senior member of the party 'fell us in' and marched us down towards the gate. The senior member was an ordinary seaman but he had been in the Navy at least two months longer than the rest of us so he was automatically selected to take charge. At the gate our route to the jetty was explained and we marched on past HMS *Black Prince*, a cruiser tied up alongside towards the motor cutter manned by sea-going Wrens. As Wrens at that time were mainly occupied on clerical, stores and communications work, it was surprising to find them manning a boat but they did so most efficiently. One of our party, who made a remark which was meant to be funny, was ticked off in no uncertain fashion so, after casting off, we set off down the Hamoaze en route for Torpoint in almost silence.

We would see the famous old battle cruiser HMS *Renown* moored near Brunel's bridge over the Tamar followed by many other warships as we travelled down. It was always interesting to me to see ships, as my home in Warwick could not be further from the sea and they were therefore such a novelty. Ship after ship lay, often three abreast, moored in mid-stream awaiting their final destination, which, in many instances, was the breaker's yard. My pencil was working overtime, jotting down the names of the ships we passed just like a small lad at a busy railway station writing down names and numbers of engines, until we came to a new-looking frigate. The officer of the day and the quartermaster were on the quarter deck looking down as we passed and I saw, for the first time, the ship's name – HMS *Porlock Bay*. "That is the type of ship I would like to serve in," were my thoughts at the time; "not too big, not too small." Little did I realise that the frigate, which had recently arrived in Devonport, would be my home for almost two years. Little did I realise too, that I would have to swing over on a stage to slap paint on the ship's side, cursing my lot at having to carry out such a boring job. Soon the motor cutter was out of sight of the frigate but, as the saying goes, it is the first impression that counts and I would never forget the brand-new vessel with her smart paintwork.

HMS Porlock Bay

2

THE GUNNERY COURSE

*"We aren't no thin red 'eroes nor we aren't no blackguards too,
But single men in barricks, most remarkable like you;
An' if sometimes our conduck isn't all your fancy paints
Why, single men in barricks don't grow into plaster saints."*
***'Tommy',* by Rudyard Kipling**

The motor cutter continued on its way past dozens of warships tied up alongside or moored in midstream past the chain operated Torpoint Ferry until we saw a small jetty that had a most inviting sign on it saying 'R.N. Property – Keep Out'. Here we disembarked with our kit, which, this time, had to be carried to the buildings forming the Trevol Rifle Range.

We were given a joining pep talk by a chief gunner's mate before being shown where to stow our kit bags and hammocks. Trevol Rifle Range was the place where, apart from the small arms range itself, we would be taught unarmed combat, go over the assault course until we knew every inch of the ground, and be initiated into the art of killing the enemy as effectively as possible with every conceivable automatic, sub-machine gun, Lewis gun, rifle or pistol. Our instructor in all this would be Petty Officer Stone, a hard nut if ever there was one, hard as his name implied but a generally pleasant character.

When the instruction came to an end on the first day, we sat down to discuss the situation over a mug of NAAFI tea. What were we doing here, in an army style camp, being taught to be soldiers when we had joined the Navy? The truth slowly became evident. Radar Control ratings were the ones who directed the guns on a ship but, if that ship should be close inshore, their gunnery control function would be reduced to such an extent that they were almost supernumerary on board, they would then be required from the landing party or assault party to go ashore and carry on the action as ground troops.

As we discussed things it became obvious that we had been somewhat naive since volunteering for the 'Y' scheme. We had been called, while still at school, to an interview at Whiteladies Road, Bristol, where a Rear Admiral and two Captains had quizzed candidates about everything in general and why they wanted to join the Royal Navy in particular. In my case, it seemed a tough interview but my spirits were raised when the Admiral told me that I had been accepted and that I was to collect my first day's pay and expenses together with a travel warrant home. How wonderful to receive six and four pence to spend on myself just for attending an interview. I couldn't wait to catch the train at Temple Meads station and get home to tell my parents. Next day I would be able to tell my schoolmates that, at seventeen years of age, I would be joining up to take part in the war which, in Europe was coming to an end but, after basic training and time in Cruisers, I would receive a Commission in the same way that so many thousands before me had done.

However, towards the end of the war in Europe it was decided that there should be a run down in recruiting, as it seemed unlikely that the newcomers would be required in the war. All those accepted into the navy would continue with their training but unless candidates were prepared to sign on for a longer period than 'hostilities only,' they would not progress towards a Commission. As a requirement for the 'Y' Scheme entry was at least a School Certificate, candidates were expected to be reasonably intelligent and it was suggested to them that Radar, which was then relatively technical and secret, would be the most appropriate branch to enter.

Having been accepted for the Royal Navy under a scheme which almost guaranteed a Commission, we were a little disillusioned when we found that, having joined as Ordinary Seamen, that was the level we would remain in, progressing ultimately to Able Seaman status but with no chance of becoming an Officer.

We had by this time become resigned to the fact that Radar was the best branch and so, after kitting up at HMS Royal Arthur at Skegness and training at HMS Glendower, another shore establishment owned by Butlin's at Pwllheli, North Wales, we were sent to HMS Valkyrie for radar training. Although I had passed the School Certificate, inter alia, in Science,

I had continued at Warwick School taking languages; French, German, together with English, dropping Science in the process. Physics in particular had been a subject in which I had struggled so it seemed that I would find the technical side of the training rather difficult, bearing in mind that several of my class, as part of their 'Y' Scheme training had spent a year at university.

The first two weeks at *Valkyrie* were spent in a classroom where the rudiments of radio, valves and radar were explained in a fairly high-pressure course. The first weeks concluded with a written examination lasting half a day. After this we did the remainder of the course at Douglas Head, marching from the former hotels on the seafront which formed HMS *Valkyrie* each day up to the Radar Station. It was during the third week of our training at Douglas Head that the Training Officer sent for me and I duly reported at his office fearing the worst from the results of the written, three-hour exam into the theory of radar. I felt I had done reasonably well but, after all, I had gone, my head still throbbing somewhat from a drinking session the previous evening, into the exam. "Sit down," he said, opening his file. As I took a seat, thoughts of interviews with the Headmaster at Warwick School gripped me and I sat in silence awaiting his verdict. "Your exam results," he began, "are most remarkable." Without doubt this meant the lowest mark ever recorded in the history of radar and I was left in further doubt while he answered a telephone call.

"As I said, your result is remarkable," he went on as he replaced the receiver. "You have a ninety-nine per cent pass in the written examination and this is the highest mark known in *Valkyrie*." I listened in almost stunned silence, half expecting him to correct himself and tell me that he had been reading from the wrong file. "With a result like that, you would be well advised to drop the Radar Control Operators Course and go on a Radar Mechanics Course," he said. "This would mean becoming a civilian for a year to attend a course possibly at Guildford or Rugby Polytechnic after which you would re-enter the Navy as a Petty Officer Radar Mechanic. What do you think of that?"

After a moment's thought I replied, "But I have set my heart on going to sea and the prospect of having to wait over a year before I get even a chance to go abroad doesn't sound very good to me." My mind was made up. Bloody fool that I was, I had opted for the sea and adventure rather than an advancement and the possibility of a good future in the radio or even television fields.

In addition to my foolishness in not accepting the Radar Mech's course, I compounded my folly by expressing a wish to go on the Radar Control Course rather than the Radar Plot Course. The latter was concerned with the navigational side of radar but I was keen to go in gunnery which meant that 'Action Stations' were in the TS, mainly operating the fire control box, or table in larger ships, rather than a radar set. It also meant that we had to go on the assault course training at Trevol.

Here we were then, wondering why we had ever been duped into coming to Torpoint or was it really our own stupid fault? Our only conclusion was that, right or wrong, we were here and we would have to make the best of it. The discussion being over for the moment, we collected our meal from the galley and sat down at scrubbed tables to eat. The evening meal was bread and cheese and a spoonful of sweet piccalilli. Very good for the forthcoming training we thought, but not very appetising.

The canteen adjoined the seaman's mess and so, as there was nothing else to do in that forsaken part of Cornwall, we all drifted in there. They had rough cider or 'scrumpy' on draught so most ordered a pint. The previous discussion was continued until we had downed the cider, which we thought tasted good despite being told that, traditionally, a dead rat had been added to assist in the fermentation process. The second pint was even better and the conversation varied from the merits of our various girlfriends to the possibility of mutiny. After a third pint the conversation became decidedly stupid and, as we got up from the chairs, our legs had great difficulty in steering a straight course. In fact, we had become virtually legless. One by one we steered through an imaginary obstacle course to the mess where our hammocks, hitherto unused, lay waiting to be slung for the first time. Fixed hammock bars were placed over the entire mess awaiting us, the clews which were already attached to the hammocks were freed when the lashing was undone and all that remained was to sling the wretched things and get in. Many of them, however, were slung too loosely, sagging a great deal in the centre, but all that remained was to lie back and sleep off the effects of the cider. However, getting in was not as easy as that. Remembering that we were nearly all legless by this time, we watched as the first would-be matelot tried to mount his stead, grabbing cach side and jumping up to get his legs inside. The result? Catastrophe, as the hammock swung though ninety degrees throwing the occupant out on to the deck. Eventually, having been keen on gymnastics at school, I hit on the idea of using another hammock bar to hang onto, then swinging both legs, and others followed my example.

As time went by we grew accustomed to slinging our 'micks' in a more professional way, fortunately before joining our first actual ship. In fact, at sea, the hammock is the most comfortable place to sleep, far better than a bunk and certainly better than the camp beds with which we were issued for use in the tropics.

We all slept well that night to be awakened by PO Stone at some unearthly hour in the morning. 'Rig-of-the-day' was overalls, the blue boiler suits with which we had been issued and, as condemned men do, we ate a hearty breakfast before starting serious work. We were all reasonably fit but, lacking the stamina required to get around the assault course quickly, we were all completely exhausted at the end of the first day. Fortunately, muscles that we didn't know existed took the strain more and more until we romped over the obstacles, finishing up with a bayonet charge on a row of straw filled hessian sacks each time.

One of the natural obstacles was a wide stream that could be crossed in one of three ways, the easiest of which was a single rope hanging from a branch of a tree. Bearing in mind the fact that the stream discharged into the tidal Hamoaze, it was a doddle to cross when the tide was out but at high tide it was impossible. Taking as long a run as possible and pulling one's knees up to the chest it still was not enough to get over and, one after the other, we all landed somewhere in that freezing cold water only to be told we had to complete the course before being able to change into dry clothing.

Other obstacles, both natural and man-made, were overcome with ever-increasing ingenuity as time progressed until the time came when we had to face the live bullets being fired, hopefully over our heads. This really emphasised the need to keep one's head down and we took the exercise very seriously from then on.

Interspersed with the assault course training was unarmed combat, firing on the range and firing along a series of mainly wooden structures, built to represent a narrow alley, with Lanchester sub-carbines. These had wooden butts and were superior in every way to the Sten gun used by the army. Ships generally carried rifles and Lanchesters for use by shore parties and I later found that HMS *Porlock Bay* was no exception, carrying twelve of each.

Although on a course, we did have to do night guard duty on the main gate and, on one occasion, clad in a long watch coat and a rifle slung over the shoulder, I watched a solitary figure approaching down the access road leading to the gate. When I challenged, he stopped and announced that he was a deserter since 1942, wanting to give himself up. Why did it have to happen to me on the very first and only occasion when I did guard duty at a gate? He was taken in, told to kip down and that he would be charged in the morning. What happened to him we never found out but it could be assumed that there would be very little leniency in his sentence.

At the end of the course we were given a long weekend leave before going back to barracks to find out our next assignment. The trip to Plymouth North Road station involved crossing by the Torpoint ferry near to which two former American lend-lease destroyers were moored and about to sink any time. However, they were still there when I returned from leave and were presumably scrapped soon afterwards.

The return journey up the Hamoaze to HMS *Drake* after leave was made in the motor cutter, again manned by Wrens. We did not have the luxury of a handcart this time and had to carry our large kit bags, hammocks and attaché cases from the jetty into barracks. However, we did have another look at HMS *Porlock Bay*, still moored in midstream, together with HMS *Roberts* as she lay alongside in the dockyard, on our way back to barracks. HMS *Roberts*, a monitor with twin fifteen-inch guns was, unknown to us at the time, to be our home for the remainder of the Gunnery Course.

On reporting to DFDO once more our draft chit ordered us to the HMS *Roberts* which had become an accommodation ship for the Gunnery School. She had served well during the war, bombarding enemy positions prior to and during the Normandy landings and also at Walcheren. She had fired her last round by the time we joined her but apparently sailed to London for the V-day celebrations before being scrapped.

As gunnery trainees we were assigned to the forward mess deck, which was immediately aft of the cable locker. Midday meals were taken in barracks or wherever we were sent for specialist training but we had breakfast and supper aboard *Roberts*. One luxury that was new to us was a canteen which sold, among other things, tins of baked beans which were still on 'points' rationing ashore. These could be heated up in a small oven in the mess after knocking two holes in the top of the tin. To be able to buy a small tin of beans any day we wanted made us feel as if we were staying in the Ritz.

Gunnery School involved 'field training', or drill, first thing every morning, and every small misdemeanour was punished by making the offending rating double round the square so many times. I fell foul on the first day when the PO Instructor on his preliminary inspection of the class ordered me to get my hair cut. I responded by saying that my hair had been cut only two days before which caused the said instructor to go a delicate shade of purple before sending me, with rifle at the slope, five times round the square. After stand-easy that same morning I had returned from the canteen caravan with my chin stay up. The result? Twice round the square.

Before the field training session on the square, we had Morning Divisions when the White Ensign was hoisted up the mast to the musical accompaniment of the band of the Royal Marines. The band then stayed for about half an hour while we, together with Petty Officers training for a higher gunnery grade, had to march around and around. The POs numbered only about ten and so they carried long poles to represent a squad to carry out their drill. By the time we started our course it was February and still very cold. After thirty minutes at the slop our arms became almost rigid, making the command to order arms a painful business. On the rainy days we had to go into the Drill Shed, a vast building on one side of the square, which, because the ends were open, was only slightly warmer than outside.

After lunch in the barracks we had training in all aspects of gunnery but concentrating on the Control Aspect. In addition we had more basic instruction in mines and torpedoes but fortunately we did not have to suffer six-inch loader drill as we had already done that under our basic training programme at HMS *Glendower*. There were occasions when we went to Wembury for high angle (anti-aircraft) training and to an old warship whose superstructure had been removed to accommodate a battery of bofors guns and which was moored just inside the breakwater in Plymouth Sound, to deter low flying enemy aircraft. In addition, we spent time in breakwater fort, a stone structure standing inside the breakwater which had been built by Napoleonic prisoners of war but which served very well during the last war as a platform for anti-aircraft guns. It was here that we met, for the first time, AB 'Bungy' Williams and AB Brenchley who, like us, were destined for service in *Porlock Bay*. 'Bungy' had only just completed a sentence of one year in the Preston detention establishment and perhaps in his exuberance at being free once more, grabbed the smaller Brenchley and held him upside down by the ankles over the side of breakwater fort, at about fifty feet above the water. He was to plague Brenchley's life aboard *Porlock Bay*, and unfortunately the lives of several others, including the Captain.

Towards the end of the course, it was announced that a revised form of rifle drill on the march had been considered for the Royal Navy and that a Vice-Admiral, the Commodore and other officers were to visit the gunnery school to see both the old and the new demonstrated. We thought that the

Petty Officers were the obvious ones to be selected to demonstrate the two methods but, they chose three trainee radar control ratings including myself. New sets of gaiters and belts were issued and we were given a short time to practise both ways, the old one being similar to the stationary rifle drill – up two three, over two three, down two three etc. – and the new way which involved a movement of the rifle in time with the right foot – up-over-down-swing etc. The three of us together with the Chief Gunner's Mate had the square to ourselves as we marched from one end to the other and back again, time after time, performing the old and new drill. No one ever told us the result but the new drill was later accepted.

With the end of the course came the exams, only practical ones this time. With memories of *Valkyrie* days, I prepared myself by going to the Plymouth NAAFI Club and drinking a skin-full of Ind Coopes best bitter the night before. Again, I headed the list and my Service Sheet was endorsed to the effect that I had been recommended for a higher gunnery rate on the basis of the exam results.

Ten days' end-of-training leave followed when I was able to discard my uniform and go around in my old school blazer and flannels. This was perhaps not such a good idea because, while in uniform my age was never questioned, in civvies I was challenged as to whether I was eighteen on two occasions in pubs. It was during this leave that my girlfriend seemed less friendly, even offhand, but it was not until *Porlock Bay* sailed for the West Indies that I found that she had ditched me. On the final day of the leave, I developed a rash, mainly on my body and arms, so I went along to the local GP who, perhaps thinking I was trying to swing the lead, told me that it was only a heat rash (there had not been a spell of really good weather so far that year). My parents were convinced it was Scarlet Fever but I had to return to *Roberts* feeling rather ill.

On arrival in the mess I was so ill that I was unable to even sling my hammock but, as it was only an accommodation ship, there was no doctor on board. In any case we were on draft back into barracks the next day so I spent a restless night on the mess-deck cushions. The journey into barracks was dreadful but at DFDO we were told by a Scots leading seaman that some of our party were going to what sounded like a 'Beer' class frigate. On looking at the draft chit we found that we were to report to a 'Bay' class frigate, none other than HMS *Porlock Bay*.

However, nothing is ever straightforward in the Navy and the next stop was the medical block where we had to strip for inspection.

As we lined up, an SBA came along with a lamp, examining each one in turn until he came to me, covered in the worst rash he had apparently seen. Muttering that I would have to be checked out in Ward Five he made out a chit to this effect and told me to report at the appropriate part of sick bay. After a short wait, a young Surgeon Lieutenant saw me and, expressing great surprise, gave me an injection in my right buttock and told me to report again the following day. My chums by this time had assumed that I would be rejoining them and continued with their draft routine, leaving me to find a billet in an old block where I was nominally on light duties. The following morning saw me waiting in the same Ward Five together with a three-badgeman who had seen plenty of service.

"Where did you catch the boat up?" he enquired, to which I replied, "I am on draft to a frigate but I haven't been to sea yet."

Thinking I was either taking the mickey or completely stupid, he then said, "I meant, where did you get a dose?" Again, mystified by his jargon, I answered that I had had an injection the previous day.

By this time he was getting quite annoyed and blurted out, "No! Where did you catch syphilis?" but when I said that I had not got VD, he replied, "What are you doing in Ward Five then?"

The truth dawned on me then and so, without waiting to be called, I barged into the same room where I had received the injection.

"Do I understand that I am being treated for VD?" I enquired in a tone perhaps unbecoming for an Ordinary Seaman. On receiving an affirmative reply, my response was, "Has no one thought of taking any tests?" to which the Lieutenant, seemingly surprised, said something about the disease being prevalent in the Navy but adding that tests would be carried out. Of course, the tests were negative and so, armed with yet another chit, I was sent in a naval truck to see the dermatologist at Stonehouse Hospital. The appropriate Medical Officer was a Dutch Surgeon Commander who examined me fully before admitting that he was mystified. "You will have to be admitted into this hospital so go back to barracks, take your baggage to the baggage store and report back here for further tests."

Accordingly, the truck returned me to Jagoe's Mansions where my kit bag, hammock and attaché case were collected from the mess to be put into storage. Under such a load and in my present state it was impossible to carry the three items and, after struggling a few yards, I had to sit down by the roadside. As if by a miracle, a passing seaman stopped and said "Roger Smith – what are you doing here?" It was Derek Southwood, who had been at school with me and who now picked up my kit and, with me following, took the two larger items, leaving me with just the attaché case. My thanks were most sincere but, unfortunately, although he lived in Claverdon, only six miles from Warwick, I never met him again. Back at Stonehouse Hospital I was placed in a dermatology ward undergoing tests until Saturday, visiting time. Several patients had visitors and everyone was speaking in hushed tones when, suddenly, the ward door opened and a doctor and several SBAs burst in and the doctor called out, "Get him out of here as soon as you can."

To my horror, they converged on my bed, then duly lifted me onto a trolley which was wheeled out of the door, into the lift and down to the ground floor. From there they wheeled me through the grounds past a sign stating 'Mortuary' towards a remote corner of the hospital where there were three wooden huts.

"Where the hell are you taking me?" was my somewhat understandable question.

"To the Zymotic Ward of course," was the answer. My vocabulary did not include 'zymotic' so, asking what it meant, I was told that it was the contagious diseases ward as my complaint had been diagnosed as Scarlet Fever, just as my parents had thought almost a week earlier. Three weeks of absolute luxury followed, looked after by a most attractive VAD Sister who always spent time with me, talking and doing the crossword. By this time the worst effects of the fever were over and, on sunny days, my bed was pushed out on to a veranda into the fresh air. One unfortunate incident occurred however, when my bed was outside and, while there, some unscrupulous person rifled my locker, taking all my money and my pay book. The Naval Police were called but the thief got away with it as he did with the belongings of other patients. The police gave me a letter to take to the barracks' pay office when I returned from the ten days' leave which resulted from the hospitalisation, otherwise I perhaps would not have been able to collect even my three-bob-a-day.

3

ON DRAFT TO *PORLOCK BAY*

> *"One road leads to London,
> One road leads to Wales,
> My road leads me seawards
> To the white dipping sails."*
> **Roadways, by John Masefield**

After my sick leave, which passed all too quickly, I had to report back to Jagoe's Mansions, otherwise the Royal Naval Barracks, Devonport. Unlike the previous occasion when I was with several others on draft, I was now on my own, feeling very apprehensive about my future and wondering if my earlier appointment to HMS *Porlock Bay* had been cancelled. The number seven double-decker bus seemed to take ages as it trundled along the road from Plymouth North Road station, stopping every hundred yards or so to pick up or set down its mainly civilian passengers. Everywhere I looked there were signs of destruction, particularly along Union Street where there seemed to be no two-storey buildings left standing after the Blitz. Several prefabricated buildings had taken the place of some of the former bombed buildings, the remains of which had often not been completely cleared. Indeed, it was a very sorry sight and would require a drastic redevelopment plan to create a semblance of order in the city.

At last the conductor of the double-decker bus called out "RN Barracks," and I struggled to get off, carrying my issue attaché case together with the parcel of sandwiches and cake which my mother had given to me as I left home. The food had not been eaten on the rail journey and I really did not want anything but as it came from the pitifully small family rations it would have been almost a sin to throw away the brown paper parcel. Protests would never stop my parents from giving me food, which was almost an embarrassment to carry back with me after a spell of leave.

The guard house situated inside the depot had many ratings waiting outside for their station cards after their various runs ashore but as I had been discharged from Stonehouse Hospital and had not yet been issued with a station card, I had to explain to the duty Regulating Petty Officer that I was to report to DFDO on arriving at the barracks. Accordingly, after checking my papers, he required to see my Pay Book, which, of course, I did not have as it had been stolen together with my money while in hospital. In order to get rid of me as much as anything else, he issued me with a temporary station card telling me to report to the drafting office at once.

As on the previous occasion, I tapped on the window of DFDO which was opened by the duty Petty Officer who listened to my tale of woe concerning the Pay Book without even a flicker of interest. He had probably heard it all before and, even if he hadn't, it was of no real concern to him.

"Which ship had you been drafted to?" he asked in a voice that indicated his complete boredom with his job.

"*Porlock Bay*," I replied, "but I expect that will be changed after a six week break." The PO sorted through his card index before stopping at my card. My fingers were crossed in hope that I would still meet up with my former mates from the gunnery training days although believing that my draft would be to another of the many vessels in Devonport Division.

"*Porlock Bay* it is and she's going to the West Indies," said the PO. "But you will have to go through the routine first just like all the others. Medical, collect your tropical kit from the stores and get your new pay book from the Paymasters. In the meantime, here's a chit for you to stay in the seamen's block until tomorrow when you report to your ship. Oh! And you will have to get your other kit from the baggage store." With that, he slid the window back with a bang and picked up his three-quarter burnt cigarette. What he muttered to himself will never be known but probably it was to curse even more these young Ordinary Seamen who interrupted his smoking and made his tea go cold. Barrack stanchions – they're all the same, thought I!

In reverse order, I did as I had been told, calling first at the baggage store where my nearly new kit bag and hammock were fortunately soon found. Heavy as they were, I had no difficulty carrying them this time together with my attaché case into which I had stuffed my brown paper parcel containing the sandwiches from home. Past Boscawen Block, or what remained of it after the Blitz, and on to the Junior Ratings Block where my kit was dumped on the ground – sorry, on the deck, outside. As a very Ordinary Seaman, I really must get into the habit of using shipboard terms at all times.

The interior of the block seemed vast with mess tables at right angles to the long, single room. Each table had the polished metal 'fannies' for rum, washing up etc. on them, together with a gash bucket underneath. Spaced out along the entire length of this rather unwelcoming room were three coke stoves, which in winter provided the only warmth to the draughty block, giving out unhealthy fumes all the time as we were to find out much later in our service career.

"Which is Number Five Mess?" I enquired from a three badge rating who was reading a magazine as he sat on the bench next to the first table. Without taking his eyes off his reading matter he answered me.

"This is Number One Mess. Count four more tables along the Mess Deck and you'll find Number Five Mess," he said, somewhat condescendingly, in a distinctly West Country accent.

"Thanks," I replied. "I should be able to find it now," trying to sound grateful and, at the same time, trying to give the impression that I knew all the time where the wretched Mess was situated.

"Stow your kit over there and come back at 1800 hours. You can fetch the meals as I'm making you cook of the Mess," said the killick of Number Five Mess.

"What a welcome!" was my immediate thought as I set off for the Paymaster's office to sort out the small matter of my stolen pay book. Fortunately, full details were in the office and, with the minimum of red tape, a replacement was issued but without a photograph.

"Get along to the photographer and get a mug-shot and report back here," were my instructions, which I attempted to obey as soon as possible. Frustrated again by the absence of the photographer, my mug-shot would have to wait until the following day, so, my next stop would have to be the Medical Department but, seeing the NAAFI van from which tea was being sold, I delayed my visit in order to get some much-needed refreshment. When the stand-easy was over for me, it continued for the young Surgeon Lieutenants and there was quite a long wait before one of them was able to put down his cup to deal with a nuisance Ordinary Seaman who had been discharged from Stonehouse Hospital ten days earlier. The young

17

Lieutenant, who appeared to be only about twenty years old but must have been at least twenty-three and just out of Medical School, read my records at length before admitting that he really did not know how to deal with a case like this. He checked with one of his superiors before signing a chit which at last enabled me to join my ship with a clear bill of health. There was now no let or hindrance, other than getting my photograph taken and getting my tropical kit, to joining HMS *Porlock Bay*.

The trip to Jack Dusty's clothing store was quite uneventful. They made a note of my draft chit before sorting out three pairs of white shorts; three white fronts; a waterproof cover for my new paybook; a white seaman's cap; a pair of white shoes, and a black steaming bag to put everything in. A signature was required and when this was given the rating surprisingly wished me luck.

"So you think I'll need it then?" I asked.

"Well, you never know," he replied as he turned to carry on with his stocktaking, leaving me to wonder if he knew more than I did about the West Indies.

That evening, I did not wish to go ashore partly because it was raining heavily, and the junior ratings' canteen beckoned. Two pints of Ind Coope's Octagon Ale were enough to relax my strained nerves sufficiently to be able to 'crash my swede' at Pipe Down in my little-used hammock. How anyone managed to get a full night's sleep in that building no one knows as ratings were arriving at all times of the night, some of them worse for drink after a run ashore and taking great delight in bumping other ratings' hammocks as they got into their own.

However, after a fitful night's sleep, reveille came almost with relief. Breakfast over and having completed my duties as Cook of the Mess, it was time to go round to the photographer only to find the building still locked. It has been said that ratings could walk about the barracks with a piece of paper in their hands for months without being found out but I felt that a visit back to DFDO was called for as soon as possible to get further instructions. Here they told me to report to my ship without further delay and without bothering about the photograph.

Accordingly, I collected my kit bag, hammock, steaming bag and attaché case and made my way to the gate between the barracks and the dockyard to be told by the dockyard police that the dockyard train would be arriving soon which would take me almost all the way to the spot where *Porlock Bay* was secured.

That excellent little train arrived and I went forward to speak to the driver to ask if he knew where Porlock Bay was lying. At that time there were dozens of ships in the dockyard but he knew precisely where she was and said he would stop as soon as the train reached the nearest spot. As the only passenger I had no difficulty loading my kit on to one of the open carriages and we chugged away through the dockyard, which had suffered greatly from the bombing with gutted buildings everywhere, leaving a most untidy effect coupled with all the cable, bits of machinery and stores standing on the uneven ground on which last night's rain was lying in puddles. Presumably there was some order in the way everything was placed but it was not immediately apparent to me.

After about half a mile the small tank engine stopped and the driver pointed to the right. "There she is, the outboard one of that pair of frigates." We would be in the part of the dockyard almost completely covered in puddles, and so this meant finding somewhere dry to put my kit down to keep the rain from soiling the almost new items. Leaving my hammock and large kit bag, I threaded my way towards the brow of the first ship with my attaché case and steaming bag and went aboard, saluting the quarterdeck with difficulty as I did so. On hearing the words "Porlock Bay," the quartermaster pointed to the second brow leading to my new home.

The Quartermaster of Porlock, who turned out to be Able Seaman Fred Amos, looked at the draft chit and said they had been expecting me.

"Get the rest of your kit aboard and the Bosun's Mate will take you to the seamans' Mess deck," he ordered and so it was necessary to cross over the other vessel, collect my remaining kit which, fortunately had not been pinched, and then cross over to Porlock a second time. The Bosun's Mate helped me with some of my kit through the midship passage, past the Regulating Office and the notice board outside until we reached a hatch leading down to the seamen's mess deck.

"Down there and number five mess is starboard side forrard," he said as he indicated downward.

It was not a simple matter to get everything down the fairly steep ladder but eventually this was achieved, my hammock stacked with others in the rack and the other items left on the seats until a locker was allocated to me. It was late afternoon by this time and the mess deck was deserted until after a few minutes, a heavily-built rating in overalls came down the ladder.

"I've just joined the ship," I told him, which was a rather obvious statement to make.

"Ugh," he replied, which did not seem very welcoming. He proceeded to get out of his overalls, speaking only in a series of grunts as he changed to go ashore. When he put his jumper on I realised why he had not been very loquacious. There on his shoulder in red was the word 'DANMARK', which made me wonder what sort of ship I had joined. It turned out, however, that he was a free Danish sailor, only a few months older than me and, as there was no free Danish Navy, he was serving in the RN. He had sailed over to Britain during the war, only to be told that he would be sent down the mines but, on protesting that he was a seaman, the powers-that-be enrolled him in the Andrew, allowing him to have the red shoulder flash as a special concession. It was, however, quite an inauspicious introduction to the ship for me, having only grunts in reply to my questions but later it became obvious that Sven Zaar was an excellent chap who took all jokes against him in good part, even to the extent of being referred to as a bloody scousewegian. His huge size made him an obvious choice as the ship's heavyweight boxer in the following months but as so often happens, the big chaps are often gentle giants at heart.

Sven left the mess deck to catch the liberty boat ashore, leaving me in sole occupation. From the start, it seemed ridiculous to have to 'catch the liberty boat' when the ship lay alongside the harbour wall in the dockyard but such was the practice in the Andrew. The liberty men would form up in ranks, be called to attention by the duty Petty Officer who would then turn to the Officer of the Day, salute and report that liberty men were ready for inspection. The Officer of the Day would then see that all were correctly dressed before telling the duty PO to carry on.

"Turn right, dismiss," would be his final words before the assembled liberty men crossed the brow on to dry land for their run ashore.

Soon the peace and quiet was broken by the Bosun's Mate calling for Ordinary Seaman Smith to report to the Cox'n in the Regulating Office. I had finally arrived.

4

JOINING SHIP

"No man will be a sailor who has contrivance enough to get himself into a jail; for being in a ship is being in a jail, with the chance of being drowned ...a man in a jail has more room, better food, and commonly better company."
Samuel Johnson

HMS Porlock Bay *proceeding along Avon Gorge after commissioning for trials in the Bristol Channel*

The Regulating Office was situated off the midship passage not far from the hatch leading down to the seaman's mess deck and it only took a minute to get there. This was the Coxwain's office from which he controlled the day to day running of the ship. Outside was the notice board and a copy of KRs and AIs. Sometimes spelt 'Cockswain' and always pronounced 'Cox'n', Chief Petty Officer Rhodes was a formidable sight. He had light ginger hair and a well-trimmed ginger beard. When he was first promoted to the rank of Chief Petty Officer he was, at twenty-three years of age, the youngest chief in the Andrew and now with his organising ability he was certainly efficient in the job. He was a 'Ganges' entrant at a very early age which qualified him in every aspect of a seaman's duties and it is on this type of person that the Royal Navy has, over the years, depended.

"So you've just joined, have you?" were his first words. "Have you settled in yet with your kit stowed away neatly? If not, the killick of your Mess will find a locker for you and put your case and steaming-bag on the racks by the ship's side." All this sounded very informal; not the sort of words that previous Chiefs had used and, although it was obvious that I would never call him 'Ginger' to his face, he was not as frightening as I would have expected from the equivalent of a Sergeant Major.

"The ship is undergoing a boiler clean at the moment and more than half the ship's company are away on boiler-clean leave," he explained. "That is why you will not see your fellow Gunnery Control Ratings for another week." It was so chatty that I was tempted to ask if I could have a similar boiler-clean leave and eventually, I did summon up courage to ask. That was a mistake!

"You've only just come back from sick leave and now you want to go home again after two days? Don't forget this, leave is a privilege and not a right in the Royal Navy," he reminded me in no uncertain terms. Those words were trotted out on many subsequent occasions and I was later to find out that, during the whole of my three years in the Andrew, leave was only given to me for end of training, embarkation and finally demob, apart from those ten days sick leave which had just come to an end. Nowadays, seasonal leave is given at Christmas, Easter etc. but we had none of these benefits and certainly service people today consider six months overseas to be the maximum reasonable period of time to be away from home. We were due to depart shortly for service in the America and West Indies Squadron for a two-and-a-half-year commission which would mean that no leave would be allowed other than a couple of days or so on very rare occasions, all subject to the 'exigencies of the service'.

All these points were put to me by the Cox'n before he reached for a blank station card on which he wrote, apart from my name and rank, my part of ship, i.e. fo'c'sle, top, or quarterdeck and my part of the watch, which was the first part of port watch.

"Here you are then," he said, handing me the small red card. "You can go ashore tonight if you want to. Fall in when Libertymen are called and hand in your station card as you go ashore. Whatever you do, don't forget to collect the card immediately you return aboard otherwise you could be in trouble." With that, the interview seemed ended and I returned to the Mess deck where by now some of the others were drinking tea.

"Are you on Number Five Mess?" asked a portly leading seaman. "If you are, pour yourself a mug of tea and find yourself a seat." They seemed a particularly tough crowd on Number Five mess and this fact was explained when they changed to go ashore as they were all Royal Navy Commandos, wearing the designatory shoulder flash. Most had served during the war in landing craft and, while waiting for their demob number to be called, they had been drafted as steaming party to prepare *Porlock Bay* for her overseas commission. They were finding it difficult to adjust to life aboard a new frigate in which discipline was far more strict – they were not used to having to wait for liberty boats for one thing and were generally aggrieved at the length of time waiting for release from Naval service. A run ashore for them meant going to the NAFFI Club for a snack before going on to their particular pub, often picking up a girl on the way. By the time they returned aboard, they had consumed more beer than was good for them unless, of course, they exercised their right of 'all night leave' and stayed at 'Aggie's', as a hostel for seamen was lovingly called after that grand old lady Dame Agnes Weston. As underage ratings, our generation of ordinary seamen should not officially have been allowed all night leave but, on a frigate, this was not enforced and so, normally, we would pay one and six pence for a bed in a tiny cubicle at Aggie's, possibly singing a hymn or two at 2300 hours before turning in.

The killick of Five Mess introduced himself as Harry Freeman and he asked where my home was.

"Warwick," I replied to his utter amazement as he came from the village of Old Milverton, only about two miles away. Old Milverton was an old feudal style village owned by the Heber-Percy family who, inter alia, never allowed a shop or pub to be opened within its boundaries and generally kept a tight reign on the activities of its residents. Harry was a regular who had served throughout the war, having joined HMS *Ganges* as a boy seaman in 1937. He was later to leave the ship to become a sailmaker, a job which involved making awnings rather than sails although ships' boats still did require sails.

The rest of the evening after a meal of 'errings-in' was spent exploring the ship and finally finding the tiny NAAFI canteen at which I bought a bar of nutty. The canteen was only open for one hour but, despite its small size, almost anything could be bought there from a tin of baked beans to a tin of boot polish. It was situated in the next compartment to the seaman's mess deck, which was very convenient. This compartment contained the ship's gyro but little else although it provided additional accommodation for the hammocks of those who wanted a good night's sleep.

At 'pipe down', the Officer of the Day made his rounds with the duty Petty Officer, preceded by the Bosun's Mate. Earlier on in the evening, the pipe was made, "change into night clothing," which meant removing the blue jean collar if one was being worn and no one ever bothered if it was kept on during rounds, such was the routine aboard a warship. With so few crew members left aboard, it was fairly quiet except for the SRE which was broadcasting either the radio or some records and so I slung my hammock for an early night.

After such an eventful day I had no difficulty in sleeping and the next I knew was when the duty PO came around bawling, "Eve Oh, Eve Oh, Eve Oh, lash up and stow," or words sounding like that, hitting each hammock within hitting distance with a stick. No one moved, whether out of tiredness or as a protest against being woken up at 0530 hours, and so, after five minutes, the PO made a second round, this time grabbing one or two hammocks until their occupants decided to admit defeat and get out.

With only thirty minutes from the initial call until "hands fall in on the quarterdeck", there was only a short time to have a wash before climbing up on the deck to the sound of the seabirds wheeling and squealing about, watching for any morsel thrown overboard upon which they would pounce, often before it hit the water. The PO of each part of the ship would then check if everyone was present, call the hands to attention and report to the First Lieutenant. It was surprising at first, how slovenly the ratings responded to being called to attention but, at 0600 hours they were only half awake and in any case we were on board ship, not at Gunnery School. This was the first time I had seen the First Lieutenant, an R.N.V.R. two ringer who was very conscious of his responsibilities and who appeared to be a strict disciplinarian. Lieutenant Digby returned the salutes of the Petty Officers without any comment other than, "very good, carry on working part of ship," before disappearing, presumably back to his cabin.

Ratings were then told to collect cleaning equipment from the buffer's caboose or a paint pot and brush from the store immediately forrard of the watchkeeper's mess deck. Others were detailed as Gunner's Party to work in the magazines or on the guns while the torpedo men went about their business with the electrical equipment. As a complete newcomer, I was provided with a tin of 'bluebell' and told to polish all and every brass plate that I could see. This seemed hardly the work I had expected to be doing and very much removed from the training that had been more or less promised when I volunteered for the Navy under the 'Y' Scheme. Anyway, in accordance with naval practice, I 'obeyed the last pipe'.

After an hour, work stopped for breakfast during which those ratings who had had all-night leave, returned and changed into their overalls, having missed the first hour of the day as far as work was concerned. At breakfast, Harry Freeman detailed two ratings as Cooks of the Mess, issuing them with two chits for food, one to be redeemed by Tanky for the meat and potatoes etc., and the other at the NAAFI Canteen. The Cooks would then prepare the food which was taken up to the galley to be heated up by the Ship's cook and in due course, the meal would be collected for dishing up in the mess. This routine was known as 'Canteen Messing' and it was the regular method of feeding the hands in the smaller ships of the Royal Navy. After breakfast, we collected our tools and equipment for further work on deck.

At 'Stand-easy', we stopped what we were doing and went below to make the tea, while most of my new messmates lit up a cigarette, not a 'tickler' now but a ready-made one from tins marked "DUTY FREE, HM SHIPS ONLY". These cost a mere 7d for twenty except Woodbines which were only 6d – the equivalent of the present two and a half pence. This was about the only 'perk' we could enjoy but, in the belief that they were getting something almost for nothing, the mess deck was subsequently filled with filthy smoke which resulted in many having respiratory problems later, including the passive smoker.

Stand-easy over, we returned to our duties until the pipe, "Clear up decks" was heard and we were able to go below for the main meal of the day while the 'G' or 'grog' ratings were able to enjoy their tot, offering sippers to the bubbly bosun before drinking the remainder. The mixture had been prepared earlier by 'Jack Dusty', the Stores Assistant, who followed the orders called out by the Cox'n who, in turn, was watched over by the Officer of the Day to ensure that the exact amounts were issued. Chiefs and Petty Officers were entitled to draw their rum neat which enabled them to store their tot if they wished although this was contrary to regulations. Little did we know at that time that our next Captain, who, when he became the Second Sea Lord, would be the one who stopped the daily free issue of rum, thus putting an end to a tradition enjoyed by generations of seamen. Such action did make sense, however, in the post-war high tech navy, particularly when ratings were operating sensitive apparatus requiring them to be fully alert. Well were we to remember later the euphoria we experienced, especially in the tropics, after our tot, although we fully realised the possible dangers which could have resulted from being in such a befuddled state.

The monotonous routine of 'working part of ship' continued for the remainder of the week when, suddenly it seemed the boiler clean leave for half the seamen was over and my fellow radar trainees appeared on the mess deck. They seemed surprised to see me; one even thought I had managed to work my ticket and another that I had succumbed to some strange, possibly unmentionable, disease as they last saw me going to Ward Five in the barracks.

They told me about the visit made by the ship to Porlock when those who went ashore became stranded overnight as the wind had freshened, making it impossible to get back to the ship. Recollections of this event were later set down by Telegraphist Victor L. Rayner who described it as follows.

> "We arrived early Saturday morning and dropped anchor in the bay. All afternoon our small boats, plus many private ones, ferried visitors to and fro.
>
> "That evening half the ship's company were to go ashore, for a reception at the village hall with the other half of us going ashore on the Sunday evening but what we didn't find out until later was that three quarters of the crew had gone ashore leaving only the duty part of the watch aboard, and trouble was brewing.
>
> "It brewed in the form of a storm which by 2200 hours had developed into a force eight gale. It was of course, impossible for our small boats to bring the crew back aboard.
>
> "The Captain in his wisdom decided to 'up anchor' and we sailed up and down the bay. He was not best pleased to find he only had the Engineering Officer aboard and he was spitting

feathers when he found that there was not one signalman aboard. That was when he summoned me to the bridge. I think it was one of the most miserable nights of my life: I had never been as wet or cold before. We did receive one signal from a coastguard station on the hill and after I made a bit of a balls of it, I managed to read it. "I have placed a red light for your assistance." "Reply, 'thank you very much'," said the Skipper. I often wondered what the coastguard thought of my performance.

"Not surprising, next morning with the crew back aboard, all the officers and senior ratings assembled in the Captain's cabin and all hell broke loose!

"We got our shore leave that night and in the village hall the Captain and the Squire exchanged gifts and we danced the night away, pausing only for the usual liquid replacements."

Souvenirs of that visit can be seen on the rear wall of St Dubritious Church, Porlock in the form of a Ship's badge which, sadly, has over the years split from top to bottom, and a plaque commemorating the visit. Exactly fifty years later we were to hold a reunion in Porlock, when during the morning service in the church a second plaque was presented and dedicated by the Reverend Barry Priory, the rector of St Dubritious.

The local people of Porlock kept in touch with the ship throughout her commission, sending copies of the local paper together with several parcels of knitted 'comforts' including socks and balaclavas to be handed out to crew members and, in return, we wrote back, thanking them for their gifts.

The ship had then returned to Devonport but instead of being moored in mid-stream in the Hamoaze, she was secured alongside making it much simpler for a run-ashore even though crew members still had to catch the 'liberty boat' in time honoured fashion.

My mates from the training days had just finished relating their experiences of the Porlock visit when a loud voice was heard at the top of the ladder leading in the seamen's mess. No! It couldn't be…or could it? There could only be one Welsh voice like that, it must be him. But why this ship? Why HMS *Porlock Bay*? Of all the ships in the Royal Navy, why did they send Bungy Williams to serve with us? Our worst fears were realised when Bungy dropped down on the mess deck, swearing loudly as he had lost his tiddy 'oggie which had fallen into a puddle on his way from the Albert Gate to the ship.

Bungy had boasted about serving a year in the Naval Detention Quarters at Preston, spinning a long yarn about returning to the ship he was serving in and finding a young Sub-Lieutenant on the dockside.

"Carry my cases aboard," were the words Bungy heard from the officer.

"Carry them yourself," was his reply. An impasse was only relieved when Bungy threw the cases into the harbour, followed immediately by the officer. We found this story somewhat incredulous until someone managed to take a peek at his records which were kept in the ship's office. It was true indeed.

Now he was a fellow crew member, allocated to Number Seven Mess, the next one to mine on the starboard side of the mess deck, a third class anti-aircraft rating wearing his newly acquired AA's badge on his arm.

"I wonder what Brenchley thinks about him being drafted to the same ship?" were my thoughts. They were soon answered when Able Seaman Brenchley descended on the mess deck, piping, "Hands clean into night clothing." The last words were uttered more in a gasp than anything else as he spotted Bungy and raced through into the Canteen Flat. Poor old Brenchley, but at least as Bosun's Mate he was in the forrard Watch-Keeper's Mess and not on ours.

The next few days were relatively uneventful, working part of the ship and generally finding my way around. It did, however, seem strange to me that ratings were not given a plan of the ship, and were not taken on a tour to familiarise themselves with the layout. They were supposed to know where each compartment was situated by being nosy and looking into each nook and cranny. What was kept in the Tiller Flat? One question for example, and we only got to know by experience as we were sent for various items of equipment.

So far, I had not been ashore in the evening and so when Humphrey Ixer suggested going into Plymouth I seized the opportunity for my first run ashore. Good old Humphrey had by this time found several 'ports of call' in Plymouth, ranging from the Corporation Billiard Saloon in Union Street and from there to the NAAFI Club where reasonable meals could be had and thence to the Royal Sailor's Rest in Octagon Square. He initiated me into the game of snooker but, try as I might, Humphrey always won. It seemed an infuriating game until someone suggested, "Hit where it shines," when my game vastly improved. The Saloon had about a dozen tables, with most of them in use by matelots from various ships in the dockyard, and all of them appeared most proficient at the game, compared with my feeble efforts. A break of fifteen was my highest achievement, thus proving that mine was not a misspent youth.

The NAAFI Club formed from a series of inter-linked Nissen huts housing, inter alia, another snooker parlour, a restaurant and a reading/writing room. It was situated on a bomb-site next to a cinema at the end of Union Street which had always had a reputation for drunken brawls and ladies of easy virtue who had little difficult in attracting lonely sailors. The Club, however, was well conducted, with no trouble from any source despite the heterogeneity of its customers and it provided an excellent 'base' for many a serviceman.

Further to the west along Union Street one came to Octagon Square, on one side of which stood the 'Unicorn' pub and on the other side, the Royal Sailor's rest. The 'Unicorn' is still standing today but the interior bears little resemblance to the pub we knew years ago with its small, intimate bars serving Ind Coope beer. Even the name has changed! The barmaid was a particularly pleasant girl who told us everything we wanted to know about the city from the destruction of its heart by the Nazi bombers to the composition of the Plymouth Argyle football team for their next match. Between serving pints to other customers, she entertained us for hours with stories of the Blitz which had, from the mere visual appearance of the city, been devastated to a far greater extent than others, including Coventry.

The ship's company had only just got used to life in Devonport when the time came to leave for Bermuda. First we were given two weeks' leave and, for me, this was granted just as my parents had arranged a holiday in Looe, Cornwall, in order to be able to make trips to Plymouth to see me. As a result, the first week of my embarkation leave was spent at the seaside with them!

However, we returned to Warwick for the final week which went by all too quickly before it was time to return to the ship. Travelling up to Birmingham to catch the Cornish Riviera train, the journey was quite uneventful until we stopped outside Bristol where we learned that a derailment had occurred to a previous freight train. Realising that my ship was under sailing orders, I rushed on to the platform at Temple Meads to get a chit from the RTO. This was given and, feeling quite secure in the knowledge that I had a good excuse for being adrift, my journey eventually continued after the obstruction had been cleared.

Arriving back on board, the chit carried no weight whatsoever! At 'defaulters' the Captain, Dudley Davenport, informed me that it was my

*Lieutenant D L Davenport RN,
1st Captain of HMS* Porlock Bay

duty to return on time and gave me a three day stoppage of leave penalty. It was of course of no consequence as we would be at sea for the next five days when no one could have any leave.

In due course, we slipped from our moorings and travelled down the Hamoaze to the Sound and thence to the open sea in rather dull weather, saluting other ships and, of course, flagstaff steps, as we progressed on our way. As the ship passed Drake's Island, the SRE was heard playing 'Home Sweet Home,' a place we could not see again for two and a half years. We were on our way to Bermuda.

5

BERMUDA HERE WE COME

*"Bermuda was a paradise
but one had to go through hell to get to there."*
Mark Twain

Settling down to life at sea was not too daunting at first. Having cleared the breakwater, the first part of the starboard watch was mustered on deck near to the whaler and given their duties for the remainder of the first dog watch. As a member of the first part of port watch, I was able to have my supper and get some sleep during the first watch and would then have to turn out of my hammock to go up top for the 'middle' – 2400 until 0400 hours.

'Errings-in' formed our meal, together with bread and a cup of tea. The tasty repast over, hammocks were slung and about three hours were available to sleep before being called for the watch to muster. Sleep came quite easily and when the first part of port were called, the seas were decidedly rougher. PO Bert Whelan was waiting for us to allocate the duties: bridge look-outs, telegraphs, bridge messenger and the remainder sea boat's crew who would be available also for any emergency. The Radar Plot ratings were operating their 293 set in the small radar office, enclosed from the inclement weather – why did I have to take the gunnery, Radar Control, course instead of the navigational side of Radar?

The rating who was given duty of telegraphsman had a relatively quiet number in the wheelhouse as there was not likely to be any change in speed or the number of revolutions. The Quartermaster was generally on the wheel, steering by the Gyro Repeat while the Bosun's Mate would be standing by to go round the ship piping the orders. However, the Quartermaster would sometimes in the ensuing weeks call up the voice pipe to the bridge to obtain permission for the telegraphsman to take the wheel as a training exercise and so many of us were able to get experience of steering the ship and several later became Quartermasters in their own right.

Bridge look-outs were, as the name implies, responsible for scanning the horizon for land, aircraft, ships, and indeed anything floating on the sea. After reporting to the Officer of the Watch that he was the relief look-out, he would take his position on the port or starboard wing of the bridge, standing just forrard of the single forty mm Bofors. He would receive a pair of binoculars from his predecessor and, on spotting anything would report Red (or Green) the degrees from the bow and a light or whatever he had seen. Quite possibly the radar plot would have already reported an echo on the PPI, making a double check on each object. In good weather conditions it was quite pleasant to be on duty as bridge look-out but, during heavy rain for example, it was necessary to stand there in oilskins and just get soaked, and in rough weather dodging the spray was the problem.

Whatever the duty it was always good to hear one's relief arrive. It was difficult to adapt to watch keeping and in fact the broken sleep every night at sea was the main reason for many of us wanting to leave the Andrew at the first opportunity during those first days of our overseas commission. No matter which watch one had had the previous night, the normal workshop routine prevailed during the day and the younger members of the crew often wondered how they would have kept going in wartime with priority calls to action stations at any hour of the day or night in addition. It must have been extremely tiring and no wonder there were lapses in concentration, often with disastrous results.

Before setting off from Devonport, the ship embarked four passengers travelling to Bermuda and one of these was allocated to Number Five Mess. He was a foreman in the dockyard in Bermuda and it was from him that we learned quite a lot about the place. Most of us knew very little about the small British Colony and several thought, wrongly, that it was in the Caribbean and some that it was in the tropics. With our passengers' help we managed to envisage life in the dockyard there and on the many islands which formed the Bermudan archipelago. The many islands were linked by bridges to make a fish-hook shape on the map, with the dockyard and HMS *Malabar*, the shore establishment, being the 'spike' on the end. About the only way to get from the dockyard to Hamilton, the capital, was by MFV, which took nearly an hour to travel across the Great Sound and which was not a very welcoming thought if we wanted a quick run ashore.

What really surprised us was the small size of the various islands – only twenty-one square miles in total and, for me, was the fact that there was a Warwick Parish, named after Robert Rich, Earl of Warwick who was one of the earliest settlers. Of more immediate concern to us was the presence of reefs almost encircling the islands on which so many ships had come to grief. We would have to approach the harbour by way of a narrow channel into Grassy Bay on our way to our base for the next two and a half years.

For the past two days, despite the inclement weather, no one had suffered from mal de mer, but then, one after the other, most of the HOs succumbed. This was one big joke as far as some of the Active Service ratings were concerned and it was necessary to keep going with the daily chores or be faced with taunts that the ship did not carry passengers (not true actually, as there were the four passengers from Devonport). Seasickness is the most ghastly feeling, which makes you want to sit or lie down until the seas calm down but that was of course impossible and with the greatest effort we forced ourselves to move around. Seasickness has affected many of our illustrious sailors including Horatio Nelson, and apparently our Captain was also a sufferer but that was of little or no consolation to us at the time.

After the third day the climate became decidedly warmer, something that encouraged us considerably. How those poor devils on the North Russian convoys survived the terribly adverse weather conditions, let alone action, which struck from below, on and above the waves, one could only guess. At least we would not be subjected to the winter in the North Atlantic – or would we?

On the sixth day, the bridge look-outs spied land during the morning watch. Soon we were able to pick out features on those islands which some people consider to be the remains of the legendary Atlantis but which we knew to be the Azores. For the majority of us, this was our first place 'foreign' as we were denied the school visits to other countries which most children take for granted today. The wartime conditions were not conducive to continental travel! As we sailed past the northern coast of the main islands of the group, San Miguel, we could see bonfires burning on the cliffs, presumably providing warmth and a means of cooking for the agricultural workers. Soon we were entering the harbour of the capital, Ponta Delgrada, where we would stay for four days, and securing alongside the jetty. No

HMS Porlock Bay *(K650)* & *HMS* Padstow Bay *(K608),*
Ponta Delgada, Azores

sooner had we done so than a Portuguese destroyer entered at great speed, bugles sounding and with a fine display of seamanship on the part of the Captain. The silhouette of the destroyer seemed familiar – it was exactly like the British A to I classes – and, as we were to find out when she secured alongside us, she was built by Yarrow on the Clyde.

For the first time, we had to paint the ship, so stages were lowered over the side and all available ratings were given a brush and a pot of light grey paint. My section was roughly amidships and, working away on the ship's side, I was suddenly aware of a discharge from the Portuguese ship about three feet away. Looking down I realised that my section was by the outflow from the heads and, there on my stage was human excreta. What a welcome!

That afternoon, shore leave was granted and together with three or four others we went to a small bar on the quayside where several locals were drinking. After two small glasses apiece we left and strolled down the main street where, as we looked into one shop window, I was thumped on the back with such force that my head hit the window. Looking round we saw two of the local girls laughing uncontrollably. Finally, one of them produced visiting cards to a place of entertainment in a road called Ruo do Beco, and they then set off, beckoning us to follow. Of course, it turned out to be the red light district, where we about-turned, heading back for the bar. Several of the active service ratings did avail themselves of the 'entertainment' with the result that a number of them had to report to the ship's sick bay for treatment about two weeks later. Matelots will never learn it seems.

Painting the ship's side continued the following day as we would shortly be leaving for Bermuda and had to be spick and span for our arrival there. When the midday break arrived we went below for a meal which wasn't there! All hands had been required to turn to with the painting and so, no cooked food. After about fifteen minutes came another pipe, "Hands to muster". The first Lieutenant had decided that it was necessary to continue without a break until the work was complete but he reckoned without some of the old salts.

"No one, repeat, no one, is to go up top," were their orders and so we just sat around on the mess deck benches. Having read about the Invergordon Mutiny, several HOs were literally scared stiff but we had to do as we were told until the Cox'n, PO Ginger Rhodes, appeared on the mess deck. He tried to diffuse the situation by asking what the matter was, and was told in no uncertain terms that we would not do any more work until we had eaten. After all, this was peacetime and there was no emergency, as the older lower deck lawyers pointed out.

HMS Padstow Bay *and HMS* Porlock Bay *at Ponta Delgada, Azores, 28th July 1946*

After only a few minutes, the Cox'n returned after reporting to the Jimmy and, as a special concession, we were able to have a cold meal before starting work again. What a relief it was that nothing more would be said about the matter and no recourse would be had to the punishments laid down in KRs and AIs. We set to with a will after that and the ship's sides sparkled like a new pin in the hot sunshine. Just a week into our two-and-a-half-year commission and we had had a mutiny aboard. Fortunately, nothing similar happened again and *Porlock Bay* became what is known as a 'Happy Ship' during the remainder of the Commission.

Just before we left Ponta Delgrada, we had a buzz that we would not be going directly to Bermuda but to the neighbouring island of Terceira in order to locate a Landing Craft (Headquarters) and tow her across the Atlantic.

Terceira was in fact the island in the Azores on which the allies were able to construct an airfield in 1943 as part of the campaign against the U-Boats in the battle of the Atlantic. The base was most successful for the coastal command aircraft to cover those parts of the Atlantic that were difficult for UK based aircraft to search in view of the distance involved, and in fact several U Boats were sunk as a result. True enough, we found LCH 75 at anchor and set about taking her in tow. This was achieved reasonably quickly and off we sailed at a much slower speed than our economic cruising speed. However, fifty years later we were to hear from Jim Blackburn, now living in Auckland, New Zealand, a telegraphist in LCH 75 who recalls his side of the saga as follows.

> "Along with dozens of other US-built Landing Craft, we were ordered to sail back to Norfolk, Virginia to be returned to the Americans as we were a 'Lease Lend' craft.
>
> "To cut a long story short, the craft was 'clapped out', the eight General Motors 250 HP Diesels were run into the ground, worn right out. However, we left Alex, sailing alone for Malta and arriving there with only two out of the eight engines working. We went up on the LC Shipway on Manoel Island for hull and engine repairs and, weeks later, sailed again for Gibraltar which we reached with three engines and a tail wind. Eventually, with twelve more LCI that had arrived from the UK and the tug Empire Rose we all sailed for the Azores with LCH 75 and two other Infantry Landing Craft, being towed into Ponta Delgrada.

"The rest of them – 261 Flight as it was known – sailed a week later leaving LCH 75 by herself working on the engines. Eventually we sailed again with just two officers and eleven ratings aboard for Bermuda but, after less than forty-eight hours we were down to four engines, three on the port shaft and one on the starboard. And there was a gale blowing.

"By the fourth day we had no engines, no generators, nothing! We were drifting on our sea anchor but luckily we had enough power in the batteries of my TCS set to get through to Gib, to tell them what had happened and where we were, roughly!

"For five days we rolled our guts out; no ventilation below, no heating although luckily the fresh water could be pumped up by hand. Still no power, no hot food and still a gale blowing.

"We tried to heat up tins of meat and veg in a stew pot by pouring diesel oil onto the sand in a fire bucket and setting it alight but the smoke got into the stew and tainted it and it made us all sick. In the end we were eating corned beef out of the tin and dried peas and beans soaked in water but still raw. We had no bread, not even any ship's biscuits.

"On the fifth day we were found by Porlock Bay and Padstow Bay who passed us over some hot soup and bread. Porlock Bay passed us a line to take us in tow and there was only a few of us to try to haul the hurricane line inboard and we couldn't manage it. So she came alongside and passed it to us – getting her stern stove in by our port ramp – and after we had secured it, she steamed slowly ahead and paid it out from her stern. We had an electric power lead floated back to us but we were 110 volts DC so it was a problem. Still we had mountainous seas running.

"After eighteen hours the tow parted and we were told to abandon the LCH and board Porlock Bay who would then sink her by gunfire. However, it was too rough for her to put her whaler down and we were going to have to jump into the sea and be picked up by lifeline as there was no way Porlock Bay could get alongside. We only had a six foot plywood dinghy.

"There were sharks around, had been for days, snapping the gash from the bucket in one gulp – some of them looked as big as whales so it was decided that we could stick it out until the weather got better – or we could walk on the water.

"The next day it was calm enough for Porlock Bay to put her boat down and the tow was passed over again and hooked up. We were all taken off to Porlock Bay and proceeded to Bermuda.

"It was a bit of a culture shock for both ships' companies – on the LCH we only wore khaki drill and canvas shoes with rope soles – never any whites. The frigate was in 'peacetime Navy routine' – all pusser and ship shape and we were like pirates and everyone did any job – if he could.

"The irony of it all was that we eventually got to Norfolk and sailed up the river to berth alongside other lease-lend craft that had been taken back and near to jetty after jetty of about twenty-four berthed aircraft carriers waiting to go into reserve. Two days after arrival we were sent up river a few miles and at full power drove her up into the river bank mud and she was left as a hulk."

Jim goes on to say that 260 officers and ratings were taken to New York and embarked in SS *Queen Mary*, arriving back in Southampton four days later. He wanted to say "thank you" to the *Porlock Bay* men because, "assuredly, if she hadn't found us there was every likelihood that we would have broken up and foundered to disappear like some others did and I wouldn't be here to tell you this."

Jim was perhaps a little wrong in saying that the tow parted as it held throughout the journey until we arrived off Bermuda. However, a few days before our arrival, we had a hurricane warning and it was decided to transfer everyone on board the landing craft to our ship, including a particularly friendly mongrel, half greyhound/half Labrador, by the name of Ponta who had 'adopted' the landing craft in Ponta Delgada.

At the time, however, we were not aware of the dire conditions aboard LCH 75 when we arrived off Terceira and it is most agreeable to discover how thankful the members of the ship's company were when we sent across food, drink and, of course, the tow.

The time taken on passage to Bermuda was greatly extended by taking the landing craft in tow as our speed was considerably reduced. A useful exercise was carried out en route when hands were piped for bathing. A Carley Float was lowered into the Atlantic and anyone not on duty was 'invited' to jump over the side for a swim while our ship and her tow described a very large circle as it would not have been possible to stop completely. Having thus jumped, the sudden realisation struck us that we would not be able to 'touch bottom', which meant that no one strayed very far from the Carley Float! *Porlock Bay* seemed to disappear almost out of sight but slowly and surely she returned with scrambling nets lowered for everyone to grab hold of and clamber aboard.

More than fifty years later at a ship's reunion in Plymouth, the First Lieutenant of LCH 75 was able to join us as a full member of our Association as he became a Watchkeeping Officer in *Porlock Bay* when we transferred the landing craft's crew to our ship. He was Lieutenant Austin Prosser, R.N.V.R. and his presence at our reunion came about as a result of a chance remark in his local pub which happened also to be the haunt of former Able Seaman John Kessell. John had mentioned that a landing craft was towed from the Azores to Bermuda whereupon Austin remarked that his vessel had 'hitched a lift' across the Atlantic. This was the first time that the two 'regulars' had realised that they had both served together, albeit in different capacities. Details of LCH 75 were subsequently given by Austin and his report is so interesting that it bears repeating verbatim.

HMS Porlock Bay *(K650) & HMS* Padstow Bay *(K608) astern of Landing Craft (Headquarters) LCH75 which we towed from the Azores to Bermuda*

"She was commissioned in the US Navy a LCI (L) 75 and was subsequently in the North African, Sicily, Salerno, Azores and D-Day landings. After I lost my own ship I took her over from the Americans in Chatham where she was converted to a Headquarters Ship for use in the Pacific landings. We were used for escorting LCTs out to the Far East but, when we got to Port Said, they dropped the atom bomb which brought the war to an abrupt halt. We sat it out in Port Said for three months while they decided what to do with us. Eventually we were sent to India for onward passage to Japan but, half way across the Indian Ocean they decided we weren't needed and were told to return to Norfolk, Virginia to pay off. That is why we finished up in Ponta Delgada. All our engines were completely worn out and, as there was nobody locally who could repair us, the admiralty decided that we should be towed as a hulk to Bermuda where some work could be carried out…we eventually arrived in Norfolk where we paid off. The old girl had a pretty hectic war and I spent nearly two happy years aboard her, the last year as First Lieutenant. Incidentally, she had eight Gray Marine diesels, four on each screw and could do you to eighteen knots."

1st part of port watch with Whelan

Before reaching Bermuda however, a radio message was received to the effect that an aircraft was missing and we were almost on the line of its flight path. Radar Plot operators and bridge look-outs were ordered to be particularly vigilant as we combed the estimated route of the aircraft from Britain to South America. It seemed very much like looking for the proverbial needle in a haystack but everyone carried out their duties conscientiously in the hope that we may be able to rescue any survivors. After about forty-eight hours we had to admit defeat as no sign could be found of any wreckage and so we continued on our twice-interrupted way. We were in fact approaching the area known as the 'Bermuda Triangle' which has, as Charles Berlitz states in his book, "an incredible saga of unexplained disappearances," but years later, in 1974 when his book was published, the story of the 'Star Tiger' was told.

This Tudor IV four-engine aircraft flying from the Azores to Bermuda disappeared on 29th January 1948, much later than our voyage, so although we must have investigated a similar disappearance it was certainly not 'Star Tiger' we searched for.

Soon after the aircraft incident came the hurricane warning resulting in the transfer of the LCH 75 crew. The news came on a Sunday morning and Lieutenant Davenport, our Captain, took a church service on the quarterdeck after divisions. He gave as much information as possible at that stage and gave orders to prepare to sink the landing craft if necessary to avoid her becoming a hazard to shipping.

The church service immediately seemed to assume greater importance, particularly for the HO ratings who would possibly have to experience a hurricane for the first time. In the RN everyone not Jewish, Roman Catholic or Free Churchmen, was automatically classed as 'Church of England', as atheists and agnostics were 'not allowed', so everyone not on duty joined in the service. It was most significant that the words of the naval hymn, "Eternal father, strong to save whose arm doth bind the restless wave," were sung with much greater fervour on that occasion.

The service over, the motor cutter was lowered and the task of collecting the other vessel's crew got under way. It took two trips until officers and men plus the dog 'Ponta' were safely aboard and the coxswain was able to make arrangements for appropriate accommodation for them. Some were allocated to the stoker's mess, the signalmen to the forward mess deck, but the remainder were given a hitherto unused mess on the port side aft.

In the meantime, the gunner's party was busy bringing up several rounds of ammunition which was fused and stowed away in the Ready-Use lockers adjacent to the forward gun mounting. This was another useful exercise as, for myself, it was the first time we had had to operate the hoist to bring a cage of four projectiles up from the magazine. The shout of our Danish crew mate, "press up on ze fingeurs," still echoes in my ears as we brought each load up from the bowels of the ship. What Sven Zaar really meant no one knew for sure but we all assumed that he was warning us of the potential danger of getting our fingers caught in the hoist. It seemed that we would soon have to put a sorry end to the landing craft and we reflected that, after all the action she had seen during the war it would be ironic to sink her by 'friendly' fire.

After a while our prayers at morning service were answered when the heavy seas eased considerably and we learnt that the hurricane had missed Bermuda and was heading out to sea having almost blown itself out. The ammunition was duly defused and struck below once more in the magazine while the crew of the landing craft took their watches with our fellows and Lt Austin Prosser took his place on the bridge as a watch-keeping officer.

Soon land was sighted; the low outline of the Bermuda Islands appeared on the horizon with no apparent outstanding features visible to the naked eye. It was then that we heard of the Captain's plans for entering harbour. We were to warp the old landing craft alongside and proceed in that way into the harbour in a way similar to that incident during the war when the tanker, *Ohio*, was taken into Grand Harbour, Valletta, by two destroyers. The sea immediately around Malta at that time was still somewhat choppy but here we were experiencing the aftermath of a hurricane which had severely whipped up the sea. On the fo'c'sle every attempt to secure the LCH alongside was thwarted by the extremely choppy seas; one minute we would be looking down on the powerless hulk and the next she would be towering above us so it was obvious that we would not be able to secure her successfully to our side. One by one the wires snapped and the broken ends came curling back, often missing crew members by a few inches. It was certainly a dangerous place to be as we flung ourselves flat on the deck to avoid being decapitated.

While all this was happening on deck, one off-duty telegraphist, Les Adams, was sleeping peacefully in Number One mess (the watchkeeper's) in the bows of the ship. Without warning, his slumbers were interrupted by metal forcing its way through the ship's side and missing him by the smallest of margins. A stanchion on the port side of the landing craft had been rammed through the flare of our bows by the violence of the seas, cutting through the metal plates like a knife through butter. Obviously Les felt shaken up, but having gone through the war earning a 'full house' of campaign medals, he soon recovered!

The Captain realised the problems and reluctantly signalled the dockyard for assistance which came fairly quickly in the form of an Admiralty tug which took the LCH in tow, astern this time, and proceeded into the dockyard. For our part, we followed at a discreet distance, saluting the Commander-in-Chief's white headquarters near Spanish Point as we passed but carefully keeping the starboard side of the ship, which had been holed and generally knocked about, away from the Vice-Admiral's enquiring gaze. Lieutenant Davenport took the ship into harbour with apparent ease where we secured alongside, kept away from the wall by means of a catamaran, a name which has other meanings today but which was nothing more than a raft of wood to us.

Both the 'cat' and the harbour wall contained the names of several occupants of that position to remind the present generation of seamen of their wartime and, indeed, their pre-war predecessors. Our position was overshadowed by a single dockyard crane on which I was particularly pleased to see the maker's name, Stothert and Pitt, Bath, England. This name-plate was retrieved later when the crane was demolished and now lies, rusting away, unfortunately, in the museum which was created out of the buildings in the shore station adjoining the dockyard.

Ahead of us in our berth lay a floating dock which we were shortly to enter and from which in the meantime we could dive into the harbour after trying out the sea water soap given to us in view of the extreme water shortages on the islands. The soap was not very successful as no lather could be obtained but at least we could wash off the scum when we swam around in the harbour.

As we entered harbour, a very large, coloured fisherman was seen with his line stretching out into the area our ship would soon be occupying but, withdrawing his line, he took our heaving line to which our bow wire was bent, and then secured the eye over a bollard on the dock side. This man was the darkest we had ever seen, slow and ponderous perhaps but friendly to a fault. He made himself known to us soon afterwards as the collector of 'edible' gash from the various messes which he used to feed his pigs. Beside the spot where he had been sitting prior to our arrival were several silvery fish which would be a useful variant to his pork diet.

After the springs had been secured and until we entered the floating dock, we carried out normal harbour duties. These would continue until our first cruise, a trip north to Newfoundland and Canada ending just before Christmas. Immediately after entering the harbour, the 'heads' were sealed, making it necessary to walk quite a long way to the toilets in the dockyard. All tin cans, and there were many, had to be carried ashore and placed with other non-pig-food gash in the bins provided near to the toilets.

We could no longer hear the BBC News Broadcasts but instead were kept up to date with reports from the local radio station – ZBM Radio Bermuda. Between times and in off-duty hours we were entertained by the latest pop tunes played over the local radio, supplemented by largely pop tunes from our own SRE. Having been brought up on a diet of largely classical music at school it was somewhat difficult to get accustomed to popular tunes and it was not long before several of us began to yearn for the more soothing sounds of Mozart etc. Station ZBM was very Americanised, catering for the locals and the tourists from the States who would soon be descending on the islands in their droves. The news broadcasts in particular were far less formal than the BBC ones read, inter alia, by Alvar Liddell, Frank Phillips and Bruce Belfrage, and it took quite a while to get used to them, making us realise that we were now quite a long way from home.

The fact that we were now on a tropical station (although not exactly in the tropics) became patently clear when the Buffer, PO Taff Alban, asked the First Lieutenant for permission to erect awnings on the quarterdeck, a practice normally adopted in hot climates in peacetime. Lieutenant Digby, a wartime R.N.V.R. Officer was not aware of this but at once gave permission for the awnings to be dragged from storage in the tiller flat and erected on the new stanchions provided for them. Taff was of course a long serving rating who had acquired his third badge long ago and so he knew the pre-war routine well whereas Digby was only accustomed to war-time conditions.

The matter of the quarterdeck raised other problems as *Porlock Bay*, along with other wartime warships, had metal decks to which slats had been welded to reduce slipping. These had to be removed before corticene decking could be laid down and this work had to be carried out by the dockyard mateys. Accordingly, a gang of workmen arrived on board with the noisiest of electrical chisels, scraping off each slat individually. The job seemed to take ages before the corticene, a type of linoleum, could be put down to provide a better surface for the feet of all the future visitors we would entertain during the forthcoming cruises. This would entail holding cocktail parties for the various dignitaries and other influential people to whom we would 'show the flag'. Peace had now truly broken out and the *raison d'être* for all ships on, or shortly to join, the America and West Indies Squadron was, firstly, to show the flag, provide a hurricane patrol and be prepared for any uprising or natural disaster which may occur.

6

PARADISE ISLAND, BERMUDA

*"Earth has not anything to show more fair:
Dull would he be of soul who could pass by
A sight so touching in its majesty..."*
William Wordsworth

These words written by William Wordsworth as he stood on Westminster Bridge, London in 1802, clearly indicate that he had not travelled very far; certainly not as far as Bermuda!

Front Street, Hamilton, Bermuda, 1946

Paradise Island, Bermuda

Now that *Porlock Bay* was firmly established as the second ship of the new, post-war, America and West Indies Squadron, we could sit back for a while to take stock of the situation as far as it affected us individually. We were fully aware that ours was a two-and-a-half-year Commission during which time we would not be able to return home to see our loved ones. For Able Seaman Slack this thought was particularly hard as he had taken the opportunity of the last weekend's leave in England to get married and, after two days, he would have to leave his new wife for thirty months before he could resume his honeymoon. For the Hostilities Only ratings, our demob numbers indicated that it would be ages before we could collect our demob suits and take up or resume our proper careers. At the time, only those time-expired regulars, those who had served throughout the war and the Class 'B' ratings were being released. We contemplated our first day after joining at HMS *Royal Arthur*, Skegness, when we were told to fall in on the left if we intended to 'sign on' and on the right if we only wanted to join 'for the duration'. This was certainly not mentioned at our Bristol interviews and the result was that no one joined the left group as everyone considered that it was rather sharp practice to dangle the carrot of a Commission as almost promised by the 'Y' Scheme and then to renege on that loose agreement. One member of our group states that he remembers an offer being made for us to go home and await normal call-up at the age of eighteen which would probably mean going into another service or, worse still, go down the coal mines as a 'Bevin Boy'. Whatever the reason, we fell in on the right, establishing our position as 'Hostilities Only' ratings.

We were now in Bermuda, confined to a monastic sort of existence, deprived of the opportunity to enjoy the company of white women for the 'duration' or at least the major part of our time overseas. Several, including myself, had been at school right up to the moment of joining and, with a rigid school curriculum, we had not had time to see life in the normal way. We had in fact merely transferred from one rigid repressive, monastic life to another – plus ça change, rien ça change.

On the brighter side, we were stationed at perhaps the most envied overseas posting, at a place which had been, pre-war, a millionaires' paradise, although that in itself was little consolation to us on our Ordinary Seaman's pay of three shillings (fifteen pence) per day. The post-war tourism from the United States had not yet fully resumed but the shops in Hamilton, the capital, were there, gearing themselves up for the eventual hordes of wealthy customers and most of the prices were out of our reach.

Temptation to spend our pittance was partially removed by the fact that we were berthed in the admiralty dockyard which meant that we had to take a one-hour trip in an MFV to get into Hamilton to see the sights and discover some of the history of the place in the city library. At least also we were able to stay overnight at Aggie Westons', a former hotel which reverted years later to its original use. We were able to have a bed for the night there for one and six pence (seven and a half pence nowadays) with real sheets and with reasonable washing facilities, although we were constantly reminded of the need to conserve water. By staying out overnight we were able to return aboard after the first work session had finished which was a real bonus as otherwise we would have to fall in for work at 0545 hours.

Soon after our arrival in Bermuda a notice appeared on the board outside the Regulating Office giving news of one of the first batches of Class 'B' Releases. Included was one of our mates from the radar training days at HMS *Valkyrie* who had managed to 'work his ticket' so early in his Naval career. As part of the Government's programme for the redevelopment of our war-torn cities they had brought out a scheme for 'Class B Release' which meant that architects, builders and planners could jump the queue to get out of the Navy by applying and, provided their former employers had signified that they were required for work of National Importance, they could go. Mike Theiss had explained to me his job with an environmental town planner, Max Lock, and naturally, having an interest in architecture myself, I had listened to the work that he had been doing prior to joining up. Now, Mike after less than one year in the Andrew, was leaving to re-commence his career and we were stuck out in the America and West Indies Squadron for the next two-and-a-half years! C'est la vie!

On the islands, the majority of which were linked by bridges, we found that every building had a stepped roof which was painted white every year. This was to enable what little rain that fell to be conducted to underground tanks for drinking water, hence the vital need to conserve every drop. It seemed strange to us that there were no rivers or even streams from which water could be abstracted and any de-salinization process was in its infancy at least as far as the general public were concerned. Water was in such short supply that beer was our main beverage ashore (such a hardship!) although Coca Cola could be readily obtained from the Phoenix Drug Store, a prominent building on the corner of Queen Street and Reid Street if my memory serves me correctly. The term 'Drug Store' meant of course an American-style soda fountain, selling, inter alia, aspirin and very mild pain killers, and was certainly not associated with the sale of narcotics which, fifty years later, have become such a menace to the world.

On landing at Hamilton after the MFV trip, several of us would stroll up the gentle slope of Queen Street, stopping at the library or the Botanical Gardens which, sadly, no longer exist in that position. In the gardens we were attracted by what we thought was the sound of crickets but we later learnt that the bell-like sounds were caused by small tree frogs about the size of a man's thumbnail. The sound seemed even greater during and after rain, a phenomenon that was confirmed by the locals.

The whole of the city was explored fairly thoroughly in our first runs ashore and we had no problem finding our way about as the road system followed a largely regular grid iron pattern. However, a certain port of call was the services canteen along Front Street where the local ladies, bless them, served tea, cakes and soft drinks which were most welcome in the hot weather. There were not many bars serving alcoholic drinks although one particular establishment, the Ace of Clubs, with its Texan style bar doors, was frequented by many despite the high cost of its beer.

Just before leaving home after embarkation leave, I remembered to pick up my camera, not an expensive one but a Kodak Box Brownie that I had received for my tenth birthday. The cost of the camera had been five shillings and the camera case was one-and-six pence making a total of thirty-two and a half pence in today's currency. The cost of a film, normally Kodak Verichrome, seemed expensive to me although by present standards one-and-tuppence (six new pence) seems quite reasonable. Just coming on to the market was Anscochrome which gave colour transparencies but obviously such films were beyond my means and in any case, a more sophisticated camera would be required for colour photography. Few other ratings on board had a camera of any description and so, as my black and white efforts were processed, the prints did the rounds of the mess-deck and often copies were requested. These were not enlargements but just small contact prints which would certainly not be acceptable by folk today. My prints were then sent home at regular intervals where they were kept safely until my eventual return, having been shown by my proud parents to other members of the family.

Another item which is nowadays taken for granted was the possession of a watch. My only time-piece had been a Mickey Mouse pocket watch which would not have been appropriate with my seaman's uniform and which, to be fair, I had not even used at school in my later days there.

Accordingly, I had to manage without, replying on other chaps having one or merely relying on the sixth sense which one acquires over time to estimate when to return aboard. It never let me down!

If we were not on duty watch aboard, a walk ashore was often taken along the chain of islands linked by bridges as far as Somerset village or even beyond there, almost to the US Naval Base in Little Sound. Before being allowed ashore however, we had to be inspected by the Officer of the Day to ensure that we were properly dressed. Most of the time the correct rig of the day was 'tropical', consisting of white shorts (almost knee length) and white fronts, a form of vest with a square blue strip around the neck. Footwear had to be our new white shoes which had to be spotless, at least at the start of our run ashore, so blanco was often in great demand. Another more irksome feature of going ashore was the fact that we still had to wait for the liberty boat to be piped despite being secured alongside the jetty. This practice was universal in the Navy and, once the Officer of the Day had completed his inspection and the liberty boat had 'gone', it was necessary to wait for the next one if there was, indeed, a next one.

The walks commenced at the old ship but there was another obstacle to be faced before we were truly 'free'. This was the dockyard gate where the Regulating Officers (Petty Officers) held sway, sometimes sending men back if they spotted an irregularity in the uniform which had been missed by the ship's OD. The dockyard itself was situated on Ireland Island North and we proceeded via Ireland Island South where the fleet canteen was situated, a very basic building which was eventually destroyed by fire. Also, off the road on the left was a cemetery which we passed with hardly a glance but which, fifty years later, I was to visit to lay a wreath on the grave of a former shipmate. From here we proceeded via Boaz Island and Watford Island to Sandys where we had a look at Somerset village before crossing yet another bridge to Southampton Parish. This was usually as far as we went because we had to retrace our steps after already walking about five miles, stopping only to take photographs of our chums as and when we bumped into them. Unfortunately we rarely photographed views of the islands or the buildings as these would have provided an excellent record as at the mid-1940s. Anyway we can console ourselves with the thought that the single meniscus lens of a box camera would not have given the definition people require on photographs today. On the return it always seemed impossible to pass the canteen on Ireland Island South where 'Lion' Brand or Budweiser Beer was sold. The rest of the walk was much easier after that but it was necessary not to show the effect of the beer too much at the dockyard gate or when one returned on board and not to forget to retrieve one's station card before going below to 'crash one's swede' wherever it was possible or convenient. Despite the heat, many still slung their hammocks although others slept on the locker seats in the mess decks at least until simple camp beds were supplied from stores.

HMS Porlock Bay *arriving at Cornerbrook, Newfoundland*

Soon after our arrival in Bermuda, the Captain, Lieutenant Dudley Davenport, had lower deck cleared to talk to the ship's company. We assembled on the quarterdeck and, after the Coxswain, CPO Rhodes reported everyone present and correct, the Captain explained our future duties in the West Indies but dropped what seemed a bombshell when he told us that our first cruise was to be to the north, to Canada and Newfoundland, while our sister ship, HMS *Padstow Bay* would be sent to the Caribbean. We had just got used to our tropical kit and we would soon have to revert to 'blues' when we travelled north in the autumn and late autumn. Fortunately, we had recently received on board some boxes of comforts, including woollen socks, balaclavas and pullovers, knitted by the good ladies of Porlock, our adopted town. My mother sent out to me an RAF blue pullover and my old school scarf which were to be most welcome in the cold weather around Newfoundland.

The Captain also told us that the present Commander-in-Chief of the A & WI Squadron, Vice Admiral Sir Irvine G. Glennie K.C.B., would be leaving for home shortly and that he would be replaced by Vice Admiral Sir William Tennant K.C.B, C.B.E., M.V.O., R.N. The latter had an impressive war record, firstly as beachmaster in the Dunkirk evacuation and later as Captain of HMS *Repulse* when she made a foray into Malaysian waters in company with HMS *Prince of Wales* without air cover in December 1941 only to be sunk by Japanese aircraft.

As far as the Squadron was concerned, we were to be joined shortly by HMS *Sheffield*, the 'Shiny Sheff', which would become our flagship. *Sheffield* was perhaps the best known six-inch-cruiser of the war, serving with Force H in the Mediterranean and Atlantic, distinguishing herself in the sinking of the *Bismark* in May 1941. She was at the time completing a three week work up programme at Malta and, later, another six-inch-cruiser, HMS *Kenya* would also join us. *Kenya* had similarly served with distinction during the war, so we would have two battle hardened veterans serving with us although it was unlikely that many of their old ship's companies would still be involved in the present commission. Two sloops, HMS *Snipe* and HMS *Sparrow* would also arrive nearer Christmas time to complete the Squadron, and the boom defence vessel, HMS *Moorpout* was already 'on station'.

Lieutenant Davenport, not unnaturally, wanted a ship which would be a credit to the Squadron in every way, a statement which sounded quite ominous although he was a cheerful personality and already much respected by the Ship's Company. He had served throughout the war in destroyers mainly and had survived the sinking of two. He began the war as a sub-Lieutenant, the navigating officer in HMS *Blanche* which struck a magnetic mine in the Thames Estuary on 13th November 1939, apparently while he was in the bath! This was the first instance of a magnetic mine sinking a destroyer and thereafter there was a race against time to discover the secrets of such a weapon in order to provide a defence against them. Sub-Lieutenant Davenport suffered a fractured skull as a result but he recovered quickly and, in February 1940, he joined the tribal class destroyer HMS *Mashona* and served in her during the ill-fated Norwegian campaign. In May 1941 *Mashona* was also involved in the pursuit of the Germany battleship *Bismark* which sank HMS *Hood*, the battlecruiser, with the loss of all on board with the exception of only three survivors.

As she returned home after the sinking of *Bismark*, the *Mashona* was bombed by German aircraft and so badly damaged that she capsized, losing forty-six of her company. Her survivors were rescued by another 'tribal' destroyer, HMS *Somali*, and Lieutenant Davenport was pulled out of the sea by none other than Sub-Lieutenant Ludovic Kennedy who later became so well known as an author as well as by his appearances on television.

After survivors' leave, Lieutenant Davenport joined the Hunt class destroyer HMS *Hursley* as First Lieutenant and later joined another 'Hunt'; HMS *Tetcott*, in which he spent the next two years in a most eventful time, also as First Lieutenant. *Tetcott* was damaged in a collision with the corvette HMS *Heartsease* in December 1941 and, in June of the following year, she picked up seventy-nine survivors from her sister ship HMS *Grove* after her sinking by a U-boat. *Tetcott* then took part in an abortive convoy to Malta which had to return to Alexandria. In May 1943 she took part in an action to stop Axis forces evacuating from Tunisia to the European mainland and, two months later, she was present at the invasion of Sicily. Later she covered the allied landings at Anzio on the Italian mainland in January 1944.

Lieutenant Davenport was then appointed First Lieutenant of the new 'C' class destroyer HMS *Caesar* which escorted Russian convoys before he was given his first command, the frigate HMS *Cotton* and later HMS *Holmes*. Eventually, he was given command of our ship, HMS *Porlock Bay*, and stood by her until her commissioning at Charles Hill's yard in Bristol. In many ways he had a profound effect on the ship, one of which was to reject the badge approved by the Admiralty Committee, and introducing the design with which we became so familiar during our time in the ship and indeed afterwards. None of us was aware of the 'official' badge until I started making enquiries in 1976, thirty years later!

Despite his exemplary war record Lieutenant Davenport was not decorated but he was twice mentioned in despatches. He had always set an example to members of all the ship's companies he had served in no matter what demands were made of them during the war. In *Porlock Bay* he continued his service in the Royal Navy as a Senior Lieutenant although we understand informally that a Lieutenant Commander's uniform was already hanging up in his day cabin! He was the son of a Vice Admiral and he had entered the RN as a Dartmouth cadet in 1933, joining his first ship, the training cruiser HMS *Frobisher* and later serving in the battleship HMS *Malaya* at the time of the Spanish Civil War. Finally, before war broke out, he served as a midshipman in the battlecruiser HMS *Repulse* in operations off Palestine in 1938 where he was mentioned in despatches for the first time.

The Captain's second in command, the First Lieutenant, was an R.N.V.R. Lieutenant who appeared to be always looking for trouble, often in the form of shipboard items improperly stowed, and he lost no time in admonishing the PO of that particular part of the ship. He was Lieutenant Digby, a ginger-haired fellow with bushy, light ginger eyebrows which always seemed to go with his perpetual frown! No one ever saw him smile let alone laugh but at least he kept a tight reign on the running of the ship which by now had developed a name for smartness during his time aboard, from her commissioning to his departure later in the year for demob.

While in Bermuda, the day began at 0515 hours when the hands were called by the duty Bosun's Mate. Normally there was no initial response on the seaman's mess deck until the duty PO came round, hitting the hammocks with a stick as he passed, shouting at the same time, "Wakey, Wakey, Rise and Shine," followed by some obscene remarks. This at last evoked a reply in the form of the usual dawn chorus from many of the ratings, breaking wind as loudly as possible, each trying to out perform his neighbour in volume.

Eventually, with only about five minutes to go before the pipe, "hands fall in," at 0545 hours men fell out of their hammocks which then had to be lashed and stowed away before staggering up top. Here, we fell in, sloppily perhaps, by division; fo'c'sle, top and quarterdeck together with the torpedo men, to be counted by the appropriate Petty Officer who would then report to the First Lieutenant that we were all present and correct. At that unearthly time everyone felt so lethargic that, when called to attention, we merely shuffled our feet in a bare pretence of any form of drill. Lieutenant Digby would return the salute and give the order "Carry On"; Cooks of the Mess were allowed below to prepare breakfast and the remainder, after the gunner's party had departed, had to 'work part of ship'. This went on for an hour when we went below to wash and eat our breakfast, listening at the same time to Radio ZBM with their programme "Reveille with Beverley" (the first word being Americanised to 'Revellee' to rhyme with the presenter's name rather than the Anglicised 'Revally').

Life at times was monotonous in the extreme despite the fact that we were constantly discovering new compartments in the ship and we began to think of ourselves as 'sailors' even though the Active Service ratings thought otherwise. Everyone of course knew where the paint shop was as we went there almost daily. It was situated next to the cable locker and reached by going though the watchkeeper's mess deck. Here, we were given a pot of paint, a brush and a rag by a former able seaman who had only recently changed his rig from square rig to the peaked cap rig of a leading shipwright. 'Spud' Murphy reigned supreme in his own little compartment, mixing paint for the various parts of the ship which was an extremely light grey for much of the paint work and a much darker blue-grey for the tops of ventilation shafts and other covers on the upper deck. Spud himself was quite a craftsman and he alone painted the named ship's lifebelts and other 'tiddly' work.

It did seem unfortunate that ratings had to find out for themselves where other compartments were located rather than by looking at plans of the various decks as, in an emergency, it could have been most important to find their way around. Perhaps the majority had no real cause to know where, say, the Asdic compartment was situated or, for that matter, the 291 Radar Office, but it seemed surprising that after almost a year these places were still unknown to most.

In addition to this, it was surprising that we had little chance to practice Action Stations, remembering that although it was peacetime there could be occasions when we would be required to put into practice our knowledge gained in the training establishments. For the Radar Control ratings this was particularly important because several never touched another radar set after training as, instead, their job was to operate the gunnery control instruments. It seemed essential that there should be an inter-changeability to enable everyone to avoid going 'rusty'. In fact, we only went to Action Stations less than half a dozen times during the entire Commission and fortunately were not faced with a true emergency, either in the offensive or defensive capacity.

As a corollary to the proceeding paragraph, escort vessels during the war were required to carry out working-up routine at Tobermory on the Isle of Mull. This was done under the watchful eye of Vice Admiral Sir Gilbert Stephenson, otherwise known as the 'Terror of Tobermory' in a book written years later by Richard Baker, the television newscaster. Over a thousand uncoordinated groups of largely inexperienced HOs, such as ourselves, were subjected to the most rigorous training programme designed to make everyone aware of the need for vigilance and familiarity with their jobs. In the space of the incredibly short time of two weeks, ship's companies were welded into a well disciplined crew, competent to face the rigours of the U-boat war in the Atlantic. The experience was quite frightful at times as Stephenson did everything possible to test the efficiency of each ship, often appearing at night to catch out unsuspecting crews to ensure that, when the time came, they acted in the most appropriate way. Stephenson himself had been recalled after retirement as one of the Convoy Commodores but he became so unpopular with merchant ship's masters that he was taken off and placed in charge of training at Tobermory, a job to which he was very well suited! *Porlock Bay* was fortunate in one respect, in not having to encounter this resolute officer, but there were aspects of his work which would have been beneficial, particularly with regard to knowing every part of one's ship together with her weaponry.

The ship was working Tropical Routine in Bermuda, meaning an extremely early start followed by a 'make and mend' in the afternoon. However, the duty watch was often called upon to work in the afternoons and sometimes the standby watch would also be required. One 'perk' that we enjoyed was the fact that postage for mail home was free at first so many of us wrote letters every day even if it meant just a single sheet of notepaper. In harbour if one was not going ashore there was also an opportunity to use time beneficially by taking some form of academic study. Accordingly, the Chief OA, 'Ginger' Ridpath, who had been appointed acting schoolmaster, made some enquiries on my behalf for further language courses. It transpired however that these would take the form of correspondence courses up to school certificate standard, a level that I had reached three years previously. In fact, before I joined up, I had been working on university entrance papers and was already fairly fluent in French and German so the chance of progressing higher was slim indeed. Perhaps it would have been to my advantage to take up another discipline but at the time, having more free time to spend as I wished seemed more attractive, particularly as conditions on the lower deck were hardly conducive to serious study.

After a week or so of the humdrum life in the dockyard it was decided that the ship should enter the floating dock lying just ahead of us, known officially as Admiralty Floating Dock Number Five. We therefore eased ourselves into the dock and stages were prepared to enable the part of the ship below the waterline to be scrubbed as the water level went down. Everyone was involved so we swung over the side with a will, clad only in bathing trunks or old shorts, some with caps on, some without, to work under the hot sun scrubbing off all the accumulation of marine growth. After a while, first one and then another 'accidentally' fell off into the water until only the complete non-swimmers were left on the stages. We had not reckoned on the number of fish, some quite large, left in the dock but, in that heat, it was glorious to swim around, trying to keep our caps above water until the ship was quite high and dry.

Back aboard it seemed strange to carry on as normal with no sea directly around us but, until repair work to the Asdic dome had been completed together with other work to the hull, we had to carry on until the ship was able to float out once more.

HMS Porlock Bay *in floating dock*

One of the main drawbacks of life in Bermuda was the fact that the heads had to be closed for the entire time that we were in harbour. Just the two urinals were still available for use on board so it was necessary to take a walk ashore if we wanted to use the toilets – fortunately, we did not have to wait for the liberty-boat each time! These toilets, still referred to as heads despite being on land, were sited in the dockyard in two rows facing each other, enabling the ratings to carry on a conversation while defecating! Presumably, the officers had to go further into the clocktower building as it would only be assumed that their heads on board were likewise roped off to prevent their use.

The washing facilities were still in use although it was impressed upon us to exercise the greatest economy in that most precious of commodities, water. The builder's plans of the ship indicated showers in the ablutions compartment but, while the fittings may have been there, no one was ever able to use them. More shower fittings on the upper deck near to the motor cutter davits were also in place but never used. There were only two baths in the ship, one in the Captain's quarters and the other for the use of the officers so the only method for a rating to have a wash-down was to strip off in the ablution compartment, soap one's self down and then empty a bucket of water over one's self. This was not universally popular if other ratings were fully clothed, perhaps merely there to comb their hair in preparation for going ashore. Many of us used to wait until the end of the middle or first watch when, before turning in, we could have a swill down without annoying our shipmates. An alternative was the use of salt-water soap but this was never really successful and it was obviously preferable to swill off the salt before rubbing down. How we longed for a good old bath tub with plenty of hot water but we could only imagine this in our dreams.

For entertainment on board we had darts, although at times it was difficult to find a clear space on the mess deck for the 'oche' between the rows of hammocks. In fact, the 'oche' was only an arbitrary chalk line on the corticene deck anyway. 'Uckers', a form of ludo, was often a popular past time although, as there was only one board, this had to be shared among the messes. The most popular form of entertainment was undoubtedly Tombola which is known outside the Navy as Bingo or Housey Housey and this was the only form of gambling allowed. For this reason, a Tombola committee had to be set up to organise the events, some of which were held on the lower seaman's mess deck (ours!) or sometimes at sea sessions were held on the quarterdeck, weather permitting. Crib was played ad nauseam either by two or four ratings, with tournaments being held always on our mess deck and with the entire ship's company (or so it seemed) watching. Bearing in mind the fact that almost everyone smoked (after all, cigarettes cost seven pence or three pence in present currency for twenty) the air could be cut with a knife at the end of a major session, when a thick layer of smoke would form just about at the level our hammocks would occupy. The air was so foul that several of us used to find a 'billet' on the upper deck to avoid breathing in such filth. At that time neither those who smoked nor those who suffered from the secondary smoke were aware of the health hazard inherent in such conditions, which was probably just as well otherwise we would have been considered hypochondriacs. It certainly explained the abnormally high number of ratings suffering from respiratory disorders in the other zymotic wards of Stonehouse Hospital, Plymouth.

The comparative cheapness of cigarettes, freely obtained from the canteen, obviously encouraged ratings to smoke not only the cheap varieties such as Woodbines at six pence (two and a half new pence) for twenty but also Benson & Hedges, Churchmans and State Express, all of which came in metal cases stamped 'Duty Free, HM Ships Only'. At that canteen price no one took advantage of the tins of pusser's tobacco for rolling their own fags which could be bought for one-and-nine pence (eight present pence) or the pipe tobacco which was only one-and-six pence for a half pound tin. Ratings considered they were almost getting something for nothing and smoked themselves virtually to death to get their money's worth! The unhealthy conditions below decks were, however, an anathema to me and it has remained my most unpleasant memory of naval life.

Another diversion in Bermuda which only took place once was a spelling bee which was held in the wardroom and broadcast over the SRE to all parts of the ship. The teams consisted wholly of HOs who had tried out words such as schism, symbiosis and, my speciality of course, zymotic, on our shipmates beforehand. However, we were faced with much simpler words, making it too easy to get everything correct and making us appear quite brilliant to those listening on the mess decks. What they could not see was a sign which appeared above our heads which read, "BORED OF ADMIRALTY," thus effectively making our protest at our exile of two-and-a-half years, the duration of the Commission. Unfortunately, the message fell on stony ground!

Time passed by until, one fine day for those concerned, the sloop HMS *Ballinderry*, the last remaining vessel from the wartime America and West Indies Squadron, left for the UK and the demob of many of the ship's company. The other sloop, HMS *Wear* had already left for home soon after our arrival. In true Naval fashion, all ships in the dockyard cleared lower deck to cheer the fortunate ship as the old stager slowly made her way to the harbour entrance and thence away into the blue yonder, as Hollywood would say. It would be a long time yet for our departure although, as events turned out, not quite as long as we had anticipated.

Going below, and for everyone to see on the notice board, were the names of those released under Class B including Michael Theiss, Ordinary Seaman. Thoughts immediately went back to our *Valkyrie* days when Mike had joined me in hiring a bicycle for one shilling each and riding around the Isle of Man before returning to Douglas where we knocked back an unbelievable amount of Guinness. What a crafty blighter he must be to work his ticket like that! Alongside the notice board were framed copies of King's

Regulations and Admiralty Instructions (KRs and AIs) together with the antiquated Articles of War. The latter gave details of the dire punishments, which could be meted out to anyone, officers and ratings, who strayed from the straight and narrow. Despite the inappropriate penalties in the modern age, the Articles of War were still apparently to be cited by Admiral Pound with the threat of a Court Martial for Admiral Wake-Walker during the war. The relevant extract in this case reads as follows.

> "An Act for the better regulating of his Majesty's navies, ships of war and forces by sea, whereon under the good providence of God, the wealth, safety and strength of his kingdom do chiefly depend; be it enacted by the lords spiritual and temporal, and commons, in this present parliament assembled, and with the authority of the same, that from and after the twenty-fifth day of December One thousand Seven hundred and Forty-nine, the articles and orders hereinafter following, as well in time of peace as in time of war, shall be duly observed and put into execution, in manner hereafter mentioned...
>
> "Every flag-officer, captain and commander in the fleet who shall not...encourage their inferior officers and men to fight courageously, shall suffer death....
>
> "If any person in the fleet shall treacherously or cowardly yield or cry for quarter – being convicted thereof by the sentence of a court-martial, shall suffer death....
>
> "Every person who through cowardice, negligence or disaffection shall forbear to pursue any enemy, pirate, or rebel, beaten or flying...shall suffer death...."

Presumably, the same Articles of War applied to Byng who was tried and executed 'pour encourages les autres' so many years ago!

The antiquity of these Articles of War made me think of the dockyard in which we lived at the present time. Many of us had thought that Nelson had used Bermuda as his main base but, after visiting the City Library we soon found out that approval for the purchase of Ireland Island was only given in 1795 and the actual purchase was not completed until June 12th 1809, almost four years after Trafalgar. Since then, much of the construction work had been carried out by convicts brought out from the UK. Some of those serving in *Porlock Bay* in fact suggested that, with the rigid regulations which existed, we were the descendants of those convicts! However, as one wag put it, fifty-seven years later, the European Court would not allow convicts to be treated so badly!

The base was used extensively during the First World War, at the outbreak of which there were five heavy cruisers including HMS *Monmouth*, the flagship of Rear Admiral Sir Christopher Craddock, which was sunk in the battle of Coronel with the loss of the Commander-in-chief. Warships engaged in convoy work used the dockyard facilities and particularly in 1917, when the United States entered the war, many vessels called there for coal and stores.

Author waiting to go ashore

In 1939 there was another build-up of warships on the America and West Indies Squadron and these included HMS *Berwick* (flagship); HMS *York*; HMS *Orion*; HMS *Ajax*; HMS *Exeter*; HMS *Penzance*; HMS *Dundee* and the Royal Fleet Auxiliary *Orangeleaf*. As history reports, the battle of the River Plate was fought by ships of the Squadron resulting in the scuttling of the pocket battleship *Graf Spee* in December 1939. The remaining history of the base is too lengthy to record here but, now, we too were members of the Squadron and we knew that we had something to live up to.

The sun continued to beat down upon Bermuda during our first summer there and, on one particularly hot Sunday, we had to parade in our full white uniforms for 'Divisions'. Fortunately during our passage out I had managed to buy a second-hand Number Six suit from one of the continuous service ratings who had become too portly to wear it himself. The alternative to wearing a Number Six suit was to use one of the white duck uniforms which had been issued to us at HMS *Royal Arthur* where we spent our first two weeks in the Navy. These suits were off-white and lacked the blue strip around the sleeves and the bottom of the jumper. The only time that we had worn these suits was when we had taken the swimming test in them at HMS *Glendower*, our primary training establishment and we soon found that they were so stiff that they restricted movement. It was therefore essential to have a tailor made Number Six suit, or in my case, a second-hand one which fitted because the ones issued were of little or no practical use as I was to find out later. However, it was necessary to carry these two duck suits around with our kit even though we did not wear them.

My newly acquired Number Six suit also had a blue collar attached, unlike the issued canvas ones, thus obviating the need for separate collars which, as in our blue uniforms, tied around the waist. The Captain inspected the ship's company, clad in their white uniforms, and he seemed pleased with the result until he noticed that, instead of white socks, I had my blue issue ones. The slightest of breezes had blown the long white seamen's bell-bottom trousers to display the offending socks.

"Why are you wearing blue socks?" he asked.

"I was not issued with white ones, Sir," I replied, whereupon the Captain called to the Coxswain.

"See that this rating gets some white socks in the next issue of 'slops'." That was the end of the matter as far as the Captain was concerned – I was not in the rattle but I had to pay for two pairs of white socks out of my KUA (Kit Upkeep Allowance) despite the fact that I, like all the others, had never been issued with any in the first place. The KUA, incidentally was six pence per day to pay for all replacement kit, an amount that was far from generous when it was considered that my new Number Six suit had to be paid for out of it. Additionally, while we were issued with two pairs of boots initially, black shoes had to be worn after training although it was necessary to keep the boots for use if one was going on shore patrol or if one happened to be a member of the guard. As a further complication, white shoes had to be worn in tropical stations but these were provided, unlike the white socks, when being kitted out for overseas duties. Kit Upkeep Allowance meant, therefore, more than the replacement of worn out items – one had to buy new items with it whenever required to do so out of pitifully low pay. At present this was still three shillings (fifteen pence) per day, but we just had to smile and accept the situation.

While still on the subject of pay, we attended a pay parade at fortnightly intervals to receive, at best, two pounds nine shillings including KUA. However, there were often 'north-easters' when money was deducted for some reason or other – such as the cost of white socks! Pay parades took place normally on the quarterdeck where we were called forward, one at a time before the paying officer to state one's official number and to place one's cap on the table. The money, in Bermudan dollars now, would be counted and put on the top of the cap. To avoid any currency notes being blown away it was often necessary to bring one's right hand down heavily, often catching the hand of the officer before he could take it away!

The resultant pay was so low that ratings were very pleased to accept hospitality from people ashore in the form of invitations to their homes or to provide transport for sightseeing which would otherwise be impossible. This was often jokingly referred to as 'Baron Strangling' but here in Bermuda the comparatively small number of indigenous people compared to the large numbers of naval personnel made the 'sport' almost impossible. Accordingly, we had to restrict our activities to going for walks in our precious free time or to catching the (free) MFV into Hamilton and getting cheap accommodation for the night at 'Aggie's'. Many years later we were to realise how fortunate we were to have been allocated to Bermuda and the America and West Indies Squadron although, at the time, we often bemoaned our lot.

By comparison, the pay of our equivalent rates in the United States Navy was almost astronomical and, because of the disparity, it seemed likely that there would be friction between us. Surprisingly, perhaps, no fights ensued anywhere where we encountered their servicemen. On the contrary, the Americans were most generous, as they obviously understood our financial predicament. Alastair Mars, a wartime Submarine Commander drew attention to the disgraceful rates of pay in the RN in his book *British Submarines at War 1939–1945* by reminding readers that unskilled workmen in the Dockyards were paid approximately five times as much as the submarine ratings including their additional allowance. He cited an AB Torpedo-man as receiving about ten shillings per day but, if he should be killed or lost at sea, his family would receive only one third of that amount in pension. Sixty years later, we can perhaps reflect upon the vast amounts awarded in the Courts as compensation for accidents or injuries but then… the British Serviceman had always been treated abominably.

Gunners' Party Members Taff Davies and Bull Reece

After quite a short time in Bermuda several of us found out that, having served in the Andrew for more than a year, we were entitled to apply to be rated as Acting Able Seamen, a promotion indeed, entailing an increase in our daily pay of one shilling. This seemed a significant increase which would enable us to enjoy our surroundings even more. As far as the Active Service ratings were concerned we were still only 'acting' and we had a long way to go before the rank could be confirmed! There were one or two of the older ratings who undertook haircutting or dhobeying in their spare time to supplement their income but the charges had to be agreed beforehand with the coxswain and, as no great fortunes were made this way, it seemed a poor way to spend one's little free time.

Other money saving ruses were tried by some of the older ratings, including growing a beard to avoid buying razor blades. It was necessary to apply for permission 'to grow' and it was fortunate that we did not have a pognophobic Captain because all applications were granted. Some luxurious growths were forthcoming, really suiting their owners, while other attempts were not as successful. Probably the best beards were grown by the GI, Petty Officer Bill Scurfield, and the PO Telegraphist, Petty Officer Bob Steane who both retained them throughout the Commission. The majority managed to retain the clean shaven look although at sea it was not necessary or even advisable to shave and most developed stubble until we entered harbour. One notable exception was the Captain's servant or 'flunky', Able Seaman Jock Cruickshanks who could be seen every morning in the ablutions compartment shaving with a cut-throat razor whatever the weather and irrespective of the movement of the ship during a storm. His service was exemplary although he did make one serious error of judgement as we will see later when our next Captain took over command!

Our balmy days in Bermuda were now coming to an end and so, with my increased pay, I was able to go into Hamilton for the last time before we set sail for Canadian waters, to buy some tinned food to send home to my parents in a parcel, sewn up in a piece of spare canvas with the aid of sailmaker's palm. We had to pay postage for parcels such as these of course but, in view of the continuing food shortages at home, we knew that the contents would be most welcome. Another thing that I bought for my mother was a pair of nylon stockings which were still unobtainable in the shops at home but plentiful where we were. Thinking that it served my former girlfriend right for rejecting me, I sent the nylons in a packet on which it was necessary to fill in details of the contents on a green label, addressed to my

HMS Porlock Bay *from mast*

mother. Unfortunately, as it turned out, an unscrupulous thief read the label and removed the contents before the package arrived at home. Several times after that my mother received ordinary envelopes without a customs declaration but with a letter which contained a single nylon stocking, saving postage at the same time. She knew that the other one would follow in the next post.

On the day that we were due to sail north, the Commander-in-Chief, Vice Admiral Sir Irvine Glennie, came aboard for a formal inspection and, after all the spit and polish, he gave a satisfactory report. This was one of his last duties before handing over to Vice Admiral Sir William Tennant, allowing him to return home soon after. The ship then sailed in the afternoon on a cruise lasting until mid-November when we would return to spend Christmas in Bermuda.

7

FIRST CRUISE – NEWFOUNDLAND AND CANADA

*"For this relief much thanks. 'Tis bitter cold,
And I am sick at heart."*
***Hamlet*, by William Shakespeare**

Having only recently arrived in Bermuda in their hot season, we were now being sent to the North Atlantic to visit Newfoundland and Canada to enjoy their autumn weather. The tropical kit with which we had been issued, or otherwise, had to be stowed away in our fast bulging lockers and, for the journey north, sea rig was once again de rigueur as we steamed on at about ten knots to St Johns, the capital of Newfoundland.

Sea mists were a general hazard at that time of the year but, thankfully, our Radar assisted greatly as we passed Signal Hill at the entrance to St John's harbour. Tony Lander, the PO Radar Mechanic was constantly required to check the calibration of the 293 set by Lieutenant Tetley, the Navigator, before we finally squeezed in and secured to the wooden jetty where we would stay for the ensuing week. Obviously, we had heard of the great part played by the people of Newfoundland in the Battle of the Atlantic and now we were experiencing for ourselves the harbour in which many of the wartime convoys assembled to run the gauntlet of the U-boats and surface raiders on their way to the old country.

By this time all ratings were wearing blue uniforms again, and Humprey Ixer and I, clad in our Number Ones, were among the first to go ashore for a look at the city. Literally as we stepped off the brow we were hailed by a middle-aged couple who asked if we would like to go home with them to enjoy a cup of English tea. So soon after arriving, here we were with a couple of up-homers who, it turned out, made quite a habit of greeting every RN and RCN warship although we were not to know that until later. Only too pleased to accept, we walked with the newly self-introduced Fred and Ethel Cotton through the city, having various sites pointed out to us. Eventually, we arrived at their well-appointed flat where their daughter, Mabel, was waiting, kettle almost boiling, to make a proper cup of tea for us. The hospitality of this working class family who must have entertained dozens of matelots before us was truly wonderful.

HMS Porlock Bay *at anchor*

After tea and cakes we signed their visitor's book which was almost full with the names of RN and RCN seamen who had called at St John's on wartime convoy duty. We also posed for two photographs taken with a box camera lodged on the sideboard, having been told to sit very still for the six-second exposure. We learned that Fred had been born in Northampton where he was involved in the shoe-making trade until he emigrated. Ethel on the other hand was born and bred in Newfy, as we always called the place. What a start to the cruise to find this marvellous couple who told us to regard their home as ours while we were there. On returning aboard later we found that several of our crew had enjoyed similar experiences in what was, then, an independent colony.

The most surprising discovery we made in Newfoundland was that mail postmarked only thirty-six hours earlier was already in our hands, thanks to the proximity of Gander Airport. Communications with the UK had always been excellent, partly due perhaps to the fact that Guglielmo Marconi had received the first trans-Atlantic wireless signal at the appropriately named Signal Hill in 1901 and, another 'first', when Alcock and Brown took off from Lester's Field in 1919 to make the flight across the ocean but ended up in an Irish bog! In our case the mail had arrived by ordinary delivery making us feel that we were not so far from home after all.

On the Sunday, the ship arranged a church parade in which about eighty ratings participated, in their full Number Ones of course. The march from the waterfront to the Anglican Cathedral of St John the Baptist took approximately twenty minutes, watched all the way by the local populace, and the cathedral constructed in the North American Gothic style was completely full for the service. Our up-homers, Fred and Ethel Cotton, together with Mabel, also attended and afterwards, Humphrey and I were invited back to their flat for a meal. What a change from the ghastly triangular-section sausages out of a tin which both looked and tasted like saw dust, accompanied by tinned peas and carrots; our regular meal on board!

Ethel wrote to my parents enclosing a print from the photograph taken in the flat and we corresponded regularly after that for the next forty-five years until she sadly died at the age of eighty-nine. After the death of Fred, Mabel apparently took annual trips to Ontario, Canada to meet relatives and, even now, I still write to Mabel as the sole survivor of that wonderful family.

We had spent seven happy days in St Johns but all good things have to come to an end as we left on the fourth of September to travel the short distance to Argentia, watched by the several local inhabitants who had 'adopted' members of the ship's company, including the Cottons. During the war a net was stretched across the entrance to the harbour to prevent U-boats from entering but naturally that was no longer the case. However, many of the convoys were observed as they left the secluded harbour and so the escort vessels of the day were required to be fully alert from the start. Happily we had no adversary waiting for us other than the sea, always lively at that time of year.

Argentia in Placentia Bay had become the United States' Naval base in Newfoundland, forming another assembly point for many of the transatlantic convoys particularly after Germany declared war on the US, soon after the bombing of Pearl Harbour by Japanese aircraft. The original settlement was a small fishing village, now completely overshadowed by the great administrative and stores buildings of the US Navy. It was here that we were to pick up the recently appointed Governor of Newfoundland, Sir Gordon MacDonald, K.C.M.G., to take him on a tour of his island, visiting many of the small communities which were often inaccessible except by sea. Before he came aboard, one or two of us took a walk through the base and, while passing one building, were accosted by a signalman from one of the upstairs windows and invited to see the communications office. Up there, we were provided with coffee from a machine and shown the teleprinter which was just printing the 'ball-game' (presumably baseball) results as we compared notes as to life in our respective services. What a difference! At that time, none of us had even seen a teleprinter so it was quite enlightening to be given a demonstration of its capabilities. When we were due to leave, the signalman phoned his MT Section and a jeep was provided to take us on a tour of the base before returning us in style to the ship. With films often depicting acrimony between our two navies and often resulting in a brawl, it *was* pleasant to find the Americans were so similar to us, albeit with more money in their pockets!

Placentia Bay was of course the place where Winston Churchill met President Roosevelt aboard the US Cruiser *Augusta* for the Atlantic Charter discussions. Churchill had travelled in rough seas in HMS *Prince of Wales* for this historic meeting which would form the basis for the future military activities of the two nations. With that in mind it seemed incredible that, in four months' time the *Prince of Wales* would be sunk by Japanese aircraft off Malaya in company with the battle cruiser HMS *Repulse*. We were told about that action by leading seaman 'Nat' Millard who survived after being rescued by one of our destroyers, HMS *Electra*. Nat, whose full name was Nathaniel Beresford Millard was a little embarrassed by his Christian names and it was not until he joined the *Porlock Bay* Association many years later that we learned what N.B., his initials, stood for!

His Excellency the Governor duly came aboard *Porlock Bay* and was given the Captain's day cabin while Lieutenant Davenport had to manage in his tiny sea cabin, just forward of the wheelhouse, for the duration of the tour. Sir Gordon had been appointed the sixty-third Governor by Prime Minister Clement Attlee following his landslide victory in July 1945 and this was to be his first opportunity to visit the many 'outposts' of the island. He had been born on 27th May 1888 in Gwaenysgor, an almost unpronounceable name belonging to a small hamlet near Prestatyn, North Wales. He had left school at the early age of thirteen to work in the mines at the Bryn Hall Colliery, Bamfurlong, where he earned ten shillings for a six-day, fifty-four hour week – even worse than a matelot, although it should be remembered that the year was 1901, the year Queen Victoria died.

Early in his career, the young Gordon became interested in Union activities, together with the Labour movement. As a result of his political interests he was selected for further education at Ruskin Hall, Oxford. He served on the National Executive of the Mining Federation of Great Britain during the 1921 strike after which he became a miner's agent for Skelmersdale and St Helens before being selected as a parliamentary candidate. He was returned with a majority of almost 17,000 to serve as an MP where he remained until 1942 when he accepted the post of Regional Controller for Lancashire, Cheshire and North Wales.

The post of Governor of Newfoundland followed in March 1946 which, in his terms of reference, included the job of persuading the local politicians to merge the colony with Canada. This was accomplished eventually in 1949, well after our time with the Squadron, but no doubt he spent much of his time with us paving the way towards this objective.

Porlock Bay sailed with His Excellency aboard from Placentia Bay on 6th September so we took a last look at the twin peaks in the distance, known to the American servicemen as 'Mae Wests' before setting off. Our original itinerary included visits to as many as three settlements in one day, several of them with French sounding names. We were to visit fifteen small fishing villages including Harbour Buffett; Burin; Grand Bank; Belle Oram; St Jacques; English Harbour; Harbour Breton; Gaultois; St Albans; Rencontre West; Ramea; Burgeo; Rose Blanche; and Port aux Basques before returning to Halifax, Nova Scotia, to refuel. However it was necessary to curtail the visits because the Governor had to return suddenly to St Johns for urgent talks with the Government.

One feature of the Governor's tour was the number of local people who came aboard while His Excellency was ashore, talking to the civic heads. Mostly they came out to where we had anchored in small boats but it seemed that the entire population wanted to look us over. The locals had probably never seen a warship before; perhaps we were the largest ship of any type, and they put a variety of questions to us, some rather naive. One particular lady wanted to know whether 'X' gun was the engine room!

We had 'borrowed' a motor cutter from the US Navy in temporary replacement for our own which was damaged and so we were able to return this somewhat ungainly object when we returned to Argentia to drop off the Governor. After taking our leave of him we continued with the pre-arranged visits to Lewisporte, Twillingate and St Anthony before reaching what was the highlight of the tour, Cornerbrook. Here we secured to the wooden jetty belonging to the Bowater Corporation, alongside piles of timber awaiting pulping for paper manufacture. On going ashore we discovered that virtually all the US servicemen stationed there had been sent to the interior of the island to search for the wreckage of an aircraft which had crashed in a densely wooded area. As they were away during the entire time we were in Cornerbrook, we had almost sole use of their canteen facilities in the form of a USO which provided unbelievably good food, together with a band that provided music for dancing. What was of even greater importance to the sex-starved matelots was the fact that there were hordes of girls who did not seem to be missing the US chaps! For me, however, it was only the second occasion when I had been in a dance hall and so, being a complete non-dancer, I had to remain a 'wallflower', although just to talk to a female seemed wonderful.

With all the temptation at the USO it was only to be expected that romances would result including one involving a two-badge Able Seaman on my mess and an attractive blonde. He confided in me that, while he had a wife back home, he was really head-over-heels in love with her and therefore wanted me to give him advice on getting a divorce. As an eighteen-year-old it seemed ironic that he wanted to discuss the legal requirements for a divorce with me, so it was necessary to pretend that my knowledge of such matters was sufficient to give him counselling. It was a truly ludicrous situation to be in but, after an hour of serious discussion, he seemed convinced that his never-ending love was mere infatuation after so long at sea without the company of women. A week later he had forgotten all about her! There were, however, several occasions later when I would have to do the Dutch Uncle act again.

The time came for us to leave Cornerbrook and it was snowing quite heavily as we slipped. After about only a hundred yards, the engines stopped, leaving us somewhat mystified on deck until an announcement was made over the SRE to the effect that we were returning to our original berth that we had just left. Many could not resist a cheer, heard no doubt by the girls waving goodbye on the jetty who would have our company for a further evening. The engine room department would not be able to join us as they would have to work increasingly hard until the fault had been rectified but we were alright, Jack! Yet another excellent, albeit unexpected, evening was spent in the USO building with entertainment hastily arranged for us.

Throughout the cruise in Newfoundland waters we were able to ditch the gash overboard via the rectangular section chutes placed over the side rather than having to take it to bins ashore. The word 'chute', usually preceded with an alliterative adjective, meant so much labour saving to the cooks of the messes but quite often items of cutlery went down with the washing-up water. Apparently, chaps on other ships, when they heard clanking of cutlery, sang the words to the tune of twinkle, twinkle, little star, as follows:

> "twinkle, twinkle, little spoon,
> knife and fork will follow soon."

It was different on *Porlock Bay* where such a sound was followed by a flow of bad language at the thought of having to pay for new mess traps out of our meagre pay.

During the Governor's tour we experienced some fairly rough weather, normal at this time of year. The seas seemed quite steep to us although conditions could not have been comparable with those existing when HMS *Roxborough* (a former US four stacker destroyer received under the same agreement when bases in the West Indies were exchanged for them) sailed with convoy HX222 during the war. On this journey *Roxborough* met such heavy seas that the entire bridge structure was stoved in, leaving eleven dead or washed overboard and several injured. The dead included both the Captain and the First Lieutenant but the destroyer managed eventually to reach England. It seemed bad enough for us because in such seas it was almost impossible to have proper hot meals and 'pot mess' had to suffice. Everything went into a large pot; meat, vegetables and potatoes were boiled up together with the result that we had a hot meal of sorts; similar, some said, to Irish stew but not by many!

Bridge look-out duty was not looked upon with any enthusiasm as the spray was constantly coming over. Sea-boats crew duties were probably the best in those conditions, the time being mainly spent in the passage leading to the galley enabling us to lean against the funnel uptake, hoping that it would not be necessary to call out the sea boat. Why had we, the Radar

Control ratings, not taken the Radar Plot course, which would mean that our place would be in the day Radar Office? Too late now although later in the Commission, two of us would get the chance to operate the 293 set but this would be in the tropics where we would prefer bridge look-out duties in the balmy fresh air. Such was fate.

HMS Porlock Bay, *Newfoundland*

One compensation for look-outs was the sight of the Aurora Borealis which lit up the sky with the most wonderful colours as we went around Newfoundland. The phenomenon was so beautiful that our attention often wavered as we watched the ethereal effect, changing colour constantly and presenting a most awe-inspiring spectacle. Admittedly, it is possible sometimes to see the Aurora Borealis in Britain but never the sustained show that we experienced in those northerly seas.

One amusing incident occurred while the Governor was aboard when, on one particular evening, that incorrigible hellion, Bungy Williams, divested himself of his overalls and started putting on his Number Ones. We were at sea at the time with no possibility of going ashore so his messmates asked him where he was going.

"To see the Governor," was his simple reply, but rather obviously no one believed his explanation. Eyes were on him as he adjusted his lanyard in true pusser style and the mystery intensified as he put his cap on at a most correct angle. Then, slowly, he climbed the ladder up through the mess deck hatch, and proceeded towards the Captain's day cabin followed by several of his incredulous messmates. At the sliding door, he knocked politely and entered the cabin out of sight of those watching.

"He's really done it this time," were the thoughts of everyone present but time went by and Bungy had not re-emerged after about half an hour. We couldn't guess what was happening but apparently Gordon MacDonald, the Governor, had lodged with Bungy's mother and the family many years previously and had particularly asked to see the most unruly member of the ship's company. His Excellency was a strict teetotaller so Bungy was not able to have an alcoholic drink with him but they were able to chat about old times over numerous cups of coffee, provided by the Captain's steward. The interview did not result in Bungy signing the pledge, sad to relate, and he soon slipped back into his old drinking habits at the first opportunity ashore.

From Corner Brook we proceeded towards the St Lawrence estuary passing Anticosti Island to starboard while watching whale spouts blown by those huge majestic creatures of the sea. Port Alfred along the Saguenay River, a tributary of the St Lawrence, was our next port of call where we secured at another wooden jetty unaided by anyone ashore. When we first arrived, we looked down on the jetty but this was to change dramatically during the night. As standby or non-duty part of the watch I had turned into my hammock, hoping to have an entire night's sleep when the Bosun's Mate woke me up with a very obvious feeling of urgency. Apparently, the rise and fall of the tide in that area was perhaps the highest in the world and, when we clambered up on deck we realised the ship was drifting mid-stream. The Officer of the Day, alerted by the Quartermaster, had ordered the ropes and hawsers securing us alongside to be slipped as a matter of urgency. If he had not done so, as the water level went down, the wires would have snapped as they were secured to bollards on the jetty high above us now. It was necessary to lower the motor cutter to take lines ashore and secure the ship once more to the jetty, an operation that took quite a time. After that a continual watch was kept on the wires, slackening them off or tightening them as necessary.

We were now truly in the French part of Canada and all notices were in that language, rather than English. One courtesy trip ashore took us to another wood pulp mill where we were able to see the stripped logs go in at one end and emerge as newsprint at the other. Further trips included visits to Chicoutimi, Jonquiere and Arvida but these could only be taken by ratings in the other part of the watch while the rest of us remained aboard.

Our next port of call where the ship stayed for five days was Quebec, the capital city of the province of that name and another place where French was the main language. Here we would be able to take a forty-eight-hour leave as a welcome respite from the almost continuous duties of the last six weeks. With so little time spent ashore other than in Cornerbrook, Humphrey Ixer and I decided that, with our accumulated pay, we would do things in style and go to the impressive hotel, the Chateau Frontenac. Still in uniform but with no luggage, we climbed the steps and went into the foyer to make enquiries as to the cost of staying there. The receptionist at the desk soon brought us down to earth when she told us that our entire six weeks' pay would not be sufficient to cover a stay of two nights' bed and breakfast. Feeling duly humiliated, we had to settle for two nights' accommodation at the YMCA near the City Gate. We reflected on the luxurious conditions we would have experienced in the Chateau, even stuck up in one of the turrets, but as we had to cut our cloth according to our means, two nights in the wonderful hotel were out of the question.

The YMCA was quite another matter as far as luxury was concerned. On the first floor was a dormitory with about a dozen beds but with no form of heating whatsoever. Outside, it was snowing slightly as about half the hostel's inmates for the night got into bed to sleep only fitfully until, one by one, we got out to put our shoes and socks back on, as well as wrapping ourselves in our overcoats before getting under the covers once more. It was really freezing and how we wished we had our hammocks with us. After a while the other inmates arrived after having a skinful of beer making it completely impossible to sleep as they switched on lights and, in their drunken state, discussed the evening's entertainment. Anyway, what could one expect for half a dollar per night ... the Chateau Frontenac?

The weather had improved by the following morning and so several of us set off early to explore the place. Quebec stands on a promontory at the confluence of the St Charles and St Lawrence rivers with an area between known as the Plains or the Heights of Abraham. It was here in 1759 that a British military force under the command of thirty-two-year-old Major General James Wolfe, assisted by a naval force commanded by Vice-Admiral Sir Charles Saunder, landed troops at a spot called the Anse de Toulon to scale the highland and to face the superior forces of the French led by Montcalm. The result had been a victory for the British but at great cost, for the British Commander, Wolfe, had been killed and, on the French side, Montcalm had been fatally wounded. Wolfe is alleged to have recited the work by Thomas Gray, *Elegy Written in a Country Churchyard*, always known as Gray's Elegy, before the battle but although some of us knew the poem, we were completely unaware that Wolfe had found comfort in it before attacking the French. He is also supposed to have commented that he would rather have written the elegy than take Quebec as he died. What a difference there would have been on the North American continent if Wolfe had achieved that ambition! Many years later, memorabilia of Wolfe was found in a house in Warwickshire, Harwoods' House, which increased my interest in his exploits.

The remainder of the city also had much to offer tourists, including ourselves. An area known as 'sous les toits' was particularly charming – why had I forgotten my old box camera!? In the city while we were looking in a shop window at a model destroyer, a lady emerged to engage us in conversation before inviting us to her home for lunch. First our host had to phone her housekeeper to warn her to prepare a meal for two extra persons after which we were taken on a tour of the city with all the important sights being pointed out to us. At the lady's house we enjoyed a wonderful lunch, eaten with silver cutlery, surrounded by objets d'art which must have cost a fortune. Words could hardly express our appreciation of the hospitality shown to us but, as all things must come to an end, we had to bid our hostess au revoir before returning aboard to continue our Spartan existence that we would have to endure until our next short leave which would be in another eight months' time, in Trinidad. Back on the mess deck we naturally compared notes to find that most had enjoyed excellent hospitality in Quebec with perhaps our experience the most pleasurable. My luck had obviously changed, or had it? Several had fallen foul of the local bylaws which required anyone drinking to remain seated but fortunately they were merely given a warning. All agreed, however, that the French language predominated among the locals, of whom there seemed to be some, while being able to speak English, nevertheless insisted on talking solely in French. The controversy continues to the present day to the extent that in the remainder of Canada, all signs must be in the two languages, and even words such as café and restaurant must be duplicated to pacify the French Canadians.

So we left the fascinating city of Quebec on our way down the St Lawrence to Charlottetown, the capital of the small province of Prince Edward Island. PEI, by which it is often known, is easily the smallest province of Canada, being only about 140 miles long with a maximum width of forty miles but we were only able to see the immediate area around the capital. We were not even able to see 'Green Gables', where Ann lived. We did manage to see Victoria Park where Fort Edward overlooks the harbour with its gun barrels pointing in that direction to ward off any possible attack from the St Lawrence. The fort was one of a series of fortifications constructed along the harbour entrance and its six-canon battery is still in good condition after all the years. The battery was the subject of one of my photographs but, unfortunately, by the time we arrived there the weather had closed in too much for a box camera loaded with a relatively slow film by today's standards.

Sydney on Cape Breton Island, forming part of Nova Scotia, was our next port of call but no one was around to secure the ship to the jetty. Some of our own fellows managed to jump ashore and do the necessary before it was discovered that we were in the wrong berth. Sydney had been the departure point for many of the wartime slow convoys but the port was not so active in the immediate post-war period. The port had the distinction of being the most easterly point at the start of the trans-Canadian road route although later, when Newfoundland ceased to be a colony and became one of the provinces, that distinction went to St Johns, Newfy. Another factor, unknown at the time, was that Cape Breton Island was the landing point of Cabot in his new world explorations.

As one of our duties was riot control in the more unruly colonies, we had an exercise in which one of the leading hands, leading Seaman Davies, had a bayonet stuck in his arm, fortunately without serious complication. At least we made the exercise appear realistic and Davies was soon patched up.

The weather had worsened somewhat for the journey back to Halifax where we were to say goodbye to some of the 'Hostilities Only' ratings and officers whose demob group had at last arrived. *Porlock Bay* secured alongside a Canadian minesweeper which in turn was lying immediately astern of the vast shape of the SS *Aquitania*, still painted grey and still on duty transporting Canadian troops back home and our own chaps back to the UK. In addition, there were also many former U-Boat crews going back to England after captivity in POW camps in Canada, including Otto Kretschmer, although, in the case of the last mentioned, he would be travelling back for de-Nazification. Kretschmer, perhaps the greatest U-Boat Commander in the Second World War, had to spend many months in England before being allowed back to Germany.

A few new crew members for *Porlock Bay* had travelled out in *Aquitania* and joined the ship as soon as we secured. These were mainly continuous service ratings who were to replace the HOs going home. Whether the mail from home arrived in *Aquitania* we did not know but anyway there was a considerable amount of it. In my case there was a parcel containing a cake to celebrate my birthday the previous month, made by my mother from the precious ingredients which were still rationed and which meant quite a sacrifice on the part of my parents. On numerous times I had told them not to use their rations so, but every few months a parcel would arrive for me. Opening a parcel on the mess deck could never be done in private as everyone wanted to know its contents and it would have been selfish, indeed churlish, to keep a cake to myself without offering it around. It disappeared very quickly, devoured by every member of Number Five mess.

Yet another parcel from home was handed to me but this did not contain food. The entire mess was looking on anxiously as the parcel was unwrapped to reveal ... a cookery book, sent by an aunt who had heard about canteen messing and the requirement to prepare all our own meals. There were many jocular remarks from the lads who were obviously hoping for some juicy reading material, perhaps even pornographic and my present was a great disappointment to them.

In addition to the parcels were letters giving news from home. Two of mine contained general news of Warwick but the third carried very disturbing news. This was a report of the death of a favourite aunt who had suffered a brain haemorrhage at her tennis club, who had been taken to hospital but had died without gaining consciousness. Her son, his wife and family, were in Alexandria, Egypt where he was serving in the Surveyor of Lands Department of the Admiralty and, as such, were unable to return home to deal

No 5 Mess plus Torpedo Ratings' Mess

with the funeral arrangements. Responsibility for the funeral therefore rested with my parents who had to obtain Power of Attorney to deal with the matter despite both being particularly busy at the time. Dealing with the matter also involved going to my aunt's flat to get everything out and put into storage to await her son's return from Egypt. Quite a headache for them.

The funeral had already taken place before I received their notification and the feeling of helplessness hit me as I realised that I had not been able to help them. In a far greater way it affected my cousin who had only recently returned from a visit to the Gaza Strip where he had just seen his father's grave for the first time. His father had been serving as a Second Lieutenant in the Royal Warwickshire Regiment and had been a liaison officer in Palestine, and had been killed on his birthday, 5th November 1917.

The date of my uncle's death was just a month earlier than the date of a very major event in the history of Halifax where we found ourselves. This was the terrific explosion which had occurred on 6th December 1917 when an ammunitions ship collided with another vessel in the harbour. The explosion had resulted in 2,000 fatalities and 10,000 injured with 25,000 inhabitants left homeless in the city. The shockwave had apparently been felt as far as sixty miles away. Halifax had indeed had more than its fair share of tragedy to record because in Fairview, a suburb of the city, are buried many of the bodies recovered from the sea following the Titanic disaster of 1912.

Captured U-boat, Halifax, Nova Scotia

When we were in Halifax it seemed that the city was still only just recovering after the massive explosion twenty-nine years earlier. It was known as the Grey City with the mainly wood-cladded buildings presenting a sombre appearance, a state which was to continue apparently until the 1960s when considerable redevelopment took place. There were no large shops, similar to Plymouth, where one could buy any 'rabbits' and for me it was disappointing checking the watchmaker's shop only to find the cost of time-pieces was still way beyond my financial means.

One rating, Able Seaman Jack Bickerton, had the good fortune to receive quite a considerable amount of back pay while in Halifax, but, on going ashore to celebrate, was mugged in his inebriated condition and lost most of his money. This was very much an isolated incident which the majority of us did not experience.

Several of us went for a walk along the harbour area where secured alongside was a captured U-boat, the U190, which, according to records, was later towed out to sea and scuttled. What a waste of a potential tourist attraction when one considers that the U534 was raised off the seabed off Denmark and is now a major attraction at Birkenhead, albeit in a rusty condition. Furthermore, it represented a great waste of good re-usable material but so many of the U-boats ended their days in that fashion. Fifty years later in fact, consideration was given to the raising of some of those scuttled in the North Atlantic after surrendering in Northern Ireland, in view of the potential scrap value of their hulls.

'Sea Boat's Crew' in the ship's dinghy

It was whilst lying alongside the Canadian minesweeper in Halifax that a local photographer came aboard to take a shot of the ship's company before the lucky devils who were going home for demob left the ship. It is interesting to see how we had to bunch up on the Quarterdeck, squeezing in between the depth charge throwers, for the photograph which obviously had to be taken with a wide-angle lens. In the centre of the photograph the ship's badge is being held by Able Seaman Taff Thomas and it was this print which I used later to convince the museum authorities in Devonport that we were never aware of the 'oak tree' badge granted by the Badges Committee for official use. Obviously, Lieutenant Davenport, our Captain, had other ideas for the badge which we all knew as one depicting an eagle arising despite the fact that this was quite unofficial.

Towards the end of our stay we received another delivery of parcels, mainly in the form of warm clothing. Several of these contained knitted garments and socks, sent by the good ladies of Porlock and which were hopefully made with wool that did not require clothing coupons. We were fully aware of the stringency of the wartime clothing regulations making it a real sacrifice for the ladies if coupons had to be handed over.

The time came to leave Halifax with the ship sailing through a plethora of small yachts and passing Dartmouth to port before reaching the open sea which was quite rough on that dull November evening. The HO ratings had fortunately acquired their sea legs by now so the regulars had no cause to make caustic comments about us. With the ship pitching and rolling badly, the logistics of getting the pot mess down two ladders to the lower seaman's mess deck seemed almost impossible at times if the contents were to remain in the pot. One slip and the boiling stew would have been spilled over the unfortunate Cook of the Mess but no such accidents occurred, enabling us to have a fairly healthy, hot meal, albeit one which would become more and more monotonous as time went by.

The following day, the old ship put into Saint John, New Brunswick, our last port of call in the Maritime Provinces. It is claimed to be the oldest incorporated city in Canada with the inhabitants insisting that the spelling of the name, unlike St John's, Newfoundland, should never be abbreviated. While we had thought the variation in tides at Port Alfred was great, the Bay of Fundy where we now found ourselves really did have the highest tides in the world. Accordingly, it was constantly necessary to keep an eye open for the wire securing the ship to the jetty as they had to be adjusted from time to time, a fact that we had learnt almost to our cost earlier. The

First Cruise - Newfoundland and Canada

Roughers, North Atlantic

hospitality extended to us by the local populace was as good as, if not better than, the other places along the Eastern seaboard that we had visited. Almost all of those going ashore were entertained by up-homers who all appeared so loyal to the British Crown. It is even said that King Square in the city had been laid out in the design of the old Union flag and a re-enactment of the Loyalist Landing in 1785 takes place each year in July, unfortunately before our visit.

Rough seas off Newfoundland

Having said our farewells to the local people, there remained one important duty for the ship's company before our departure and that was to attend the Armistice Day parade to which we sent the ship's guard together with all available ratings not actually on duty aboard. It was a most impressive ceremony, similar to that performed each year in Whitehall and it felt a privilege to take part.

Eleventh of November generally seems to be a sombre day weather-wise and so it was as we left Saint John in the afternoon to sail back to the open sea through the Bay of Fundy, passing settlements with such English-sounding names as Weymouth and Yarmouth on our port side. Soon the ship was heaving up and down in roughish weather, heading south towards our base in Bermuda. Each day seemed to get warmer as would only be expected and our newly acquired 'comforts' were slowly stowed away to be used at a later date, in fact a year later when we unexpectedly returned to the UK.

The dark clouds gradually gave way to brighter skies until we eventually sighted Bermuda, having completed the first post-war cruise of the America and West Indies Squadron. Although we were the first ship home, our sister ship *Padstow Bay* arrived the following day and our flagship *Sheffield* entered harbour soon afterwards. We were the junior ship of the Squadron, this status being due to the fact that we had a mere Lieutenant in command whereas *Padstow Bay* had a Lieutenant Commander. We were indeed the 'canteen boat'!

What pleased us as we entered harbour was the sight of Ponta, the dog carried across the Atlantic by LCH 75, which had by now been returned to the US. He was on the quayside wagging his tail in greeting at our return, a true survivor having lived on scraps in the meantime. Near to Ponta was the coloured fellow, still fishing in the harbour, who would resume his gash collection once again to feed his pigs. It begged the question; how had they survived during the cruise without our gash?

8

CHRISTMAS IN BERMUDA

*"He will not, wither he is now gone, find much difference,
I believe, either in the climate or the company."*
Dr Samuel Johnson

It seemed quite a relief to arrive back in the Ireland Island harbour once more after the cold conditions of the North Atlantic. Not that it was exactly hot in Bermuda at that time of year but at least we could shed some of the woollen garments sent over from England. One noticeable feature on board was that the cockroaches were travelling about more, sometimes dropping on to the mess tables while we were eating, from the asbestos-clad pipes overhead. During the cold weather they had tended to cluster on the other side of a bulkhead where one of the lights permanently switched on had provided heat for them. While they were there we could exterminate them but it was an endless sport as the survivors soon started to breed again. In Northern waters, the draughts from open hatches made life quite miserable at times although our experiences were nothing compared with life on Russian convoys. We had something to be thankful for but moaning or 'dripping' is, after all, the prerogative of the seaman.

From the harbour we were able to hop over to Hamilton in our off-duty hours, chugging over in the MFV crammed with similar-minded ratings from the other ships. Once we were there we could take a trip on the so-called railway which ran along a spinal route almost to the extremities of the islands. This was quite an experience in itself, to catch the train as it stopped in Front Street for passengers to climb aboard and settle themselves into the wickerwork seats. The rails ran along the street with no protective barriers, reminding us of a tram rather than a train, until the outskirts of the city were reached when the rails continued along through cuttings and in parts on elevated stretches. We were able to see other parts of the islands of which we were told there were 365 – one for every day of the year, – although some of these were mere rocks sticking out of the sea and many of the larger ones had been joined by bridges thus destroying their claim to be separate islands. The controversy over what constitutes an island was to come to a head in 2003 when the European Community Authorities decided in their 'wisdom' that Britain was not an island, so who were we to express an opinion on the matter?

Several of us took the first opportunity once in Hamilton to buy groceries to send home to supplement the meagre rations there. Tinned meats and fruit were in good supply where we were so we bought up several of them together with butter and, a commodity missing from British shelves for years, rice. All the items were then packed in a cardboard box which in turn was stitched into pieces of canvas with the aid of a sailmaker's palm. With our previous experience of the nylon stockings, the canvas seemed a sensible precaution against theft, as such a parcel must have been quite a temptation to some at home. The cost of postage was fairly reasonable at the time unlike today's rates which would be quite prohibitive. With regard to the rice included in the parcel, my mother, who had regularly asked our grocer if he had any, was able to take a few ounces to *him* to make a rice pudding for the first time for several years. How pleasant it was to deal with a small grocer, than having to buy foodstuffs from one of the wretched impersonal supermarkets.

Soon after we arrived back in Bermuda we heard some earth shattering news – Lieutenant Davenport, our Captain, was to be transferred to the flagship HMS *Sheffield* and, in his place, we were to get a Commander, recently promoted to that rank, who had been a Prisoner of War of the Japanese. We learnt that his name was Frank Twiss, the holder of a Distinguished Service Cross and that he had been the Gunnery Officer of the heavy cruiser, HMS *Exeter* when she was sunk by the Japs in the Far East. At the time, he had been in the Director Control Tower when the cruiser had met a superior force soon after leaving Surabaya on her way to Colombo. Apparently he had been swimming about in the Java Sea, hanging on to a ping pong table which had floated clear, when he was picked up by the Japanese.

In his book published many years later entitled *Social Change in the Royal Navy 1924–70* he described briefly his experiences as a POW, first at

Macassar Camp, then at Zeulsuji Camp followed by Mitsushima on the Japanese mainland. It was while he was here that the atom bombs were dropped at Hiroshima and Nagasaki in August 1945, following which the war ended abruptly. His report of treatment as a POW makes light of the conditions, although one guard in particular, Sergeant Watanabe, must have been a sadistic lout, hitting his charges with a bamboo cane and generally behaving in a most inhumane manner. With so many of our prisoners killed, starved or beaten in captivity it seems unbelievable the British people almost fell over themselves to buy Japanese cars, TVs, Hi-fi sets, motor cycles and cameras only a few years later, completely forgetting the atrocities that had been committed by them. After the pyrrhic victory gained by the Allies our country seemed hell-bent on self-destruction economically. Memories are certainly very short!

Porlock Bay was soon to be commanded by a Gunnery specialist who, we surmised, would be a strict disciplinarian and would run the ship with a rod of iron. Having been on the instructional staff at the Whale Island Gunnery School he was bound to be a strictly 'pusser' person, dealing with any miscreants without mercy and keeping everyone on their toes at all times. How wrong we were!

At the time we were only in the fifth month of our thirty-month Commission in the America and West Indies Squadron with no immediate hope of returning to the UK until the bitter end. It seemed that only a small handful of time-expired ratings, together with a few HOs who had served throughout the war, were being demobbed. Just how much longer would we have to serve before we could start our civilian careers? Writing to one's Member of Parliament was a punishable offence but it did not stop the parents of ratings making representations and so mine contacted Mr Anthony Eden about the iniquitous 'Y' Scheme we had joined at seventeen, only to find that advancement was barred to anyone not signing on. Possibly as a result of these representations, the 'Y' Scheme was abandoned shortly afterwards but this was little consolation to us because we were well and truly 'in'.

As we mulled over our fate, unable to even contemplate our future civilian life, Commander Twiss was sailing out in a sloop, HMS *Snipe*, which was to join the Squadron on arrival in Bermuda. In a letter he wrote to me many years later, Admiral Sir Frank Twiss was also very apprehensive, in his case at the prospect of taking over his first command from a well-respected and experienced senior Lieutenant whereas he had only a series of refresher courses at Greenwich Royal Naval College after three years as a Prisoner of War. He also later confided that he had been terribly sea-sick on the journey across the Atlantic which surely was not a good start.

Describing his arrival aboard *Porlock Bay*, Commander Twiss wrote as follows:

> "Arriving of Five Hundred Fathom Hole in Bermuda, it was arranged that I should transfer by whaler to the Porlock Bay which was exercising with a submarine (HMS Token). In due course, feeling rather like Hornblower, I was pulled across to my new command and boarded her by jumping ladder.
>
> "The Captain, a senior Lieutenant, was on the bridge taking charge of the morning's exercises and he received me civilly enough but not perhaps with enthusiasm at the idea of giving up his lovely command to this, a new and inexperienced gunnery chap. I watched proceedings from the bridge, trying to observe how skilful or otherwise were the operators, aware that the ship's company probably shared their Captain's reservations about the new boss."

Submarine 'Token' alongside PB Bermuda *after exercises, Dec 1946*

The exercise with HMS *Token* continued and after a few more runs, Lieutenant Davenport asked his successor-to-be if he would like to take charge of the ship for the next, an invitation he accepted gladly. To indicate where it was thought the submarine was, hand grenades were lobbed over the side and thanks to the leading submarine detector we were often on target, making quite an impressive show of anti-submarine work. The Leading Asdic Operator was Leading Seaman Shortle who soon afterwards was sent home for demob, to be replaced by Leading Seaman 'Pat' Melia. My job was to fuse the grenades and, if there were any left over at the end of the day, to defuse them.

With his first 'attack' completed successfully, the Captain-to-be was feeling mildly elated when the leading torpedo-man "came clattering up the bridge ladder, calling out, apparently in some panic … that he had let go a depth charge." Everyone on the bridge froze at the thought of what might happen. Hearts stood still. The story continues in Commander Twiss' words:

"Was the safety pin in? Would it explode at any second? What in any case might happen to a depth charge dropped in such terribly deep water? We waited tensely but, by the grace of God, nothing happened. The explanation was all too simple. The afternoon exercise included firing a whole pattern of depth charges and these were being prepared for the event. Hearing the fire buzzer sound off on the quarterdeck, the leading hand panicked, thought it must be the moment for the full pattern, for which he and his mates were not ready, and dashed to the stern to remove the retaining rails, thereby letting one charge roll down the shoot (sic) into the sea. It was certainly an ugly moment. Over lunch, the Captain and I pondered over who would have faced the Court Martial, he or I, one or both. What too if the submarine got to hear of it. We decided that, above all, the incident must be kept secret, the leading seaman in no way punished and that on our return to harbour the Captain and I should invite the submarine Captain aboard to take a very strong drink or two."

To most of us the whole incident went on without our knowledge but, over the next day or so, garbled reports circulated, becoming more dramatic by the hour, despite the fact that the torpedo-men's mess was situated on our mess deck and we could have asked for their account. Incidentally, although we had torpedo-men aboard, we had no torpedoes but we naturally had the depth charges which could be fired from four DC throwers and two chutes to roll the charges over the stern. In addition they were responsible for the electrics of the ship including the maintenance of the telephone communications, throughout the ship.

It occurs to me that a short digression on the topic of telephones should be told here involving a leading torpedo-man on the bridge as we were about to leave our anchorage on one occasion. I happened to be on the fo'c'scle on the other end of the phone waiting to pass on orders from the bridge when Able Seaman Cathcart, a broadly spoken Scot, suddenly said, "We," full stop, nothing more. Thinking that there must be something further, I asked him to repeat.

"Wee," to which I again asked him to repeat.

"Weeeeee," he went on in desperation.

My thoughts were, "why should I want to urinate – did he mean over the side?" Then, it suddenly dawned on me he had said 'weigh' but, not being used to the Scot's accent, I had misinterpreted the order. The result was that the ship weighed anchor – only about one minute after the order was first given but a delay all the same! Fortunately, the time of our departure was not critical so nothing further was said about the matter.

Soon after Commander Twiss assumed command, the coxswain came down to all mess decks to ask members of the ship's company to muster on the upper deck by the brow to bid farewell to Lieutenant Davenport. To a man, we acceded to his request in view of the popularity of our departing Captain and, when he appeared, CPO Rhodes called for three cheers. Lieutenant Davenport returned the salute, crossed the brow on the quayside to leave for the final time, never to return.

We now had a full Commander as Captain of *Porlock Bay* which meant we were no longer the 'canteen ship' of the Squadron. This was to manifest itself a few weeks later when we left for our next cruise, the entire squadron leaving harbour in line ahead, with *Sheffield*, the flagship, first, followed by *Kenya* and then ourselves. Seniority and the correct 'pecking' order was always observed in the Royal Navy.

The day following Lieutenant Davenport's departure, Commander Twiss took the ship to sea for the first time but only for a short distance. We had to replenish with oil from an oiler lying in the small St Georges harbour which we approached slow ahead in calm weather conditions. However, going alongside for the Captain's first attempt was fraught with much difficulty, in the new Captain's words:

> "I took the ship slowly and carefully through the narrow channel and was happy to find the harbour calm and the oiler lying waiting for us. We glided along – bows pointing in what I estimated to be the right spot, speed just enough for steerage way, the men on the fo'c'sle at the ready with heaving lines and apparently all set for a good alongside. Alas, pride comes before a fall. Just as I reached the oiler I realised for the first time that there was a marked flare to her fo'c'sle and her bow overhung considerably. From the way I was going, my awning stanchions were going to foul her fo'c'sle and we were clearly in for trouble, but too late to check the way. With a nasty rending noise the stanchions bent and broke and then, in one of those moments of utter silence which usually follow disaster, I heard a sailor's voice from somewhere aft shout, "away stanchions". I never forgot that cry. It said everything the ship's company thought of their new Captain: cack handed, no ship handler, spoiling our nice ship, not what we expected of you, sir, not what we look for at all."

Commander Twiss was too self-critical but it proved to everyone aboard that he was human and not the Gunnery automaton that we were expecting. These words of his were copied from a report that he sent me many years later entitled 'First Command'. The report had been prepared for his grandchildren with perhaps a little 'embroidery' that comes from writing descriptions of events from memory. I am more than likely to have written in a similar style!

To return to the events in St George's harbour, our stay there was quite a bonus. For one thing, the town had been the capital of the islands until the Government transferred to Hamilton and consequently the town had a greater historic impact than Hamilton. Secondly, and to us perhaps, more important, we were able to go to the USO stores in the American base there. We were able to buy a pair of black shoes, without toecaps, at the remarkable price of four dollars which at the current exchange rate was just under one pound sterling. Not only were they cheaper than the ones we could get from 'slops', they were far superior; quite a bargain indeed.

Other items of clothing were similarly of exceptional value, so all our KUA was spent on buying caps (for fun only), towels and underwear etc. It is hardly surprising that fifty-seven years later, our troops in the Gulf, are buying, out of their own pay, equipment from the Americans in preference to their own issue!

Our stay at St George's was all too short as we had to put to sea in order to carry out a survey of the seabed around the islands, supervised by the Navigator, Lieutenant Nigel Tetley. For the Engine Room the job must have been a nightmare, stopping and starting off again while the Asdic operators took readings of depths. Everyone was aware of the reefs surrounding the islands together with the danger to shipping as evidenced by the vast number of wrecks that had occurred. Plans of these could be seen in the Hamilton Library which I visited after our survey and these brought home to me the importance of charting accurately the depth of water, particularly at the relatively narrow channels into the harbours.

Captain's uniform, Christmas 1946, Bermuda

The survey work meant that we were involved until Christmas Eve when we eventually returned to our normal 'home', the Ireland Island harbour, to consider the prospect of having nothing for Christmas lunch other than possibly corned beef. However, the thickset figure of Tanky was seen going ashore to return with turkeys which were prepared and cooked by the new leading cook, always known as Jake.

Christmas Day in the Royal Navy has its own particular traditions. Even during the war the practice whereby the most junior rating takes over as 'Captain' often continued and now, despite the fact that I was not exactly the youngest on board, the Captain's second best uniform was handed to me by his servant, the three badge Able Seaman Jock Cruickshank. Having donned the uniform complete with the ribbon of the Distinguished Service Cross together with both the silver jubilee and the George VI coronation medal, I was required to accompany the Captain on his mess deck rounds, preceded on our way by the coxswain and the Bosun's Mate. As we went

Able Seaman Smith in the Captain's uniform – Christmas Day, Bermuda Dockyard

from mess to mess it was a tradition to take 'sippers' until by the end of the tour, I was very decidedly drunk but this did not stop me from going up on deck to salute the Captain as he went ashore, across *Padstow Bay* to church.

Everywhere, photographs were taken of the genuine and 'temporary' officers who by now included the irrepressible Bungy Williams, resplendent in the uniform of a Lieutenant R.N.V.R. and my fellow Radar Control rating, Humphrey Ixer in the coxswain's uniform. Having reached the bridge, I tried to take the ship to sea, thwarted only by the fact that the Engine Room staff were not at their posts before going below in my drunken state to enjoy Christmas lunch. The vast amount of rum had taken effect by now so the lunch was eaten slowly until sleep caught up with me, sitting at the mess table with my head resting against the storage racks where I remained in a drunken stupor for the next hour. After that, my lunch was brought back up and deposited in the harbour.

While all of this was going on, festivities aboard our sister ship *Padstow Bay* were taking a slightly different form in that a giant 'tiddy oggie' had been made, paraded around the upper deck and then carried across the brow to *Porlock Bay* for us to see before being taken on the *Padstow Bay*'s motor cutter. The 'oggie' was then displayed to other ships of the Squadron but at that point, the high spirits of the cutter's crew prevailed and they proceeded to paint the side of the flagship. The story is best described by Commander Twiss who writes in his report as follows:

> "Hardly had I emerged on deck when the First Lieutenant came up and said, "Sir, have you seen the Flagship's side?" I looked across the harbour when there, to my consternation, I saw my own ship's pendants painted in black figures on the cruiser's spotless side.
>
> "It wasn't long before the flagship signalled "Commanding Officer to report on board wearing sword and medals". I was clearly in for the high jump. Indeed this was an underestimate. Received on board HMS Sheffield, I was taken to the Flag Captain who was standing glowering at the after end of the quarterdeck and here I was treated to a tremendous round of abuse, anger and recrimination. What kind of undisciplined ship did I command? The incident was a disgrace and immediate steps were to be taken to remove all the black paint and repaint the flagship's side a beautiful grey.

"Very shaken, I returned to my ship to confer with my First Lieutenant and tell him what he had to do. He reported that the Ship's Company were extremely angry at the officer and denied vehemently that it was in any way the doing of HMS Porlock Bay. They were horrified, too, that their Captain should have to face such indignity and, above all, on Christmas Day. In fact, it began to look as if any working party sent to put the flagship's side to right would be a pretty bloody-minded lot. We were debating this situation when the coxswain came along to report that he had irrefutable evidence that it was our opposite number, the Frigate lying astern of us, which was the culprit."

Shortly afterwards, the Commanding Officer of the other ship apparently came aboard and offered to put the record straight. The matter all blew over in the end but our Captain, newly appointed as he was, had been absolved and he said that it did, in fact, blow him some good. He considered that, to some extent, his initial poor ship handling had been forgiven for standing up for his ship's company.

Commander Twiss returned to his day cabin and found that a treasured bottle of Drambuie had disappeared and on Boxing Day his three-badge servant did not appear for duty. On enquiring of the coxswain, he was told that Able Seaman Cruickshank was extremely under the weather. Several had seen him in his paralytic state and were fearful as to the consequences and, eventually, he appeared before the Captain who asked him where the bottle had gone.

In the Captain's own words:

"Yes, Sir," he replied, "I took it."

"And did you share it with your messmates," the Captain enquired.

"No, Sir, I drank it all myself."

This was such an honest admission that the Captain considered whether it was another case of discipline or discretion and he chose the latter. This was a wise decision and indicates the wonderful nature of the Captain who said that he never had a more loyal or honest cabin hand. Jock Cruickshank had indeed got off lightly but it was his only and last indiscretion in all his naval service.

Commander Twiss' troubles that Christmas were still not yet over as the secret code wheels disappeared and despite a complete check of all compartment and individual lockers, they were never found. During wartime this would have been a disaster and it was dreadful for us now, even though the war was over. The missing code wheels must have disappeared overboard although it is difficult to envisage how this could have occurred as they were kept at all times in the 'sparker's' office, or rather, should have been. The first days of his first command must have been a nightmare for Commander Twiss but he was not deterred and, as we all know, he had an excellent career in the Royal Navy, later becoming an Admiral and Second Sea Lord.

However, at the time, he had more pressing matters on his mind, the most important of which was to take our ship on her second cruise, this time to the warmer climes of the Caribbean.

9

THE SPRING CRUISE

"The year is dying in the night;
Ring out, wild bells, and let him die."
Ring out, wild bells, **by Alfred, Lord Tennyson**

America & West Indies squadron leaving Bermuda on Spring cruise.
Taken from HMS Porlock Bay *as we followed HMS* Padstow Bay
past Flagship Sheffield

The Spring Cruise

On the morning of 31st December, we slipped and proceeded out of the harbour into Grassy Bay. This time we were no longer the 'canteen boat' as our new Captain was senior in rank to the Lieutenant-Commander-Captain of our sister ship Padstow Bay. As we passed the harbour entrance, I glanced at the NE Breakwater where, in 1926 during a particularly violent hurricane, the light cruiser HMS Calcutta had almost come to grief and would have done so but for the action of the Executive Officer and several officers and seamen who leapt ashore and secured the ship.

Calcutta sustained only superficial damage before she was able to sail, against the terrific force of the hurricane, back to her original berth where she was finally secured. It was particularly interesting to discover that *Calcutta*'s commander at the time had been Captain A.B. Cunningham, a destroyer man from the First World War and, as Admiral Cunningham he had been C-in-C, Mediterranean during the greatest part of the Second World War. How fortunate that he, together with the ship's company, had not succumbed to the violence of that storm.

In Grassy Bay the ships of the Squadron filed out past the flagship, *Sheffield* and no doubt the eagle eye of the Commander-in-Chief, A & W.I. Squadron watched us as we left. We had to wear full Number Three uniforms and this would have to be the rig of the day until we left the company of the flagship. The weather was freshening as we bade farewell to Bermuda and the seas would become increasingly rough as we sailed south.

The first watch (2000 to 2400 hours) saw me as bridge look-out, standing in front of the starboard forty mm Bofors with powerful binoculars and thinking of the folks back home between sweeps of the horizon. Would I be able to hear the traditional sixteen bells hammered out on the Quarterdeck? However, just before the New Year was ushered in, my relief arrived in the form of 'Ginger' Faulkner, another Able Seaman Radar Control Rating so we very solemnly wished each other a happy new year, spoilt only by Ginger adding, "I hope I won't see your ugly face up here next New Year's Eve." Ginger, who many years later became Secretary of the *Porlock Bay* Association, was not being derogative but merely expressing the hope that we would both be demobbed before 31st December 1947. At least I hoped so!

The 'pleasantries' over, I made my way below to the ablution compartment to swill myself down with a bucket of warm water before turning into my hammock for the remainder of the night until "call the hands" was piped at 0530 hours. For me, watch keeping was never easy as it meant being on deck for four hours each night unless one was fortunate to have one of the dog watches of two hours. The working hours regulations came in some fifty-five years later but they would not have applied to a ship at sea.

During the voyage we carried out exercises with the other ships and went to action stations on two occasions. By the second day the seas were decidedly rough and, in keeping up with the two cruisers, the frigates were covered in spray for much of the time. It was satisfying to see that the larger ships were bouncing about as well as us with the screws racing away as their sterns were one minute left high, if not actually dry, as their bows plunged into a trough. Next minute the bows would rise, throwing spray over the ship and the screws would once more bite into the sea to send us on our way.

By 4th January it was definitely much warmer as we entered harbour at Kingston, Jamaica, to anchor for a few days while the ship remedied the action of the sea by yet another coat of paint in preparation for the tour of the Turks and Caicos Islands and the Cayman Islands by His Excellency, the Governor of Jamaica. On the Saturday afternoon some of us drifted ashore and proceeded to one of the major hotels whose manager had extended a welcome, the Myrtle Bank Hotel. Here we met a group of former RAF chaps who said they were there for a few days while flying round the world – or were they shooting a line?

Perhaps we had imbibed just a little too much that evening because we were a little jaded as we swung over the side on stages to paint ship the following morning. As the ship was anchored, the gash chute was used to dispose of the waste and, hearing a sound just below me, I looked down to see a large shark swim past and return moments later to half turn and seize a mouthful of the vegetable peelings. Remembering our experiences in Bermuda Floating Dock when almost everyone fell off the wooden stages, it occurred to me that it would not be in anyone's interests to do the same now! As the stages were lowered to just above the water line we were particularly vigilant to see that no part of our person could be grabbed by one of the marauding creatures for its breakfast.

On 6th January, *Sheffield* left for the Panama zone and the cruise to South America which our new First Lieutenant had so looked forward to before being transferred to *Porlock Bay*. The newly joined *Snipe* also left for the Canal zone and *Padstow Bay* set off for Antigua, leaving *Kenya* and ourselves in Kingston Harbour where we would stay until 8th January.

His Excellency the Governor of Jamaica, Sir John Huggins, K.C.M.G., M.C., then embarked at the Myrtle Bank pier in a police boat at 1600 hours, accompanied by Lady Huggins and the Colonial Secretary, the Hon. H.M. Foot, C.M.G., O.B.E. Lady Huggins and the Hon. H.M. Foot, after only a brief visit to the ship, went back ashore while we set off for Grand Cayman Island, the first of the Governor's dependencies. In addition to the Governor, we had also embarked a correspondent and a photographer from the Kingston *Daily Gleaner*, His Excellency's A.D.C., Captain Young, and also a Jamaican valet! Our visitor accommodation was sorely stretched almost to bursting point with all the extra passengers. There was a heavy swell as we left Kingston but we never learnt how our visitors fared on their first night afloat as no one saw them.

Some fifteen hours later we approached Georgetown, Grand Cayman, and proceeded with great caution to our anchorage because of a dangerous reef. With the aid of both the Asdic and a leadsman in the 'Chains' to make sure there was sufficient water beneath the hull we safely arrived at the appointed spot. The ship's guard went ashore by motor cutter which returned to take the Governor and the Captain to Georgetown pier while a seventeen-gun salute was fired from the ship. The Governor spent the rest of the day ashore and, next day, continued with his inspection, returning in the evening to host an official cocktail party on board. Later in the evening we sailed and proceeded to Cayman Brac where we arrived early morning. This was to be the routine on so many of our visits during the cruise. Apart from the guard and certain officers, no one from the ship went ashore and all we could see of the place was the low outline of the land. However, not many people can claim to have even seen Cayman Brac! At least the Governor was able to make his inspection of the island, going ashore in pretty rough seas and having quite a difficult time jumping on to the landing stage.

Porlock Bay continued her cruise from Cayman Brac to Grand Turk sailing north of the Caicos group in a force five and heavy rain squalls and, again, encountering anchorage difficulties when we arrived. Here, not only the Governor and his party went ashore but also our soccer team which played against the locals and won quite easily. In fact, during the Commission many football matches, both soccer and rugby, together with several cricket matches were played by our ratings who had had little opportunity to exercise on board and many stiff limbs were felt afterwards as a result. Ratings off-duty were also able to get ashore in Grand Turk and, returning later in the evening when there was not even moonlight to guide us, let alone street lighting, on what was only a beaten track, we found numerous glow-worms darting about us which made us forget the darkness. This was our first experience of such ephemeral creatures which, apparently in their quest to find a mate, give off a significant glow for about a second or so.

At the next place, Salt Cay, (pronounced 'Key') the ship had to remain under way, without anchoring, while the Governor et al went ashore for a brief visit and, on his return, we proceeded to Cockburn Harbour in South Caicos. Here, the sea conditions were again rather difficult and so the Governor reluctantly decided not to try to get ashore, perhaps also to the relief of the motor cutter's crew!

We therefore returned to Grand Turk where the Governor gave another cocktail party. The work was largely carried out by the officer's stewards, dressed in their Number Sixes, while the rest of us had to keep well out of the way. In fact, although the cocktail party was given in Government House, the refreshments were provided by the stewards, on board using the minimum of facilities in the wardroom pantry and carried ashore for the event.

Apparently, disappointment was expressed that the ship had not been open to visitors but we, the ratings, were happy! It was here that the ship's doctor, Surgeon Lt Kirk was landed to assist at an operation at the local hospital and the Navigator went ashore to check the coding agreements. The operation could not be carried out quickly and the doctor was late in returning aboard to the annoyance of the Captain.

Grand Turk was the final island on the Governor's tour and we were not sorry that it was now coming to an end. At least at our final call there was a hospital of sorts but in many other islands there was no doctor or dentist to care for the population. The main industry appeared to be the preparation of salt for export to Canada and the US and large mounds of salt were seen along the foreshore awaiting transport. What a change was to occur in the next fifty years! In our day there were only two cars on the island.

His Excellency embarked in the early morning and, after a ship's company photograph with the Governor, we weighed anchor and proceeded to Port Antonio, Jamaica. Whether the photographer had had a drink or two before taking the exposure we would never find out, but the resultant photograph was sloping badly with the horizon most certainly not horizontal. To keep my parents happy however I did buy a copy but not only was there a horizon problem but the sides of the print were somewhat unsharp.

Our passage to Port Antonio involved passing along the northern limit of the practice area of the US base at Guantanamo Bay where we were challenged over the radio. The large US base had been established during the war and was to become quite a thorn in the side of the Cubans, particularly when Fidel Castro came to power. The American authorities have since made maximum use of the base, principally as camp for the incarceration of the terrorists responsible, or suspected of being responsible, for the September 11th attack on the New York twin towers.

We arrived at Port Antonio early the following morning and secured temporarily at the United Fruit Company's wharf where the Governor disembarked for the last time. He was received by a group of dignitaries before boarding a special diesel coach for the journey to Kingston, the island's capital, perhaps relieved that his trip aboard was over! No sooner had we landed the Governor than we had to move from our berth to anchor off the port to allow a banana boat to take our place alongside. This did not stop a group of important local people coming aboard to be entertained in the wardroom while quite a crowd of the general public arrived in droves, brought over by two small motor boats packed to the gunwales. The Captain in the meantime had gone ashore to lay a wreath at the War Memorial, a ceremony which was to be enacted, with or without the guard, at numerous places later.

As non-duty watch several of us were able to go ashore with the aim of finding the Tichfield Hotel on the hill overlooking the small harbour. We had been invited there by the manager to enjoy the swimming pool and bar facilities of the hotel but there was an added attraction in the form of Errol Flynn who was there with three remarkably attractive young ladies. He generously paid for a round of drinks for the impecunious ratings but did not join us, nor did he allow his female entourage to leave his side. This was perhaps not surprising as he certainly would not want any of his 'birds' to disappear with a crowd of sex-starved matelots, all of whom had been cooped up on the lower deck for so long without any female company! Errol had arrived at Port Antonio in his yacht which was lying in the harbour, apparently with the intention of buying the hotel, which he did later.

At one time, Port Antonio had been the second largest port in Jamaica until the reduction in the banana trade to Europe and, in particular, the British Isles. The local people were extremely pleasant and the police, resplendent in their uniforms and white pith helmets were most tolerant of our fellows who had had too much of the local rum. On one memorable occasion, one Able Seaman staggered back to the ship and saw two members of the local constabulary approaching, whereupon he hailed them and asked them to stand to attention in front of him while he took their photographs with his box camera. They readily acceded to his request, and were patted on their backs before he resumed his unsteady course to the jetty. Strange to relate, the resultant photograph was quite good.

Two R.N.V.R. officers were embarked at Port Antonio; Lieutenant Commander MacDonald and Lieutenant Thompson who remained aboard for our cruise around Jamaica. The ship then sailed for Savanna La Mar with Lieutenant Thompson responsible for making the arrangements ashore. There was a slight hiccup at Savanna, however, as several small boats came out with visitors who were shown over the ship only to find that the small boats had disappeared when they wanted to return. The only answer was to convey them all ashore in the motor cutter involving several trips to do the mile-long journey.

A party of about seventy from the ship managed to get ashore themselves to visit the West India Company's sugar factory at Frome and to be entertained by the local people. Sugar is of course one of the main crops of Jamaica and forms, together with the associated production of rum and the banana trade, the main exports from the island.

Our next port of call was Black River, the highlight of the Jamaican part of our cruise. The Captain laid yet another wreath on the memorial plaque in the Old Court House and then a party of about seventy drove up to Malvern where football and hockey matches were played against Munro College. In addition there was a miniature rifle (.22) match and golf for the Officers. Malvern, at just over 2,000 feet above sea level was apparently very pleasantly cool, something that the duty watch, including myself, were unable to enjoy. We learnt that the last RN warship to visit Black River had arrived in 1908 and, perhaps due to the infrequency of our visits, hundreds of people came aboard to be shown around by the few ratings left on the ship.

Finally, we proceeded back to Kingston to take on fuel oil and, in the evening, the ratings enjoyed a dance given by the British Sailor's Society while the officers with the sole exception of the Officer of the Day dined with the Governor at King's House. Only a few chaps were proficient on the dance floor with large numbers preferring to remain in the bar. This resulted in the Chief OA, Ginger Ridpath, being given further extra-curricular duties in the form of dance teacher with quite satisfactory results, as most of his class were quite anxious to learn. However, one of our number was very good at dancing the jitterbug and every time he took to the floor a large audience was attracted, whether to see the girl who was partnering him or, more likely, to see the underwear she displayed as she was swung over his head with great regularity.

The Captain's Report to the C-in-C records that Able Seaman McConachie was adrift when we sailed from Kingston and we heard later that he had reported at the Naval Office ashore very soon after we departed. It was a most serious offence to be adrift when the ship was under sailing orders so no doubt he had the full force of KRs and AIs thrown at him before ending up in 'chokey'.

Soon after leaving, the gunner's party were required to prepare ammunition, both Bofors and 4" for the main armament in readiness for daylight and night action. 'Evolutions' were fully practiced in fairly rough weather conditions, including the calling out of the whaler in a mock 'man overboard' exercise. Of course, this event had to take place when the first part of Port watch were the duty watch and I had to take my place as bow oar. The whaler was gently lowered until just above the waves when the boat's cox'n released just at the correct time as a wave appeared beneath us. Leading Seaman George Evans was very experienced fortunately, and the whaler veered away from the ship in copybook style for us to pull round to where a lifebelt and flare were bobbing about in the sea. As bow oar, it was my job to retrieve these items but, in doing so, our boat was caught by a wave, soaking me completely. We then pulled back to the ship, by which time lower deck had been cleared to hoist the whaler back to its position on the davits.

Having attached ourselves to the falls, orders were given to those on board to hoist and up we went until the order was given for the four crew members in the centre to clamber aboard leaving the cox'n and myself to attach the lifelines. At no time during our training had we been instructed how to do this and so it was necessary for PO Merryweather to shout instructions to me in order to ensure that the whaler did not drop back into the sea with disastrous results. It did prove the importance of these exercises which, in this case, would forever remain in my memory. As it transpired, the order, "ease to the lifelines," was given and my handiwork held, enabling the falls to be secured to the cleats on the davits, and the next order, "light to," was given. George Evans and I were then able to clamber back aboard.

The winds increased further as we approached Vera Cruz, Mexico, and strong currents were experienced as we reached Isla Verde and passed the breakwater to the large harbour. A salute of twenty-one guns was fired to be answered by guns of Fort San Juan before a pilot was embarked to take us to the passenger jetty. We secured to the jetty but with the starboard anchor down and five shackles out as the jetty was less than half the length of the ship. This became increasingly necessary as the winds freshened again, making it important to retain steam as a precaution.

In harbour was the USS *Tanner*, one of two modern surveying ships in the US Navy which was carrying out a detailed survey of the harbour. Also in harbour was the Mexican gunboat *Orizaba* but she was refitting at the time. As we had entered harbour we passed a rowing boat, the single occupant of which ran his hand across his throat, shouting, "Inglese," which we assumed was his way of saying that he did not like the English! This did not seem a warm welcome but three of us, John Stoker, Michael Sheppard and I went ashore, passing the bullfighting arena where there appeared to be some activity although we had no wish to attend. After a few drinks John was persuaded to do his version of the Mexican Hat Dance, carefully making sure that no locals were watching, thus ensuring our reputation as 'Ambassadors'.

However, other crew members were not as circumspect and, the following morning, it was a case of 'on belts and gaiters' to collect a messmate, 'Geordie' Sparks, from the local gaol. He had been arrested, having drunk too much of the local Cerveza and fighting anyone who stood in his way. Geordie was only about 5'4" in height but he usually picked tall opponents to fight with the inevitable result. What a sorry sight he appeared when we collected him but he gave a toothless grin as we arrived and we duly matched him back to the ship. He was 'weighed off' in due course and a warrant issued which had to be confirmed by the C-in-C. His main worry was that he had lost his dentures in the fight and, with no dentist on board he would have to wait until our return to Bermuda before he could have replacements made. He was lucky. During the afternoon, a Rolls Royce was seen approaching on shore and the uniformed driver of the Vice Consul's car came aboard to hand to the Quartermaster a small brown box containing his teeth!

During our run ashore in Vera Cruz, it was noticed in the shops that the 'best buys' were leather goods and so I was easily tempted to buy a leather covered box which had the Mexican Calendar stamped on the top. It was comparatively inexpensive but not only did it look attractive it served as a box for my studs and cuff links for many years after demob, standing on the mantelpiece of my bedroom at home. However, it was possibly the appearance of the box that was its undoing as a particularly unpleasant drug addict burglar by the name of Glen D. Anderson spotted it when he broke into my home some forty-five years later and took it with the rest of the swag. Anderson was apprehended the following day by the police but all the stolen articles had already been whisked away to a 'fence' by that time. At least he admitted the offence and was sentenced to one year in a Young Offender's Institute but my nice box was never retrieved. It did occur to me to sue the burglar and after contacting the police, his name was given to me in order that I could write to the Governor of Olney Young Offender's Institute, which I did only to be told that Anderson had no money. If I had carried on, it was extremely unlikely that any good would come of it other than seeing the burglar face to face. Little wonder that people have little respect for the British Legal System. Other items which were not retrieved included my identity disc which had hung on a chain around my neck during the entire time in the RN.

The ship was open to local visitors while we were in Vera Cruz and it seemed hundreds came aboard despite such adverse weather conditions. Winds gusting at fifty-five mph meant that the ship suffered chafing against the wooden structure of the jetty and most of the fenders put out were the worse for wear before we departed. Worse still, the chafing against the ship's side meant that more painting would be required before our next port of call as we had to appear 'Shipshape and Bristol fashion' at all times.

As the weather forecast predicted a further gale, the ship was moved to a new berth by the breakwater and, with two anchors down and wires securing us to the breakwater, we maintained steam in one boiler as a precautionary measure. Special sea duty men were closed up throughout the night when the wind reached force eight on the Beaufort scale but by morning this had reduced to force four. With the seas still fairly rough, the two anchors were weighed after a pilot had been embarked but he obviously considered that discretion was the better part of valour as he left while the ship was still well inside the harbour. Notwithstanding that, a large pilotage fee was charged despite the fact that he had done virtually nothing to earn it.

We had a fairly rough ride to our next port but, with the seas easing somewhat, the ship arrived off the entrance to Tampico to be met by crowds waving union flags, surely a good sign that the natives were friendly! Having passed the breakwater, the ship proceeded up river, firing a twenty-one gun salute as we went but no return salute was heard despite the fact that the British Consul there had informed the authorities ashore. Our gun salute at least succeeded in stampeding horses and cattle in the adjoining fields but we did not find out the reactions of the local people. On the forecastle we had our guard in full Number Six suits and, on the bridge, Humphrey Ixer was pressed into service as the bugler to sound the General Salute. Furthermore, the SRE was turned up to maximum volume to play mainly Souza marches as we made our way towards the city of Tampico.

As the guard was only required to parade on board, I decided to use one of my brand new white uniforms which had been issued to me on joining up at HMS *Royal Arthur* at Skegness. This was partly because my best Number Six suit needed dhobeying after the run ashore in Vera Cruz and it seemed crazy to have to include an issued white uniform in my kitbag if it was never to be used. The canvas material was very stiff and the jumper required a separate blue jean collar but, with belt and gaiters donned, I was confident that there was no difference between my uniform and those of my colleagues that could be detected by anyone ashore. It was noticed however by Lieutenant Tetley, the Officer of the Guard who asked me why I was so attired.

"This is the suit which was issued to me," was my reply to which he rejoined, "Please ... avoid wearing the regulation uniform if you are with the Guard ashore – only wear it on board; if you must!" The situation seemed farcical because, having been issued with items of kit, we were only required to keep them for kit inspections with no intention on the part of the Navy that they should ever be worn. It was ludicrous that we should have to conform to such Naval 'bull' and, hopefully, this is no longer the case in the modern Service.

By the time we were allowed ashore, my Number Six suit had been dhobeyed and ironed, a laborious job when one considers that it involved getting a bucket to do the washing, drying the items, claiming the sole iron on the mess deck and waiting until the mess table was sufficiently clear to spread the clothing out to do the ironing. Fortunately for the present day matelot he does not have to worry about such matters as washing machines are now provided and, in many ships, Chinese dhobey wallahs are there to do the entire job.

Clad therefore in pristine white uniforms, two of us who had declared an interest in tennis were invited to a most select club for a game. Rackets and a box of new tennis balls were provided by the Club and we were able to enjoy some exercise which manifested itself in stiff muscles the following morning.

No 5 Mess plus Torpedo Ratings' Mess

Later we went to the house of some English up-homers living in the city and it so happened that our host was an enthusiastic philatelist, a hobby that I had enjoyed from an early age, albeit in a small way. In fact, with Leading Torpedo-man Temperley who hailed from South Africa, I had been buying sets of stamps (the lower values) in each of the colonial ports we had visited. 'Temps' was a highly intelligent rating who had signed on for twelve years during the war and was now regretting his decision to do so. Nevertheless he faced the situation philosophically, spending much of his spare time poring over his stamp catalogue and comparing notes from time to time with my basic collection of British Empire stamps.

The stamp collection of our host in Tampico was far more impressive than any I had previously seen, with entire volumes devoted to single colonies and, as for the Mexican stamps, he had several volumes which we examined enviously. It was a pity that Temps was not with us to partake in the enjoyment of looking at page after page of valuable pieces of paper but, if he had been present, we might possibly have missed the excellent meal provided by our host's wife, due to his overriding interest in stamps.

Back on board, the Captain and officers held a cocktail party for the local dignitaries, consular staff and certain British residents living in the city. Over the grapevine we heard that the local people in accordance with custom had thrown their empty glasses over their shoulder and, although this was not confirmed, an urgent order was sent out from the Consul for a supply of glassware.

The following day the ship was visited by a Mexican General accompanied by two staff officers and fortunately my Number Six suit was still reasonably presentable when the guard was turned out for his inspection. The General seemed delighted with the reception and positively glowed with pleasure as he inspected us, watched by quite a large crowd that had gathered in the quayside. One advantage that RN ratings had over our counterparts in the army was that the rifles, bayonets, belts and gaiters were not issued to individuals but were maintained by the gunner's party. The result of this was that everything was in first class condition, bayonets in particular sparkling after regular rubbing with a chain-mail type of pad. Of course, drill on board was carried out from the shoulder arms position whereas ashore it was always done from the slope, a fact that was always necessary to remember. A smaller guard of five ratings was formed about this time to act as colour guard which was formed up each morning when we were alongside under the overhang of the four-inch gun position and marched to a central point on the quarterdeck to present arms as the white ensign was raised by two signalmen. For this event, we were required to wear Number Tens; shorts and white fronts, belts and gaiters.

Yet another Mexican General wearing riding boots and spurs appeared on board the following day, requesting to be shown over the ship. His request was granted and he was duly escorted over the upper decks and then, after expressing satisfaction, he announced that he would like four more of his officers to be taken on a similar tour. Again this request was granted in the interests of maintaining good relations between the two countries.

A football match was arranged for the ship's team and after accepting we learnt that it was to be a top class event at the city stadium against a crack Tampico team. The home team were apparently the current Mexican champions and our fellows were totally outclassed by their regular full-time players who were in peak physical condition in comparison with our team, the members of which had had little opportunity for training.

Afterwards, at a party at the Casino Club, two ratings became completely legless and, although the local people there were making complimentary remarks about the behaviour of the British seamen, the local paper *Mundo* raised the matter in the morning addition, complaining bitterly at the drunkenness of our people and generally stirring up trouble beyond reasonable proportion. The ratings concerned managed to walk back aboard but because of the newspaper article they were placed on Captain's Report and duly received their punishment of 'jankers'.

The fact that the ratings had walked aboard unaided, raises a point about the sobriety of sailors as they cross the brow. It is often possible for a chap to be completely 'gunnels (gunwales) under' and yet manage to pull himself together for about one minute while he salutes the quarterdeck in view of the Officer of the Day; collects his station card and goes below. He will then throw up and collapse on the mess deck to be there until the hands are called the following morning. What a sobering effect the quarterdeck has!

The hospitality in Tampico had been almost overwhelming and almost everyone was sorry to leave but we had to 'show the flag' further and so we departed, seen off by large enthusiastic crowds who obviously did not agree with the reporter of the local rag. A pilot had been embarked for the journey down river and out to sea where we dropped him to set course for the Texan port of Galveston. Incidentally, for the journey down river the coxswain was on the wheel, unable to see ahead in the enclosed wheelhouse and steering solely from orders from the open bridge above. Nothing to port, nothing to starboard!

There were strong winds as we set off for Galveston, Texas and most vivid flashes of lightning en route accompanied by heavy rain squalls which made the job of everyone on the open bridge most unpleasant. The first part of port watch had the 'middle', and the bridge lookouts, forewarned by their predecessors, took the precaution of wearing full oilskins with towels over their heads and some even had steel helmets as protection against the incessant rain.

Bad weather was nothing new to Galveston because, in September 1900, the most devastating storm in American history reduced many of the buildings to matchwood, killing as many as 10,000 inhabitants. The city at the time was becoming extremely wealthy with new electric streetcars, an electricity supply for the whole area, three large concert halls and some twenty hotels. The hurricane struck on 7th September, bringing with it a wall of water estimated at twenty feet high which left most of the clapperboard housing in ruins, and only a few of the more substantially built houses remained. The entire city was low lying and so all parts were affected to a greater or lesser degree. A century later, with some alarming reports of the possible affects of global warning it poses the question as to whether catastrophes of this nature are really a modern phenomenon or whether they have been with us over the years.

For me a minor accident occurred which meant losing most of my front teeth. As a youngster of around eleven I had lost my two front teeth which had been crowned, causing me nothing but trouble thereafter. Always conscious of the need to avoid any blow to the face, the teeth had nevertheless been knocked out on two further occasions playing rugger and had been re-crowned. With these two knocked out again plus three other damaged it seemed that I would have to have the remains of the five teeth removed and have a denture. How to do this was another matter as there was no dentist on board and so it was necessary to suffer in silence until the ship returned to Bermuda where it would be possible to receive treatment in the dockyard dental surgery.

My troubles were minor however, compared with those of Able Seaman McDonald, a seasoned rating who had survived the war unscathed but now he suddenly developed abdominal pains, diagnosed as appendicitis. He was in agony but an operation on board during the night with the ship rolling badly was impossible. We were all very concerned at his predicament, so much so that progress reports were posted at regular intervals outside the door of the sick bay. If he could hold on until we arrived in Galveston he would be likely to survive but every extra minute that we took getting there seemed to lower his chances.

There was poor visibility as the ship approached Galveston, reducing our speed but, with the assistance of the 293 Radar, the Asdic and soundings taken by a leadsman in the chains, we safely arrived at the spot where a pilot was embarked to take us into the port. An ambulance was waiting to take McDonald to the General Hospital where his operation would take place. Having secured to a pier it was realised that a deputation of locals was waiting to come aboard before the Captain had had a chance to shave and smarten himself up. As he was always so correct in his dress and general appearance he was somewhat embarrassed by the early appearance of the visitors but with the poor weather conditions, the Vice Consuls of Galveston and Houston quite understood his difficulties. Two hours later he managed to present himself with the Vice Consul at the City Hall, resplendent in his best uniform to meet a crowd of civic dignitaries. In fact, the entire day was spent meeting people and making, as well as listening to, numerable speeches. He impressed us as a natural diplomat and it later came as no surprise to all who served under his command that he was appointed Black Rod at the Palace of Westminster after his retirement from the Royal Navy.

As far as the ratings were concerned, the entertainment was equally lavish with a dance at the YMCA attended by almost half of the ship's company. Despite the efforts of Ginger Ridpath in teaching dancing, many like myself were somewhat shy when it came to asking the girls to dance but others more than made up for our lack of social grace. With all the entertainment ashore, readers could be excused for thinking that life was just one round of pleasure on a cruise but nothing could be further from the truth. Honestly!

We were surprised when, on the day after arriving in Galveston, A.B. McDonald *walked* back aboard after his acute appendix operation. In the US, surgeons had developed new techniques involving only small incisions and consequently used only a couple or so stitches, almost like the pin-hole microsurgery used in our hospitals today. Mac appeared quite well, so well in fact that he was put on light duties immediately on his return including some watch keeping duties and, within a week, he was considered fit enough to resume normal duties. As we were reminded, *Porlock Bay* carried no passengers.

The usual, or perhaps on this occasion, unusual, football match was held against a local team which we won 3-1, cheered on by a crowd of women. These turned out to be G.I. Brides, married during the US 'occupation' of Britain during the war. The Brides, probably beginning to feel homesick, made such a fuss of our matelots that we gained the impression that they would have returned to the UK aboard *Porlock Bay* given half a chance. Fortunately, their husbands must have been at work otherwise there may have been a display of jealously at the way the girls flung their arms around our players.

Church parades in the Andrew were, by now, no longer compulsory so the good reputation of British seaman was raised considerably by the voluntary attendance of most of the off-duty officers and about forty ratings at Trinity Church on the Sunday. Perhaps some had ulterior motives in going because the chaps were invited to the homes of the parishioners afterwards but, as the hospitality had not been offered beforehand, the lads must be given the benefit of the doubt! In my case, used to going to the school chapel every morning, it seemed natural to attend the service where the welcome was extremely warm, both from the Minister and the congregation. The people were most generous and we began to wonder whether they regarded all of us as victors of the Battle of the Atlantic which, in fact, some were although not the Radar Control ratings. Perhaps it was the ribbon of the War Service medal which gave them that idea as the ribbons had just been handed out to all those who had joined up before the end of the war.

Life seemed to be improving for the lads. Not only had we enjoyed a good time in the last two ports but the weather was brightening up. Four of us went ashore for the last time before sailing, for a quiet 'run' and were walking along the main street looking for a bar, not realising that Texas was a 'dry' state, when we were accosted by an attractive girl wearing a grass skirt. She was standing outside a club and invited us inside where there seemed to be a well-stocked bar serving alcoholic drinks. Other grass skirted girls were dancing with the local males in the dimly lit room when we suddenly realised that the 'girls' were in fact males and that we had unknowingly got ourselves into a homosexual den. As the truth dawned upon us, we drained our glasses and made for the door as quickly as possible. It seemed so strange to think that, in a State where we had always believed that men were men, we had found a club where this was certainly not the case.

With that episode behind us, the ship sailed next day bound for Mobile, Alabama. We were by now fully aware that the cost of living was very expensive in the United States where the rate of exchange was, at that time, over four dollars to the pound. Our two weeks' pay had been paid in US dollars using a conversion rate of 4.06 dollars to the pound which turned out to be over generous as a nought had been omitted and the correct rate should have been 4.006. A corresponding reduction was made after we had left Mobile for converting the money back into Caribbean dollars but the Captain had to explain in detail to the Admiralty why the *Porlock Bay* ratings had been so "grossly" overpaid. Although we had received the unexpected 'bonus', costs ashore were so high that our money was soon spent despite the generosity of the local people who provided entertainment in the form of dances and sightseeing tours. As an example of the costs ashore, a visit to the cinema was equivalent to more than two days' pay. We were certainly the poor relations.

As sea, we were able to enjoy occasional film shows on the quarterdeck subject to reasonable weather conditions prevailing. One film in particular, entitled 'The Bridge of San Luis Rey,' was a popular choice but cartoons were also in great demand. It was only possible to have a film show when the seas were extremely calm, as the deck was often awash, apart from the possibility of the screen being blown away in anything other than windless conditions.

It was on one such hot afternoon that the off-duty members of the ship's company were summoned to the quarterdeck for a Forces Educational Lecture. The officer giving the talk was Lieutenant Tetley who began, most apologetically, by saying that he had been lumbered with the job but that he was about the only member of the Wardroom who had never been to India, the subject of his talk. Details of the situation there had been supplied to the ship in the form of notes and he had studied these to give a reasonable account of the present difficulties occasioned by partition. Granting self-government to India had presented more problems than during Colonial Rule, particularly with regard to religion, the source of so many conflicts in the past and in the future.

We were told of the ghastly bloodshed as Pakistanis left to go to the north west of the Indian Sub-Continent or to the east centred on Calcutta, a city in which the parents of a friend of mine were serving in the Civil Service. The Jenkins' had spent most of their adult life in Calcutta but their future was now far from clear and, in fact, they were 'required' to leave the country soon afterwards to make way for indigenous people to take over. It was difficult to return, aged in their early fifties, and to find alternative employment in England, particularly as so many Service people were also coming on to the labour market. The word 'racism' had not been heard at that time but, in retrospect, how strange it is that employers here today would not dare to deny a job vacancy to any immigrant for fear of being taken to court under the Race Relations Act.

A 'sods opera' was also held at sea under calm conditions although we had to admit that there was not much talent onboard. The upright piano was manhandled on to the quarterdeck to be played by PO Bert Whelan; a stand up comedian in the form of PO 'Taff' Alban cracked a few jokes and the Canteen Manager played his clarinet. Many years later when this was mentioned to can-man Alan Barnard he denied all knowledge but as we had three can-men during the Commission it is quite possible that one of the others was responsible. Whoever played the clarinet he seemed to know only one tune, 'In a Monastery Garden' and we always waited for the wrong notes which cropped up with monotonous regularity. The certainty was that Bert Whelan played his party piece ... "I want to be happy but I can't be happy till I've made you happy too oooo", with the assembled company joining in, accentuating and prolonging the final syllable.

It was always a relief when tombola (known as Bingo here) was played on the quarterdeck rather than on the lower seamen's mess deck because sleeping conditions down there were undesirably horrible after about 500 cigarettes had been smoked in such an enclosed space. The 'houses' were not very great but the gambling instinct of the matelot was such that many of the participants bought as many as ten cards each time with their precious cash in the hope of winning a maximum of five pounds. Because of the stifling conditions during these tombola sessions, one or two of us preferred to remain on the upper deck watching the flying fish leave the water in the ship's bow wave to fly for as much as a hundred yards alongside the hull dropping back into the sea. We were surprised when one misguided specimen landed on the quarterdeck and, in the belief that it had not intentionally tried to commit suicide, we carefully lifted it up and dropped it over the side. Dolphins were also a great pleasure to watch, accompanying the ship for miles as they played around in the bow wave and jumping out of the sea in apparent *joie de vivre* to keep up with us. It was always a strong temptation when on look-out duties to watch the dolphins, a temptation that was often indulged in when in an open expanse of sea but not in a busy seaway for obvious reasons.

Another 'divertissement' that we were able to enjoy in calm seas was pistol shooting, using the twelve revolvers (always known as pistols in the Andrew) which were normally kept in the wardroom under lock and key. These weapons were kept in immaculate condition by the gunner's party and only allowed out under strict supervision. The two quarterdeck bearing-off spars were secured over the side with a line stretched between them and from this were hung bottles as targets. Boxes of .45 ammunition were fairly freely available but all under the critical supervisory eye of Bill Scurfield, the G.I. At Gunnery School we had been taught to fire pistols from the hip but here it was from the shoulder which seemed a more practical way. We soon learned that hitting the bottles from a short distance was not as easy as it appeared and few of the bottles were actually smashed, clearly giving lie to those Wild West films in which the cowboys could fire their revolvers and hit the target from a range of a hundred yards or so.

The inclement weather throughout much of the cruise meant that our hammocks were the best place for sleeping despite the fact that camp beds had been issued to anyone wanting one. In any case, camp beds took up more deck space and consequently making one's way across the mess deck when going on watch was made more difficult and often resulted in a flow of strong language from anyone disturbed by an ill-placed foot. Later on we would be very grateful for the camp bed which enabled us to 'crash our swedes' on the upper deck away from the ghastly cigarette smoke. The smokers themselves were totally unconcerned at conditions which would be considered a major health risk today, so much so that many offices, aircraft and train operators ban smoking altogether and it was later prohibited in bars. Perhaps it was my experience in the zymotic wards of Stonehouse Hospital that made me dislike cigarettes so much as patients there were often a sorry sight, suffering greatly from respiratory troubles. Many could still not give up with the result that so many who served in the Andrew were later unable to breathe due to advanced emphysema.

With only one dartboard there was only an occasional opportunity to play, often with badly damaged flights to the darts. Each time we played, a lightly drawn chalk line on the cortisene served as the oche; lightly drawn because it was always necessary to erase any sign of it for the Saturday rounds. For this latter ritual, the duty Cooks of the Mess were required to spring clean their section, scrubbing the tables and deck, polishing the mess traps until they had achieved a mirror-like surface and generally stowing away all personal gear ready for inspection. Having thus gained a spotless environment, Captain's rounds would be piped. The Bosun's Mate would precede the Captain as he piped the 'still' and the Captain would then follow, accompanied by the First Lieutenant, the coxswain and the Mess deck PO. Hopefully the Captain would just pass through and express his satisfaction of what he saw.

Another unexpected form of amusement was to ride the gunner's bicycle along the midship passage while the ship was at sea, rolling and tossing about in the prevailing weather conditions. The bike was normally lashed to a rail in the passage, an open 'invitation' to any member of the ship's company to try rough riding. To walk along the midship passage was often difficult enough without staggering from side to side but riding a bike was well nigh impossible without crashing into the sides. It was similar to riding a bike for the first time when the balance had to be mastered before attempting to go on the road, but here we were, one minute going uphill as the bows lifted and the next going hell for leather as the ship dipped into a trough. At the same time the ship was often rolling, not in a regular movement but as it was affected by the sideways buffeting it received from the rough seas. Fortunately, the Gunner, Mr Ulyett, never learnt of these activities or at least we hoped that he was unaware of them although the slightly bent forks of the frame caused by hitting the end of the passage at the door into the watchkeeper's mess bore enough evidence for him to be suspicious. At least no bones were broken and Mr Ulyett managed to continue riding his bike ashore, quite oblivious of our activities.

The approach to Mobile, Alabama was made difficult by poor visibility and was under the pilotage of the oldest of the port's pilots. Fortunately the fog cleared and courtesies were exchanged with two destroyers, the USS *Willard Keith* and USS *Shannon* together with the minesweeper, USS *Mojave* which were proceeding to sea via a channel marked with poles. Eventually we secured at the Louisville and Nashville Railroad Company Wharf for a stay of seven eventful days but arriving a day late to enjoy the Mardi Gras celebrations. The reception party who were welcomed on board included the usual civic dignitaries and serving officers, all of whom apologised for looking jaded as they had been up all night taking part in the celebrations.

We lay immediately astern of another destroyer, the USS *Ludlow* which was being preserved on a care of maintenance basis as a Reservists' Training Ship. The usual visitors came aboard although the weather was far from good. Among a small group was an English speaking gentleman who enquired about life below decks and whether we were able to enjoy good music. My reply was somewhat guarded as far as his first question was concerned but that we were restricted to a small number of records of the 'pop' variety and that I longed to hear some decent classical music. He then told me that they were putting on a concert at the Assembly Hall of a large high school here in Alabama and offered me a couple of tickets if I wished to go. My knowledge of music was not great although in my last year at school the music master, Martindale Sidwell had held music appreciation classes for an hour each week and these had been of great interest to me as I had not taken up any instrument. He did not have the tickets but said that if I applied at the Hall I would be able to collect them there.

A difficulty suddenly struck me – I was duty watch and would have to get a 'sub' before I could go to the concert. This was possible and I managed to find someone to go with me, A.B. Atkinson, who had similar tastes in music. Accordingly, we caught a bus, asking the driver to drop us off at the nearest point to the school and arrived in good time before the start. Having collected our tickets we were ushered to the best seats in the Hall to await the appearance of the orchestra.

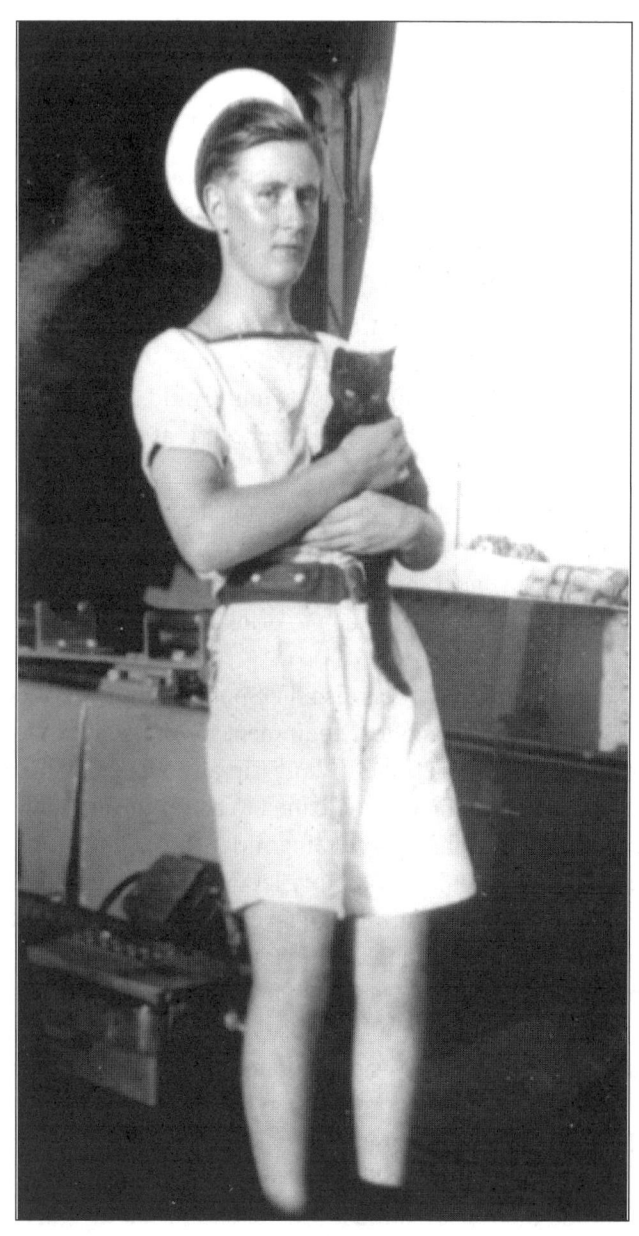

Roger Smith with 'Sippers', a kitten adopted by the ship

One by one the musicians walked on to the stage but, try as we could I was unable to spot the benefactor who had provided us with the tickets.

"Probably he is the chap who opens the lid of the piano," suggested my companion as we watched the leader make his entrance and take his bow. Then the conductor came on; Eugene Goossens, the Musical Director of the Cincinatti Symphony Orchestra, the person who had provided the tickets! Eugene Goossens was later knighted and became the Director of the fabulous Opera House in Sydney, Australia, having insisted on separate Halls for Opera and Concerts as the acoustics were so different.

The concert was the most memorable that I had attended, opening with the Overture from Wagner's *Tannhäuser* and continuing through a varied programme until no less than five encores were played; the last, a piece by the American composer, Morton Gould. What a magnificent experience to listen to such a fine orchestra at the invitation of the conductor himself.

While we were enjoying the concert, most of the off-duty ratings were at a dance which lacked sufficient young partners and many spent the evening in the bar. The next morning there were several glum faces possibly because they had had a drop too much to drink but Atkinson and I felt on top of the world!

The Gunner, Mr Ulyett, was also the Sports Officer, who sent me to the US Navy's Sports Centre to collect equipment for our stay in Mobile. A jeep was provided for the comparatively short trip and I came away with shorts, shirts and hockey sticks which were loaned to us for the duration of our stay. When he saw the shorts which were rather brief, Mr Ulyett almost exploded.

"Disgusting, we couldn't possibly let our team play in those," was his immediate response, giving an order that HMS *Porlock Bay* must play in regulation shorts, tropical issue, knee length, white, seamen for the use of! In deference to our hosts, the shorts were retained on board and finally returned with the other sports items just before we left Mobile. At least, identification of the two teams was facilitated by the fact that our hosts wore their extremely short garments, rather than by the colour of the shirts which were similar to those of our team.

The receipt of mail was always a source of excitement and, when we arrived in Mobile there were quite a few letters for me together with copies of the overseas *Daily Mail*. It seemed unbelievable that the cold weather at home which had started on Boxing Day was still continuing and the snow had not even started to thaw. To add to the troubles, coal was in short supply, making life pretty miserable in the home. Fortunately, the water pipes had not frozen and my parents were not plagued with bursts as so many others were.

On the Sunday, the Ship's Company were again invited to church so, together with about forty others, I attended and, afterwards, was invited for lunch at the house of a former US sailor, Harry Noble. His family was so hospitable and, anxious to dispose of his uniform jumpers, these were parcelled up and put into my hands. As part of my 'sea rig' these proved very useful! Writing 'thank you' letters was beginning to take up a lot of my spare time, let alone the postage which, as the letters were not going to the UK, had to be paid for.

HMS Porlock Bay, *Key West, Florida, March 1947*

All good things come to an end and we slipped to retrace our passage through the fairly narrow channel, marked by poles, out to the open sea. We then proceeded to the end of a string of islands linked by bridges to the southern tip of Florida. Here lay the naval port of Key West which was so important as a staging post for the east coast convoys during the war. Several years later when speaking to someone who had visited the place in the 1990s, I learnt that there was now no sign of any Naval presence.

We secured alongside in the basin at Key West Navy Yard and, on going ashore we were to find that the US Navy had regular shore patrols which even stopped some of our chaps to correct their dress. The commonest thing that the patrols picked up on was the cap, often worn flat-aback in the heat of the sun, but this was really no problem and no incidents occurred. Typical of the US people, they had arranged a coach trip for us along the linked string of islands, including the so-called seven mile bridge although perhaps it should more accurately be called a causeway.

The following morning, Key West was hit by a very large squall, with lightning and heavy rain and a wind force of seven which eased in the evening. Florida was uncommonly cold and so the officers' cocktail party attended by all the Senior US Naval Officers and their wives had to be held in the small wardroom rather than on the quarterdeck.

On our trip ashore we had passed the home of Ernest Hemmingway without realising its significance and had, surprisingly, passed the bar in which he was so well known. The port was far too 'pusser' for our liking and apart from the coach ride to so many of the linked islands, we were not very impressed with the place.

As we slipped after a couple of days we were assisted by a US Naval tug and a civilian pilot came aboard to disembark at the Sea Buoy. We experienced strong winds and heavy seas in the Florida Straits as we set course for Nassau in the Bahamas. Most people think that, apart from some bad spells in the hurricane season, the Caribbean had all round sunshine and calm blue seas but we could certainly dispel that impression!

The ship eventually arrived off Hog Island with several of the awning stanchions twisted out of all recognition by the heavy seas. With Lieutenant Fenton, a former submariner, on the bridge, some wag suggested that he may still think he was serving 'in the trade' and was trying to submerge our frigate!

It was not known until the pilot came aboard where we were to secure. Owing to a merchant vessel occupying a berth at Prince George jetty we had to stay off Nassau with both anchors down and the stern secured to a mooring buoy just off the jetty. The ADC to the Governor of the Bahamas – newly appointed following the departure of the Duke of Windsor – arrived on board and the Captain went with him to Government House to meet His

Excellency, Sir William Murphy. When the merchant vessel, *New Moreland* left Prince George's jetty, we were able to weigh anchors and proceed to the jetty that she had just vacated. Two Royal Marines were then able to join the ship for passage back to Bermuda with us.

In the afternoon, matches were held against the local hockey and shooting teams and, for the others, there was a bathing party on Hog Island, a truly delightful place despite its rather unfortunate name. A notice had appeared on the ship's notice board placing out of bounds an area beyond a range of low hills and we thought at the time that this sounded too much like an invitation to visit the low dives! There was so much to do in Nassau however that most, if not all, ratings followed the advice.

The following day the Captain returned to Government House to discuss with His Excellency his forthcoming tour of the major islands of the Bahamas Group. At that time the Duchess of Marlborough was staying at Government House on her way to Trinidad in the course of a tour of the West Indies for the Red Cross. In the afternoon the ship turned out a Rugby Football team to play the Nassau Club in a match that started quite well but, by the end, the locals were almost literally walking away with it. The score was irrelevant but it proved the necessity to keep in training, particularly in hot climates, when playing a fit team in such heat.

The ship was open to visitors who appeared in great numbers having seen an announcement in the local press. We used to dread taking people around because it meant keeping an eye on everyone to ensure that no one went to those parts of the ships that were out of bounds to them and making sure that they all left at the end of the tour.

Because the berth at Prince George's wharf was required for another merchantman, we had to slip in the early morning and we proceeded out of the harbour on course for Bermuda. On our way 'home' we staged a full power trial, steaming at nineteen knots for about three and a half hours before the Engineer reported bearing trouble and the trial had to be abandoned. After about four hours the spare bearing was fitted and we were able to continue on our way to Bermuda at twelve knots. The economical cruising speed for the ship was eleven knots and that was our normal speed for most of the time.

We experienced strong winds and a long swell on the journey and Gibb's Hill light was sighted early in the morning, enabling us to enter through the narrows and go into the Dockyard at 1000 hours, having saluted Admiralty House on our way. Hopefully the C-in-C was watching.

Thus ended our second cruise, and the first in tropical waters. The ship had handled well and in fairly rough seas as she had done in the North Atlantic. The builders had done a pretty good job, assembling a ship which had been pre-fabricated to quite a large extent. The design for frigates had developed from the wartime corvettes, then the 'Castle' class and the 'River' class through to the 'Loch' class. The 'Bay' class had developed from the 'Lochs' which were essentially for anti-submarine duties and, when the War in Europe was coming to an end, greater emphasis was placed on anti-aircraft capabilities for the war in the Far East. In fact, although our ship had been launched and commissioned as HMS *Porlock Bay*, the hull had originally and provisionally been referred to as HMS *Loch Muick* and HMS *Loch Seaforth*. These were matters that we had gleaned so far but many details came to light later including the design for the ship's badge which remained a mystery until 1976.

At the present time, though, we were in Bermuda and a trip to Hamilton was called for to buy food items to send home. This completed, my purchases were stowed in a cardboard box which was then stitched in pieces of canvas before sending by parcel post to my parents. "And she was fayr as the rose in May," wrote Geoffrey Chaucer and, in many respects, these words could have been applied to Bermuda.

10

BERMUDA IN THE SPRING

"Oh to be in England now that spring is here in order to see a host of dancing daffodils."

With apologies for mixing up two quotations but those were our feelings on returning to Bermuda. However, we were not in England and Wordsworth's host of dancing daffodils were nowhere to be seen on the Island. In any case, the folks back home were only just recovering from the longest known spell of cold weather whereas we were experiencing the finest time of the year in Bermuda.

If anyone aboard thought that our return to Base would be synonymous with a life of comparative leisure in the beautiful islands, he would be sadly disillusioned. Admittedly, we did not have the dreaded watches to keep and we were able to go ashore in the MFV to Hamilton when off duty to spend the night at the Sailor's Rest, alias 'Aggie's'. During the day there was much to be done, painting ship in between chipping off paint, painting our work with red lead and washing down paintwork. It seemed a never-ending cycle which, years later, made me detest the sight of a paintbrush but the exercise was necessary as we were always under the watchful eye of the Commander-in-Chief, just across the water in Admiralty House.

We were able to have some spare time to consider some of the experiences we had had since joining the ship and contemplate our various futures when we were eventually released from Naval Service. Some ratings would depart for home during our stay in Bermuda, including Jim Cretney who really had a raw deal from the 'Y' scheme as he had almost finished his training for a Commission and had indeed bought his sub-Lieutenant's uniform before the end-of-the-war cutbacks brought an end to his aspirations. He was accordingly reclassified, sent to HMS *Valkyrie* for a radar course and emerged as a Radar Plot rating. He was now being sent home for demob. But there was to be yet another unfortunate twist to his Naval Career as his demob group number had not actually arrived and, in the meantime, he was drafted to HMS *Illustrious*. He therefore spent several months as an AB before finally leaving the service in March 1948, three months after the majority of the Radar Control ratings had left. It always seemed possible to find someone worse off than oneself despite thinking that we had had a raw deal! Jim, however, took everything in his stride and, when he was eventually released, he studied medicine and achieved his ambition to be a doctor. Many years later after retirement he joined the HMS *Porlock Bay* Association to become one of our more active members.

HMS Porlock Bay *reunion 2002. Dr Jim & Mrs Jeanne Cretney, County Hotel, Llandudno, Oct 2002*

Another well-known personality, the Cook, Byron Davies, left to open a pub in Newport, Mon, and he became a valued member of our Association in later years. He was replaced by a most colourful character by the name of Jake whose surname no one can remember but who ruled his domain with a rod of iron. No one dared to question his ability as a Chef and, as leader of the football cheering party, no member of the opposing team's supporters was advised to cross his path! As far as the preparation of the food was concerned all this was carried out in each individual mess, relying largely on the ingenuity of the mess caterer who was normally, but not exclusively, the killick of the mess.

Food was mainly distributed by Tanky from the beef screen or the potato locker in exchange for a chit, which was passed on for the preparation of the mess accounts to the officer concerned. An allowance for food was made by the Admiralty which, if exceeded, resulted in mess bills to be paid out of the meagre pay of the ratings. If there was a surplus in the mess account, mess savings were paid although questions were asked if the amount suggested that ratings were being deprived of their full rations by an unscrupulous mess caterer. Also taken into account were the chits for food obtained from the tiny NAAFI store, such as baked beans and other tinned foods. Ratings could buy these items out of their own pocket to supplement the mess rations, together with chocolate, mainly peppermint creams.

The empty tins had to be carried ashore for disposal as we were not allowed to use the gash chutes while in Bermuda. The large coloured fellow came aboard to collect the pig food although no one knew whether the scraps were boiled up in the approved manner. However, foot and mouth disease was apparently unknown in the islands so we could only assume that the correct procedures were carried out.

The title 'pigs' we learnt had another connotation and this term was often used by the 'regulars' when referring to the officers. When we joined ship it soon became apparent to the HOs that there was some enmity on the part of certain ratings towards the 'upper deck' which made us wonder at times how we ever won the war. One incident in particular remains in my mind and this concerned a water polo watch against the wardroom when the two bearing-off spars were rigged outboard to provide the goals. As the topmen had so few swimmers, I was pressed into service, with no knowledge of the rules. The advice given to me was to ram an officer's head between the goal posts rather than the ball, but, if this was not possible, force their heads below the surface and keep them there! While this advice was given in a reasonably jocular way the underlying intention was to give our opponents as rough a time as possible, whether within the rules or not! For my part however it was a matter of keeping my own head above water which was my main concern as swimming was not my strong point.

Another incident which illustrated the attitude of the lower deck towards the officers took place when a parade was arranged to celebrate the King's birthday. Each ship in the Squadron provided as many ratings as possible, the numbers being dependent upon the number of rifles available in each ship. *Porlock Bay* had only twelve with the other escort vessels having a similar number while *Sheffield* and *Kenya* were able to supply about fifty each making a total of 148 for the guard. The Gunner's party was responsible for the maintenance of the rifles together with the webbing equipment which was spotlessly white on the morning of the parade.

The ship's guard before setting off for Hamilton for the King's birthday celebrations

The problem came when parading on the dockside together for the first time as each contingent was accompanied by its Gunnery Instructor with the result that conflicting orders were given by NCOs to the general annoyance of the Lieutenant Commander in overall charge of the parade. Fortunately all this took place in the dockyard with no one watching before we embarked in the MFV which was to take us to Hamilton, because it was a complete shambles. So much so that the Lieutenant Commander, becoming redder in the face every second, finally exploded and screamed out his opinion of the lower deck generally.

"Seamen of the Royal Navy are, and always have been, the scum of the earth!" were the words he bawled out for everyone to hear. Now these words, with a slight variation, were said by Wellington in the first instance but the Officer of the Guard omitted to complete the quotation by saying, something to the effect, that with thorough training and experience, they were second to none. Unfortunately, without the qualification, the words were somewhat harsh and the repercussions were soon to be made apparent.

Everything was soon sorted out and we duly sailed over to Hamilton where everything went according to plan. The local press made most complimentary remarks about the smart turnout of the guard and their immaculate drill. Whether the smartness was due in part to the admonition received in the dockyard earlier or not, the *Porlock Bay* lads returned to the ship feeling quite content with the proceedings and no further thought was given to the outburst by the Parade Commander.

However, this view was not shared by the ratings on the flagship and it was not long before a deputation arrived to speak to our 'twelve'.

"You're not going to put up with words like that, are you?" were their first words. "We want everyone to put in a request to see the Commander-in-Chief, through the Captain, to state a complaint. We will get that bastard!"

Not wishing to be the only ones not in step, we all duly complied with the demands of the dissidents and put in our individual requests, as petitions were not allowed. In due course, Commander Twiss arranged to see all requestmen on the port side of the deck, outside his day cabin. As we were requestmen and not defaulters, we were called, one by one, with our caps on to appear in front of the Captain where, after saluting we awaited his words. Commander Twiss, ever the diplomat, said to each one that he had been told of the incident about which we were making representations and asked for our views. My personal attitude was that it was largely a storm in a teacup but, as it was necessary to back up the ratings in the flagship, I had to say that the remarks by the Lieutenant Commander seemed somewhat over-the-top. My response referred to the acrimony which seemed to exist between officers and ratings and that it could be that the words uttered voiced the opinions of the officer class towards the lower deck. The Captain seemed quite concerned at this and hastened to assure me that, in his view, every member of the Ship's Company had a job to do whether that person was an officer or rating. There was certainly no ill feeling on the part of any officer as they relied upon the seamen to carry out their normal seagoing duties in addition to the specialist work required from every non-substantive rate. He hoped that the members of the guard would accept the fact that the offending words were uttered in the heat of the moment and that the officer concerned deeply regretted that he had caused any slight on the ratings.

The Captain's remarks were at once accepted by myself and the other eleven ratings, and we came away from our interview feeling that honour had been satisfied, if there was indeed any strong feeling in the first place. After all, the instructors at Gunnery School, being NCOs, were constantly casting doubts as to our parentage without any offence being taken so why all this bother now? However, we heard later through the grapevine that the officer concerned had lost all his seniority due to his outburst and this was likely to affect his career prospects in the Navy. It did seem a very harsh punishment for a few ill-chosen remarks and most of us later felt some guilt for our part in the episode.

Ratings in the other ships were not so generous in their opinions, some saying that the officer should have been dismissed from the Service, "pour encourager les autres", if they had known what Voltaire meant by the expression. For our part we had, in supporting the others, perhaps made an impression on the Captain who, when he became Second Sea Lord, was responsible for all personnel matters.

Porlock Bay had indeed been fortunate in having two Captains who, being quite different in character, were both highly respected by the Ship's Company. Lieutenant Davenport was a generally jovial personality although we understand that he was none too pleased when the ship visited Porlock in the early days of his command. As mentioned earlier, a large proportion of the ship's company were actually encouraged to go ashore leaving a small skeleton crew to hold the fort when the weather worsened and the ship had to steam back and forth while those ashore were enjoying themselves. Under normal circumstances, there would have been no problem but conditions can change rapidly in the Bristol Channel and the Captain apparently showed his displeasure at having so few left on board.

Lieutenant Davenport's ability to bring the ship alongside was admired by everyone as it demonstrated his very real seamanship qualities and it came as no surprise to all who served under him when he became a Rear Admiral, Commander-in-Chief in the Mediterranean. He was the son of a Vice-Admiral but his father's position undoubtedly played no part in his advancement as it was purely achieved on merit. How unfortunate that with his exemplary war record he did not receive a gallantry award and all he had to show for six years continuously at sea were his campaign medals. As Commander-in-Chief, Mediterranean, he was later responsible for handing over the harbour at Malta when the colony achieved independence.

Commander Twiss on the other hand made light of his ability to bring the ship alongside as his memoirs, which he sent to me, describe and which have been reported on earlier. In writing to me many years later he referred to his first attempt to go alongside an oiler with flared bows and other instances where he made miscalculations. He was however a fine diplomat who was especially suited to flag-showing duties. We were extremely apprehensive when he was first appointed as successor to Lieutenant Davenport as he had been trained in Gunnery, a branch which required strict training. In short, we thought that he would be something of a tyrant, similar to Admiral Vian and others who drove everyone into the ground with their strict application of KRs and AIs. Fortunately, our initial assessment of him was totally wrong and we found him generally lenient and understanding towards the ship's company. His experiences as a Prisoner of War of the Japanese, after his ship, the cruiser HMS *Exeter* was sunk, did not affect his judgement in any way, despite the ill treatment he received at their hands. Apart from being kept on short rations, he was beaten about the face by one particularly unpleasant guard who, hopefully, was a candidate for the War Crimes team after the Japanese surrender. Personally, there is nothing that would persuade me to buy Japanese items although the memories of the average person in England must be remarkably short as the import of goods from Japan has meant the cutback or closure of many of our industrial companies.

We were also able to compare the two First Lieutenants who served in the ship. To start with we had an R.N.V.R. Lieutenant by the name of Digby who, being a strict disciplinarian seemed to go around looking for faults and making his displeasure known to the divisional petty officer. Many years later, we learnt that he rather fancied himself as a singer in the wardroom, pressing into service as a pianist, another R.N.V.R. Lieutenant, John Burman. Despite this more pleasant attribute, he always appeared unsmiling and severe to the ship's company. He had left the ship just before Christmas to be replaced by an RN officer, Lieutenant John Fenton, a former wartime submariner who had been awarded a Distinguished Service Cross for his service in one of the 'U' class boats in the Mediterranean. He was not nearly such a captious character and he came to us from the Flagship HMS *Sheffield* with a strong recommendation from the Editor of the *Sheffield Salvo*, a magazine produced at irregular intervals for their ship's company. He was totally different from his predecessor and, at first seemed somewhat remote. We learnt many years later that a possible reason for this was that *Sheffield* was about to set off for an interesting cruise, taking her through the Panama Canal to the Galapagos Islands, round Cape Horn to the Falkland Islands and visiting several of the larger South American ports before returning to Bermuda three months later.

Instead of enjoying that cruise, he would now be with *Porlock Bay*, which was required to host another Governor, this time Sir William Murphy of the Bahamas, to visit all the major islands in the Group. One could understand his disappointment at having to sail from island to island, rarely putting his foot ashore – little consolation for having to miss such a high key cruise around South America.

The Navigating Officer, Lieutenant Nigel Tetley RN remained with the ship throughout the entire Commission. He was a most talented officer, almost boyish in appearance and conscientious in the extreme. His attention to detail when entering harbour almost drove Petty Officer (radar) Tony Lander to distraction and on one occasion when we approached St John's, Newfoundland, he was continually calling on him to re-calibrate the 293 Radar to get accurate readings for the ship's position. This was not a bad thing, however, as it is a very narrow entrance and it was foggy at the time. He was assisted in keeping the Admiralty Charts up to date by his Yeoman, Able Seaman Jamieson, a quietly spoken Scot who remained in that job throughout.

Lieutenant Tetley was a keen yachtsman so he was able to keep a small sailing boat on board, stored just aft of the port twin Bofors mounting where the ship's dingy should have rested according to the builder's plans. The dinghy was in fact always kept underneath the whaler on the starboard side. Lieutenant Tetley reached the rank of Commander and took part in a Round-the-World race which had a most controversial finish. In addition, he was an experienced deep sea fisherman and, on one occasion, landed a shark off Bermuda which was dispatched by Tanky with the salvage axe but although the creature was cut up into small pieces, not many fancied shark meat to supplement their diet.

Two R.N.V.R. Lieutenants left during the Commission to travel home in order to continue their civilian occupations. Lieutenant John Burman, who has already been referred to, was a 'Y' Scheme entrant who 'made the grade'. He was apparently 'head hunted' by the first Captain, Lieutenant Davenport, after serving with him under a previous command. Lieutenant Don Brindle was the other R.N.V.R. officer, presumably with a similar background although we have little other information about him. For a time we had two

Canadian Officers seconded to us, one a Lieutenant and the other a Sub-Lieutenant but over the course of time, their names have been lost.

Two further members of the Wardroom were the Commissioned Gunner, Mr Ulyett, and the Engineer, Mr Barry. In addition to his duties as Gunner, the allocation of duties required the former to be the Sports Officer, a job which was not made easier by the lack of storage space for sports equipment and it sometimes meant borrowing kit from a variety of sources including the American Naval Authorities. Boxing gloves were no problem and, for a time, we had some fencing equipment but, with no one to instruct, there was little demand for it. Years later, fencing became my main sport and it is always a matter of regret that it was not possible to make a proper start with the sport in those early days.

Obviously, soccer and cricket were the main source of recreation and, in both, the regulation shorts were worn instead of purpose made kit. Also, there was a Rugby Festival in Bermuda in which all ships participated together with teams from Yale University and the local militia. It did seem ludicrous, however, to expect the chaps to play a full-time match after being cooped up for weeks on a ship having no uncluttered deck space on which to get into training. In addition the enervating conditions out there made the games very tiring, and it seems surprising on reflection how the players could last the course.

HMS Porlock Bay – *rugby team*

Our Rugby team was a mixture of experienced players and others co-opted into the team. Of particular note was the G.I. who had played throughout his life. Short in stature, Bill Scurfield was an outstanding NCO who, coming from Pembroke Dock, had also represented Wales as a schoolboy International at the Cardiff Arms Park. He took his place as scrum half in the ship's Rugby Football Team and in so doing denied me my normal position – in those days substitutes were not even considered in Rugby circles. As G.I. he was responsible to the Gunner for all matters relating to the armament including the magazines and the small arms and also for the selection and training of the guard. During one run ashore, he bought a live turtle which he decided should be taught to swim! This was kept briefly in the CPO's bathroom until the animal escaped during one swimming lesson! On another occasion he was handed a parrot which had been presented to the Captain by one of the visiting dignitaries, but the Chief Stoker, thinking of the possibility of Psittacosis, objected so strongly to it being kept in the mess that it had to go.

There were others of CPO rank but these were the Engine Room Artificers who had a separate mess. Among them was C.E.R.A. Philip Coulson, a survivor from the battlecruiser Repulse and also from the minesweeper *Dundalk*. He was a native of Bristol where our ship was built. By coincidence, when we visited Belize which was, at the time, the chief port and capital of the former colony of British Honduras, he was able to meet his brother, George, serving with the Gloucester Regiment. Another C.E.R.A. was George Badland, a former submariner who came to us in an exchange from HMS *Moorpout*, the Squadron's boom defence vessel. He had agreed the exchange with an original member of the ship's company whose wife had travelled out to Bermuda and wanted to settle there. As *Moorpout* was stationed more or less permanently there and did not go on cruises it seemed an admirable swap! George Badland hailed from Wolverhampton but he had had a particularly tough time during the war and had quite a drink problem. Commander Twiss was, however, quite sympathetic to George and although he appeared on defaulter's parade on one or two occasions, he normally got off lightly!

The Seaman Petty Officers remained very much in the same jobs throughout the Commission while the junior ratings were regularly changed around. The Buffer was Taffy Alban; PO Merryweather was in charge of the fo'c'sle; PO Taff Penney looked after the top division and PO Bert Whelan the quarterdeck. PO 'Buck' Ryan was in overall charge of the below decks area and PO 'Lofty' Fern was a more or less supernumerary PO. The latter, when he first joined the ship, was an acting PO wearing seaman's rig but when his appointment was confirmed he was able to change to the more normal PO gear of peaked cap, collar and tie etc. The Yeoman of Signals was PO Trotter and the Telegraphist PO was Bob Steane while the Electrical Artificer was Bob Atkinson. The two Radar Mechanics were PO Tony Britton and PO Tony Lander, the former being responsible essentially for the gunnery 285 set and the latter taking control of the navigational sets 293 and the little used 291. The Petty Officers were totally different to those in the training establishments and particularly those in the Royal Naval Barracks, Devonport, where discipline in its most bullish form was the watchword.

Soon after our return to Bermuda we were issued with new cap tallies bearing the name HMS *Porlock Bay* to replace those with which we had been issued on joining up which merely had the initials HMS. The original tallies were worn as a wartime measure presumably to hide from the enemy the names of ships in any given theatre of war and the issue of the new ones was a clear indication that the war was now over! As several of us had only volunteered for the 'duration' we were cheered somewhat by any indication that demob could not be far away and that we may soon be able to start or resume our peacetime occupations.

In addition, everyone was supplied with a new type of working rig, to be known as Number Sevens, which consisted of dark blue trousers and light blue shirts to be added to the kit in our already bulging kit bags. Seamen now had to maintain at least two blue serge suits (bell bottoms); three tropical white uniforms (two of canvas duck material which were never to be worn!); three sets of white shorts and white fronts; the two new working uniforms; overalls; boots (for guard duties); black shoes and white shoes and gym shoes; together with so many small items such as the collars which fastened around the waist; blue, white and football socks, silks and several lanyards. All these together with blue jerseys, blue overcoat and oilskins had to be carried around with both blue and white round caps in the large orange coloured kit bag, supplemented by a black steaming bag. To ease the storage problem we were able to buy from naval stores, on presenting a slop chit, a green canvas covered suitcase at a cost of 27/6d or one pound and thirty-two pence in today's money. It was perhaps fortunate that we were not often required to transfer permanently from ship to ship or ship to shore because it now meant carrying so many items, not forgetting one's hammock, with every move. The hammock, incidentally, when lashed up for stowage or when on draft, consisted of a spare hammock, a horse-hair hammock 'bed', two bed covers and a cream blanket plus two sets of clews, one for each end. It was always a matter of pride to have one's hammock well lashed because, apart from professionalism, it was always possible to distinguish the newly enlisted rating by a slovenly lashed hammock!

One of the real advantages of being in Bermuda in the spring was being able to sleep on the upper deck at night. This seemed sheer luxury to me in view of my dislike of tobacco smoke which was all pervading on the lower mess deck and was possibly my main reason for wanting to leave the RN. The collapsible canvas camps beds were put together with four legs which were inserted into the main frame and the whole could be condensed into a cylindrical shaped package for storage with the hammocks. It was a delight to crash one's swede on these beds under the open sky, covered with a blanket or, if conditions were particularly favourable, with no covering at all. My chosen position was on 'X' gun deck, out of sight, and where those returning from shore leave would not disturb me whatever their inebriated condition, unlike the situation on the mess deck where returning libertymen regularly bumped their heads on the hammocks or tripped over the camp beds, waking their occupants in the process.

There was a double attraction in going ashore to Hamilton however as, by catching the MFV to the capital, it was possible to book a bed at Aggie Weston's for the night and avoid the dreary first work session on returning aboard. The returning libertymen would have the sleep firmly driven from their eyes by the sea breeze on the return journey and would arrive just in time to have breakfast in the mess, feeling much fitter even when suffering from 'the morning after the night before' than those who had chosen to stay aboard or who were duty watch.

The SRE blasted out pop music but it also broadcast the Z.B.M. Radio Bermuda news reports giving a brief outline of world news together with the mainly local Bermudan news. My parents had also arranged for the weekly edition of one of the national newspapers to be sent out to me and these kept me, together with my associates, reasonably well informed about current affairs. Several of the ratings on the other hand only received children's comics from home and these were much sought after, to be read avidly to the exclusion of the world news. It did seem unfortunate that these ratings were completely unaware of the world about them in carrying out their daily tasks, living for the day but having no interest in their future or, indeed, anything that might affect them other than their next run ashore.

One particular item of news which did reach everyone was the fact the field gun competition back home had been won by Devonport, our own port division.

As the demob numbers slowly advanced, people were leaving for home from time to time. For the remainder of us, time rolled inexorably on. Able Seaman Jim Cretney of whom reference has been made earlier was a radar plot rating and his departure together with that of Walter Nield meant that, unless replacements for their radar duties were sent out, the ship would be without full coverage of navigational radar people. This was only realised just before the ship set off for the third cruise, this time to the West Indies and South and Central America. As a result, two radar control ratings, Humphrey Ixer and myself, were hurriedly given a refresher course on the 293 set by Tony Lander before we left. There was no mention of extra 'badge' money for the responsibility – we were just given the job! The full implications of the new job were not immediately apparent because we were still in Bermuda and still 'working part of the ship' during the day. However, it was not long before we discovered how hot it became in the 293 Radar Office when we reached the tropics and we would have to watch the PPI for any echoes for four hours at a time. As deck seamen it was quite pleasurable to stand on deck, even when on bridge look-out duties, to watch the flying fish and dolphins playing in the phosphorescent waters at night in between scanning the horizon for ships or shores. As the ship steamed on at its regular cruising speed there was always a breeze but shut away in the radar office immediately behind the bridge, there would be little fresh air to keep us awake. Conversely, how wonderful it would have been to sit in a warm radar office when the ship was in northern waters around Newfoundland and the spray and heavy rain were soaking us to the skin. It is the seaman's prerogative to grumble and we grumbled! Fortunately, the 293 radar was only in use at night as visibility during the day was excellent for the naked eye so, with the outer door open, conditions were reasonable. The radar office was on the upper deck but sufficiently out of the way of most of our colleagues so that we had few 'visitors'. If one did appear we used to impress him by putting a finger across the spark gap which would produce an effect similar to lightning; it looked quite spectacular but only gave a slight tingling sensation in the finger.

With an open sea and no other ships or land anywhere near, watching the PPI screen was boring in the extreme and the circular movement of the trace had a most soporific effect on the operator. So much so that my oppo

HMS Porlock Bay

HMS Porlock Bay in Nassau, Bahamas with the Governor; Sir William Murphy, Lady Murphy & Commander Twiss, DSC, RN

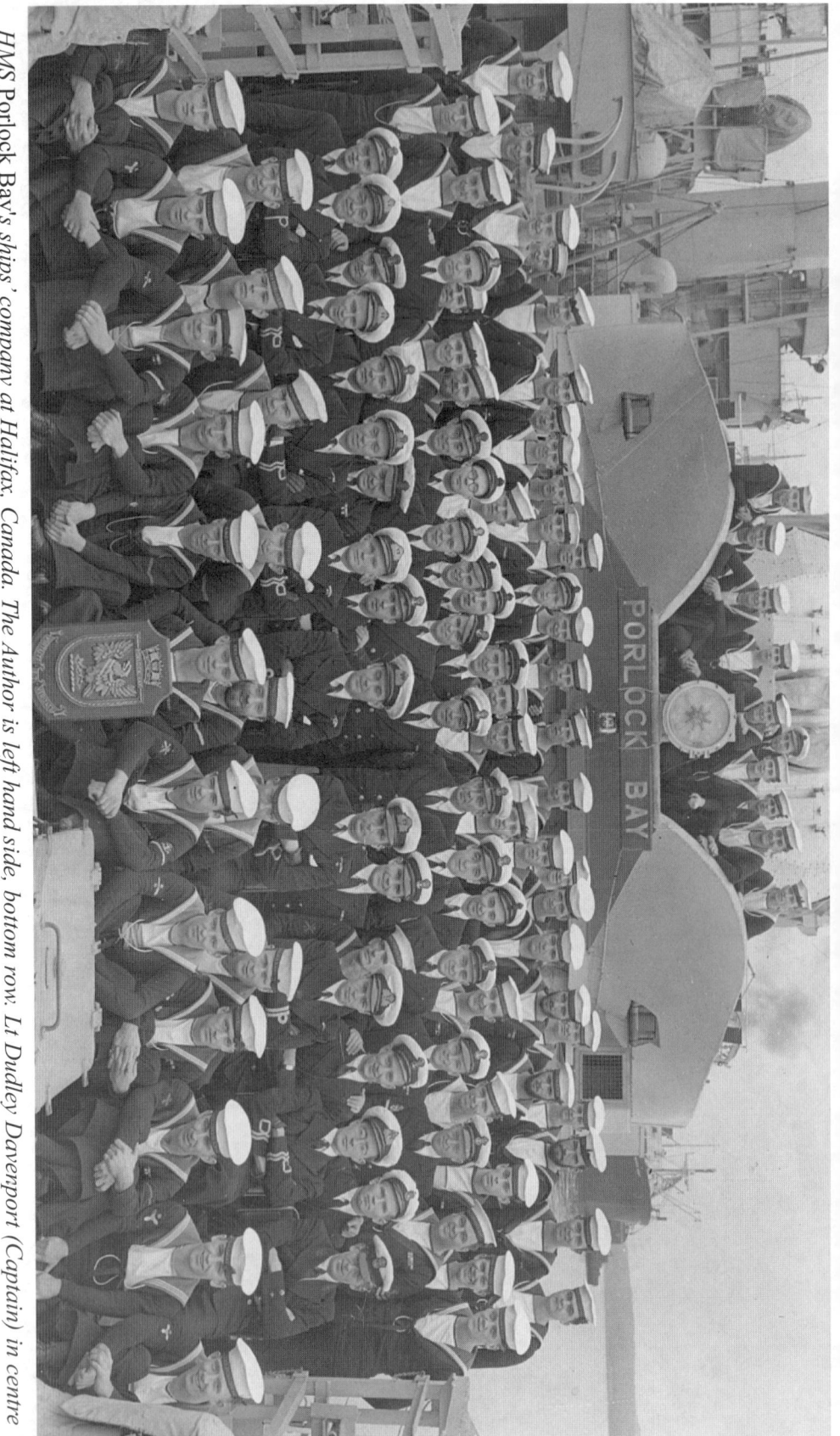

HMS Porlock Bay's ships' company at Halifax, Canada. The Author is left hand side, bottom row. Lt Dudley Davenport (Captain) in centre

*Gunnery Instructor, PO Bill Scurfield
(Welsh school-boy Rugby International)*

Komm. Kapt Visa, Captain of FNS Matti Kurki, *1975*

Admiral Klenberg having invested Roger Smith with a Naval Cross in the Radisson Plaza Hotel, 2004

HMS Porlock Bay Reunion - Porlock 1995 at the Ship Inn where the AGM was held al fresco

Ilkka Ignatius, Chairman of the FNS Matti Kurki Association

and I had an agreement that, for half an hour at a time, one would watch the screen while the other closed his eyes, perhaps even to catch up with a little sleep. On one of these occasions, during the morning watch, I 'dropped off' for a while to awake suddenly to find my oppo fast asleep with the time being 0700 hours, a full hour after we were supposed to 'close down'. Waking my oppo we decided to brazen it out, calling to the Officer of the Watch, "Radar / Bridge," and, when the reply came, "Permission to close down 293 Sir?" The Officer of the Watch, probably because he was not fully alert at that time in the morning, apologised for not giving the order earlier, adding as usual, "scrub out the office before you go". This we did willingly as the remainder of the ship's company had by then completed two hours' work!

Uppermost in the thoughts of the 'hostilities only' ratings were our future careers when we were eventually demobbed and, in retrospect, why we had joined the Navy in the first place. With regard to the latter thought, the general feeling was that we had been finagled into enlisting by the prospect of a Commission after the necessary basic and sea training, usually in cruisers. The stark disillusionment when, after joining, we were told that, unless we signed on for a longer period than 'the present emergency' we would have to remain on the 'lower deck', irked us considerably.

In my case, a career in architecture after demob beckoned and it was frustrating that there were no Forces Educational Courses available to make a start at least with the studies. Most of the HOs seemed to be earmarked for future careers or the resumption of their pre-service jobs including one called Purcheon who had been in banking and thought it a wonderful job. My father was also in banking and, at each interview with the inspectors, the inevitable question was asked, "You have a son. Could you persuade him to join the banking profession?" Having experienced the late hours that my father had worked particularly at the end of each year I was not inclined to follow up what did not appear to be a reasonable job opportunity despite the encouraging words of Purcheon who later became an important banker in Canada and the US.

Anyway, civilian life was still only a pipe-dream and, in the meantime, we would just have to 'soldier on', if that is the correct expression for someone in the Navy.

11

RECREATION IN BERMUDA

"And she was fayr as is the rose in May."
Geoffrey Chaucer

Although there was plenty of work to do while in Bermuda, there was also time for play. Reference has already been made to water polo and the almost 'free for all' that took place during a match. At least it got rid of much of the aggression in us in a similar way to boxing although there were obviously fewer participants in the latter sport.

Chief Stoker Giles, G.I. Bill Scurfield, Cox'n Rhodes, Chief OA Ridpath

Another sport which was enjoyed by even more people was preparing for the annual regatta held in Grassy Bay just outside the harbour. It could be said that it was an extension of our normal duties to get into the whaler with five others including the coxswain and practice pulling an oar over a course of approximately one mile. Each 'division' was allocated a time for practice during working hours but it was not necessary to volunteer for Racing Whaler's Crew as it was a case of "you, you and you" will take part! The topmen's crew of five plus PO Taff Penney as coxswain became really adept at pulling those ash oars and we began to fancy our chances on the Regatta Day. All went well until the day before the Regatta when PO Taff Penney was rushed into hospital with appendicitis leaving me to take over the tiller while another topman was pressed into service as bow oar. At least the course was well known to me and we duly lined up on the Day against a team of Royal Marines from the flagship. The course was a 'dog-leg' one, turning at a buoy roughly half way along the course. My intention was to start as quickly as possible to get to the buoy first and so we did just that with the RM team about three quarters of a length behind. My next, more evil, intention was to round the buoy closely but not to turn too sharply making our opponents swing out further. The language of the Marine's Sergeant could probably be heard in the harbour as he swore as only a Marine Sergeant can, calling me all the names possible while I merely raised two fingers to him and continued on our pre-determined course. Fortunately, the two coxwains did not meet after the race as we went our separate ways but I have often wondered what he would have done if he had realised that I was only an Able Seaman, put into the position of coxswain at the last minute.

Other events in the Regatta were the centipede race in which teams of about a dozen with paddles instead of oars raced the same whaler over a course inside the harbour. This was accompanied by much shouting both from those taking part and the grandstand spectators on the various ships within the harbour. Following this was a Carley Float race with teams paddling the floats, making much splashing both to propel their own flat and to soak their opponents at the same time. It was all good fun.

Finally, there was the more serious dinghy race in which our coxswain, CPO Rhodes, was entered by *Porlock Bay*. Rhodes put in a tremendous effort, standing up to row with two oars to win handsomely, cheered on by the lads standing at the guard rails along the ship's side.

During our stay in Bermuda, we saw several 'Woolworth' aircraft carriers which were being returned to the United States, their duty fulfilled.

In turn, the MAC ships, *Atheling*, *Rajah* and *Patroller* anchored in Grassy Bay while equipment was transferred to the dockyard and the ships' companies had a short respite before continuing to the States and to their ultimate destination, the scrap yard (the ships of course – not the ship's companies!). It seemed a rather ignominious end after such sterling service in the Battle of the Atlantic but their usefulness was now over.

PB crew, centipede race, Bermuda

Another visitor to Bermuda was a Training Cruiser which also anchored in Grassy Bay. While there, the cadets were sent out in whalers for sailing exercises but unfortunately, the weather was not suitable for such training and one of the whalers capsized. All other small boats were alerted and a thorough search was made for the occupants, some of whom could not be found despite star shell being fired into the failing light. Later, the upturned whaler was towed into the dockyard where a body was found, caught beneath the thwarts. What a tragic end to a young life but that was part and parcel of our nautical existence.

While we did not actually have leave, there were two occasions when certain ratings were away from the ship for a time. The first occasion only involved sleeping away from our normal 'billets' when we had to move into buildings in HMS *Malabar* to do fire duty there. Here there were beds for us together with basic toilet and washing facilities which were better than those on board. They obviated the need for the long walk to the toilets but of course the distance to the Fleet Canteen was longer so we generally remained where we were during off duty hours.

The second occasion was when the mess decks were painted which required the occupants to vacate them for about a week. Most the seamen went over to Ports Island by the MFV but some of us had to go in the ship's motor cutter, which took longer. The result was that those who travelled in the MFV were able to claim a 'billet' in one of the five large bell tents, leaving the rest of us no cover at all. We had our portable camp beds which were erected at night wherever we chose to sleep, always under the stars. The trouble was that our stay on Ports Island coincided with a spell of particularly bad weather from the second day onwards and, when it rains in Bermuda, it really does rain. On the first day there, several of us found a clearing which contained about a dozen graves and so we settled down among them for the night. It seemed very strange to be sleeping in a graveyard but at least it was quite restful! There was not much to do the following day except swim around the island although at least one, the newly promoted leading seaman Nat Millard, spent much of his time fishing, using a line and hook but no rod. He had little luck despite the fact that the sea was teeming with fish as the swimmers could testify.

It was spotting with rain as we went to the sleeping area but, as we had our oilskins, it didn't unduly worry us. However, it soon started to rain in earnest, so, sitting on shortened camp beds, we drew the oilskins up to our heads which were covered by the only other item of equipment we had; our towels. Very soon, the heavy rain came through the towels, literally soaking us to the skin and making life pretty miserable. After a while we could stand no more so we made our way to the caretaker's wooden hut where the overhanging roof offered just a little protection from the elements. Here we spent the rest of the night, miserably wet and hoping for dawn when we could perhaps dry out. Some had even considered 'island hopping', making for the 'mainland' where we could see the lights of those fortunate enough to have a proper roof over their heads. However, swimming between the islands at night in those conditions seemed somewhat hazardous so we remained on Ports Island until morning, despite the rats which came out from the hut to search for food!

On a later visit to the library in Hamilton, the 'secrets' of Ports Island became known to us. Apparently, the Admiralty had established a quarantine hospital on the island in the mid-1800s and this was used to isolate yellow fever patients, some of whom died there, hence the graveyard. One ship sent several patients to the island and when the epidemic was over, the island and its hospital remained unused for about a year when a party of Royal Marines was sent to renovate the building. All these men contracted Yellow Fever with two dying almost immediately together with the ship's doctor. As a result of these deaths, the building was burnt to the ground and never rebuilt, as a new Isolation Hospital was then built near Grey's Bridge. This was known as the 'Zymotic', the first time I had heard the word used since leaving the Zymotic Ward at Stonehouse Hospital, Plymouth some fifteen months earlier. At no time was any mention made of the past history of the island before we went there, otherwise it is certain that those who could not be accommodated in the bell-tents at least would have opted to stay at Aggie's in Hamilton while the mess decks were painted.

It came as a relief when the day arrived to return to the old ship in spite of the smell of fresh paint on the mess deck but, by then, the weather had improved, enabling us to sleep on the upper deck with the chance of going below if a repeat of the storm occurred.

Back on board, the old routine continued – washing paintwork, scraping paintwork, painting red lead before painting with the very light grey of the America and West Indies Station. One wag suggested that prisoners in the gaols at home enjoyed better conditions and another suggested that if they treated prisoners as badly as seamen they would have a riot on their hands! At least prisoners had regular visits from their loved ones. We were however fortunate that war time conditions were a thing of the past and we would, hopefully, never have to experience the horrors of the Russian Convoys or the deleterious effect of the seemingly endless Battle of the Atlantic, to say nothing of the Kamikaze attacks of the desperate Japanese. At least we should be grateful that all we had to endure was a boring existence.

There was much discussion about the conduct of the war and how, in retrospect, some of the mistakes could have been avoided by the allies. It was sheer hypothesis but one particular subject was whether lives could have been saved if the proposals by Rudolph Hess had been taken more seriously in 1941. Had he acted on his own initiative in flying to Scotland or was he an emissary of the Führer, suggesting an armistice with the Western Allies? The Nazi's main opponent was the Soviet Union and a break in hostilities with the other allies would have enabled an all-out effort against a Nation led by a dictator as ruthless as Hitler. At home, propaganda had represented 'Uncle Joe' Stalin as a benign leader who would have as much support as possible in the form of ammunition, aircrafts and tanks which involved conveying these supplies by ship through waters menaced by U-boats, aircraft, and the threat of the Nazi surface fleet operating from Norwegian ports. Having arrived in the Russian ports, the crews of the supply ships, when they had evaded all the hazards and shocking weather conditions, were often denied any chance of going ashore. At the same time Stalin was calling for a 'second front' when preparations for it were at an early stage and to have acceded to his request would have been catastrophic. All these things exercised our minds particularly when we thought that, if the two giants, Hitler and Stalin, had been left alone to fight it out, we would not be in the Navy at all – a far too simplistic thought!

Another matter which we discussed at length was whether the allies had lengthened the war by insisting on unconditional surrender and by refusing to consider any form of armistice as happened in the First World War. Talk passed the time away but one thing was certain – we were serving in the West Indies and nothing would change that situation.

While in Bermuda one of the strangest coincidences occurred with the arrival of post from home. Able Seaman Atkinson, the chap who came with me to the concert in Mobile, Alabama, had been sent home for demob, but before he was given his papers for his release from Naval Service he was given two weeks' leave. He had told me that he lived within the confines of Catterick Camp, the base for the Royal Armoured Corps and, having passed the main gate, he was seen by one of my school friends who just happened to be on a course there. Atkinson was wearing his new HMS *Porlock Bay* cap tally and this immediately caught the eye of Tom Flynn who wrote to me to ask if the ship had returned to the UK. My reply stated that unfortunately this was not so and that we were still sweating it out in the West Indies. While a matelot in uniform would have stood out like the proverbial sore thumb in an Army Camp, Tom's eagle eye had also noticed the cap tally but he was so surprised that he failed to ask Atkinson about the old ship.

Time in Bermuda was fast running out before we left on the third cruise which would include a mini-cruise with the Duke of Windsor's successor as the Governor of the Bahamas, Sir William Murphy. We heard with some incredulity that he was to be accompanied by Lady Murphy, his wife, who would be the first lady ever to travel with a warship of the Royal Navy in peacetime, a worrying thing for the more superstitious members of the ship's company.

Another feature of spring in Bermuda was the Annual Rugby Week, held near Hamilton and contested by all the ships of the Squadron together with teams from Yale University and units of the Gloucester Regiment which were stationed in the West Indies. As on previous occasions, the heat and the fact that insufficient facilities for practice had been provided were hardly conducive to first class matches but the players were able to let off steam and everyone enjoyed the event. Another important factor was that members of the teams had perhaps never played together before but one participant, a member of the Padstow Bay team, went on to captain England, leading them to win the Triple Crown no less in 1954/55! He was Peter Young, who kept in touch with a member of our team, Ken Faulkner, who, many years later became Hon. Secretary of the HMS *Porlock Bay* Association. Peter unfortunately died aged 74 in Eire where he had also, inter alia, set up the Dublin Indoor International Horse Show.

Before our departure for the summer cruise there was time for a last game of cricket, Seamen versus Stokers, on the usual hard concrete pitch covered with coconut matting. In addition, another trip to Hamilton's small supermarket for a selection of groceries to send home, including more rice which was still unavailable in the local shops in England but which was sold in vast quantities in Bermuda.

Two days later came the pipe, "Hands to Stations for leaving harbour. Special Sea Duty Men close up," and we slipped out of the dockyard, first for a firing exercise after which we proceeded south to the Bahamas.

12

SUMMER CRUISE

"Old and young, we are all on our last cruise."
Robert Louis Stevenson

On 26th June, HMS *Kenya* left the dockyard for her summer cruise and, on the following day, the rest of the Squadron left, passing through 'the narrows' into the open sea. Here an old tug, the *Sandboy* (formerly *Strenuous*) was waiting for us, padded out to withstand gunfire from all ships which passed in line ahead, firing as they went. In the Transmitting Station it was not possible to see the target but our four-inch guns made a terrific noise as we let fly with our main armament, bringing down cork and more than a little rust overhead. Apparently our target was reluctant to die and our following run was designed to try out the ABU, my action station. Ratings on the bridge said later that *Sandboy* was repeatedly hit but still remained afloat so we were sent in to administer the *coup de grâce* with our Bofors to make sure she was not a danger to shipping.

The firing exercise over, our flagship, *Sheffield*, accompanied by *Padstow Bay* sailed away north to Halifax, Nova Scotia, while we set off for the Caribbean. Just before our departure, it had been decided that everyone should have a yellow fever injection, but it was too late for it to be administered while in harbour and so a doctor was given a 'pier head jump' to join us specifically for that purpose. Now, it just happened that the doctor had broken his arm during the Rugby tournament and this was in plaster so we became a little worried as to whether he would be able to carry out the injections. At the time, the weather was worsening and we encountered a bad patch of 'roughers' just before the ratings were lined up for the 'treatment'. Fortunately it was the Surgeon Lieutenant's *left* arm that was broken so, wedged in one corner of sick bay, he pinched everyone's arm with the fingers of his plastered left hand while he plunged the needle of the largest syringe anyone had seen into our arms. Painful was hardly the word but no one refused, probably because they had seen the graves on Ports Island and knew just how deadly yellow fever could be. The rough seas continued unabated and several of us, including myself, began to feel decidedly unwell with our red arms swelling up to at least twice their normal size. In my case, the pain was almost unbearable but we had a night exercise that night to add to our problems and after about one hour of fitful sleep, the alarm sounded and we had to go to action stations. Going up to the TS with the ship pitching and rolling quite considerably meant that arms were knocked on every obstacle making our discomfort complete.

When the night exercise was finally declared over, we made our way below with great care but, in my case, I was unable to get into my hammock so I lay on the cushioned seats on the lockers in the mess deck to await the call for my watch, the morning watch. Sleep came quite easily but, a few minutes before 0400 hours it was necessary to, once more, go up top for whatever duty was allocated to me. The only good thing was that my clothes had not been taken off that night so I was already fully dressed when the time came to start my watch.

By the time we arrived in Nassau, the seas had become calmer and my arm was just getting back to its normal size, although it was still quite painful. However, the sun was shining and so it seemed a good idea to go swimming. In those days it was necessary to cross over to Hog Island by a small ferry which several of us took to what we considered was the most ideal spot to go into the sea. Life at last appeared to be worth living.

After two days in Nassau, we embarked the Governor, Sir William Murphy and Lady Murphy, who brought with her sewing machine which she offered to the ship's company although little use was made of it. As soon as they were aboard, we departed for the first Bahamian Island to be visited, which was San Salvador. The departure went off apparently unheralded at 1100 hours which was somewhat surprising considering that we had the new Governor aboard who was going to visit the majority of the larger islands in the group for the first time.

Early the following morning we arrived off San Salvador where the first of many guard duties took place. The guard, spruced up in Number Sixes with spotless white belts and gaiters, went ashore first to line up for the arrival of the Governor who came over in the second trip by the motor cutter. After a 'present arms' in his honour, the Governor inspected us before going off inland with the civic dignitaries. This was to be the routine for all the other islands although, in San Salvador, the guard were able to see the alleged spot where Christopher Columbus landed in 1642, only 305 years before. After ten hours lying at anchor there, we then departed for another ten-hour stay at Ragged Island, followed by a nine-hour stay off Fortune Island followed by an extremely short stay in Crooked Island. At each island we marvelled at the clarity of the sea through which we could see our own anchor and the multitude of fish, mostly brightly coloured, swimming around below us.

The next island was Acklin Island where the normal formalities were carried out but the return to the ship was completely different for some of the ship's company. Most of us were quite unaware as to the drama which unfolded and so it would be best described by one who was directly involved, Chief Engine Room Artificer Philip Coulson. He related the incident as follows:

"...We visited the islands of San Salvador, Ragged Island, Fortune Island, Crooked Island and, on 7th July, Acklin Island. 'Awkward Island' might have been a better name, due to Porlock Bay having to anchor sixteen miles off the landing stage because of the extremely shallow water. This perforced the Governor and his retinue having to be landed in our one and only motor cutter – and thereby hangs this tale.

"The wretched boat had a troublesome two cylinder diesel engine and the electric starter was u/s. Consequently, the Engineer Officer detailed me to take my tool kit and go inshore with the boat. This tickled my sense of humour and I jokingly said "Tell them to load a whaler's mast and sail as well!" I was surprised and amused on manning the boat to see that they had in fact done just that.

"We shoved off at about 0900 with a pretty full load of people aboard, including a Telegraphist, complete with walkie-talkies. A local pilot was put in charge on the boat to and from the island which proved to be a very memorable trip. The course steered seemed to be very winding and eventually the telegraphist reported that he had lost contact with the ship. We were now in quite shallow water, it being gin clear and we were able to study the array of marine life below.

"Having made good time, we were approaching the landing stage but we grounded some hundred yards short and a rowing boat came out to land our passengers.

"They returned again by rowing boat in the late afternoon and were safely embarked and so the return trip to Porlock Bay got under way. Some half hour had elapsed when the killik stoker on the engine called to me that the gearbox was overheating. The pilot gave permission to stop the engine. We checked the cooling water inlet and also removed the reverse gear top cover and added fresh lubricating oil and allowed a short while for it to cool. We got underway again but overheating occurred again after a short while, whereupon the pilot said ... "Leave it! Up mast and sail."

"The light breeze was in our favour and we made steady progress. The telegraphist made frequent attempts to raise the ship to no avail. Darkness overtook us as we cruised silently on – it was a most pleasant experience. Eventually, contact was made with Porlock Bay and our predicament explained. Almost at once, the ship's searchlight blazed forth, directed vertically skywards, making an excellent homing beacon. We hoped to be able to use the engine to go alongside but the wretched heap of old iron refused to start. However, our pilot, being an expert, put us alongside most handsomely.

"On entering the 'tiffies' mess to some ribald jesting from my messmates, I was most gratified to find that they had saved my tot for me! Altogether a very pleasant adventure. I wonder sometimes what the Governor and his Lady thought of it all?"

As I re-read his account, I can vividly recall the wonderful Bristolian accent of Philip Coulson who had been a survivor from three ships during the war, including *Repulse* and *Dundalk*, telling us about the incident when we were chatting at one of our reunions some sixty years later. Unfortunately, Phil, who had contracted cancer through handling asbestos during his long time in the Navy, died early in 2003 and, at his funeral, his coffin was draped in the Association's White Ensign.

From Acklin Island we visited Great Inagua followed by Rum Cay (pronounced Key) both for seven and a half hours each before our last island on the mini-cruise, Cat Island, where the Governor landed at Port Howe. The 950-mile cruise was completed when we arrived back at Nassau where Sir William and Lady Murphy disembarked. However, that was not the last we saw of the Governor because he was photographed with the ship's company before leaving and then, most generously, invited as many as possible to a garden party at Government House.

Leaving only a skeleton crew aboard, the rest of us made our way along the main street of Nassau, clad in our spotless Number Sixes and entered the gates of the House. Here we were greeted by our recent passengers and lavishly entertained with the type of food we had not encountered for years. Some of the most attractive young ladies were also in attendance making the event seem so unreal that many of us had to pinch ourselves before believing we were really there. One charming lady to whom we were talking suggested that we may like to see around the house which the Duke and Duchess of Windsor had so recently vacated. This was an extra bonus which six of us accepted and we were taken from room to room including the Windsors' bedroom which was air conditioned, a luxury I had not experienced before. In terms of the English stately homes, Government House was not large but it was most interesting bearing in mind that the general public would not have had access to the entire house which was also the Governor's home.

The following day in Nassau was not so pleasant however. Arthur Stelfox, another HO rating, and I were put on shore patrol duties with Petty Officer Bert Whelan. After dark we marched along the now familiar main street, looking into the bars where the lads were soaking back the booze but generally behaving themselves as we were required to do as part of 'showing the flag'. At the end of the evening, we all assembled on the jetty waiting for the motor cutter to take us back to the ship, when we were joined by the Captain, Commander Twiss, and two of the officers who had been attending a function ashore. They were standing about ten yards away from the main group when along came the staggering figure of none other than Bungy Williams, very much the worse for drink. Spotting the Captain, Bungy, who was already serving two months 'Two and Two' punishment, started shouting abusive and obscene threats. Bert Whelan and Arthur and I told him to be quiet but this made him worse, so much so that he pulled a knife and said he would 'get' the Captain. Whether this was said in bravado we were not to know so Bert stepped forward, disarmed Bungy and kicked the knife into the harbour. This made Bungy even more abusive, leading to Bert landing a punch on his face and knocking him on to the wooden jetty. He

SUMMER CRUISE

Chief ERA Badland with the Governor Sir William Murphy & Lady Murphy

The Governor's Garden Party, Nassau, Bahamas

The reception given by the Governor of the Bahamas following the cruise

161

staggered back up, still shouting abuse to be met with a series of blows to the head until he was finally subdued. The problem was, we had no handcuffs and so it was necessary to twist his arms behind his back and more-or-less throw him into the motor cutter which had by this time arrived.

Back on board, it was decided to put Bungy in the tiller flat to cool off as the ship did not have the 'luxury' of cells to keep miscreants. In the Navy, the job of guarding a prisoner falls to his messmates and, of course, he happened to be on Number Five mess, my mess. I therefore took up position on the outside of the tiller flat hatch which had four clips, standing by the closed hatch down to the aft four-inch magazine. Soon, one of the clips started to move, whereupon I immediately put it back but another clip came off as Bungy attempted to get out of his confinement. This stupid situation went on for quite a while; Bungy trying to open the hatch but as fast as he did so, I put the clips on again.

After quite a while, he appeared to give up and things quietened down so I was able to sit on the magazine hatch to keep my lonely vigil. Not for long, however, because soon a shout from the quarterdeck was heard.

"Bungy's got out!"

True enough, when I reached the quarterdeck he was standing there, swaying on his feet, but upright! Everyone had forgotten that there was another exit from the tiller flat – upwards on to the quarterdeck and Bungy, despite the drink and the knocks he had taken, had found that hatch which was unguarded.

The Bosun's Mate who raised the alarm had meanwhile disappeared to get help, leaving me to reason with Bungy. He then made for the starboard side aft towards the short boom to which the motor cutter had by now been secured, climbed over the guard rail and shouted out that he was going to swim for shore. My response was to encourage him to do just that, adding … "either sharks or the barracudas will get you before you get very far. The blood on your face will certainly attract the sharks." This response was perhaps not the most sensible one but fortunately it worked and Bungy came back over the guard-rail onto the quarterdeck where, by this time, the duty watch were waiting for him. He had completely lost face in more ways than one because by now, he could hardly see through the puffed up bruising on his face. He was led, quite meekly this time, down to the tiller flat where he lay on some of the awnings which provided a make-shift bed for him until the morning, allowing me to have some sleep too while he was guarded, this time, by two other members of Number Five Mess, much to their annoyance.

The following morning, his face hardly recognisable, Bungy was led to the Captain's table on the starboard side of the fo'c'sle where he was charged and received a 'Remand'. This meant a punishment which had to be authorised by the Commander-in-Chief and the verdict was duly delivered … an extension of his 'Two and Two' punishment. He was extremely lucky not to have received a harsher sentence, a sentiment that was agreed by just about everyone on board. Commander Twiss, who had originally been expected to be a severe disciplinarian was, in fact, a humanitarian who went up in everyone's estimation. Bungy became much quieter; admittedly he was only allowed ashore once during the term of his punishment but this time his run ashore passed off quietly. He was a changed man!

While still on the subject of punishments in the Royal Navy, the case of the killik of Number Six Mess was somewhat severe. He had received news of the birth of his first child and went ashore to buy presents. Unfortunately, some mess savings were paid at the same time and so he used the money for his purchases. He was found out, hauled before the Captain and reduced to Able Seaman. At the same time, as the charge against him was one of theft, he had to leave the ship and in fact, he was sent home for re-deployment. Theft from one's shipmates is a serious crime and punishments always severe but there were members of his Mess who were prepared to take a lenient view in the circumstance even though it involved their money.

Author at X gun

To return to the cruise, *Porlock Bay* sailed to Kingston, Jamaica where she was met by remarkable thunderstorms. Here, we refuelled before proceeding to Belize which was the capital city of British Honduras at the time. Today, Belize is the name of the Central American Country and has been since independence. Word soon got around that British Honduras was about to be invaded by their neighbour, Guatemala and we could possibly expect trouble. Rumour had it that the Guatemalan Air Force had six aircraft which just might make a surprise attack on the capital so some rounds of ammunition were brought up from the magazines and placed in the Ready Use lockers, just in case! It was, however, not an idle threat because not long afterwards the flagship *Sheffield* was detached from the Squadron to carry out 'gun boat' duties, and landing a party of seamen and marines in a show of force.

However, our stay in Belize went off extremely peacefully and many of us went ashore to see the mainly wooden houses in the capital but little else as the country is covered in trees including Mahogany. The Chief Electrical Artificer, Bob Atkinson, took advantage of the situation by buying a log of mahogany which was kept in the Quartermaster's lobby until our return to the UK. Far from adopting a belligerent role, some of us were able to take a banyan party on a small island lying just off the channel we had gone through to reach Belize. The small cay was only a few feet above sea level as, in fact was Belize itself and the only man made structure was a metal tower holding an automatic light to guide ships along the channel but the food was good and we enjoyed ourselves there. In the meantime, C.E.R.A. Philip Coulson was able to spend a few hours with his brother, George, who was serving with the Gloucester Regiment's small detachment in Belize.

Our return journey along the channel took us past the little cay, where we had so recently enjoyed our banyan, out to the Caribbean once more on our way to La Ceiba in the Republic of Honduras where we spent four days, in my case without going ashore. Our next port of call should have been Greytown, Nicaragua but news came through that a revolution was taking place there so *Porlock Bay* gave it a wide berth and nipped back to Kingston, Jamaica once more to take on fuel.

Refuelling complete, we set off south for Barranquila, Columbia for a seven-day visit to this South American port. The country which later became notorious for supplying drugs to the US and Britain was certainly pro-British at the time and we were made to feel most welcome. On one occasion, our guard was turned out for a wreath laying ceremony at a memorial by the Captain, and the twelve ratings plus Petty Officer Penney and Lieutenant Tetley paraded about a mile away to march through the city. We had donned our spotless Number Sixes and the belt and gaiters of each rating had recently been whitened so that, with the sun shining on our bayonets, we presented an extremely smart appearance. This view was expressed by the chap who had taken my little box camera to get a few shots of the lads as we marched away. What we had not realised was that the Colombian Army were turning out in force for the occasion, almost a thousand of them, which completely overshadowed our twelve-man guard.

Crowds had turned out along the route but whereas the people applauded their local soldiers, the sound reached a crescendo as we passed. We rose to the occasion and the folks loved it as we made our way to the memorial where we lined up for the ceremony. As the Captain stepped forward to lay the wreath, we presented arms to even greater applause before marching off. By this time the local military had disappeared and we were alone to savour the adulation of the crowd all the way back to the ship.

During our week in Barranquila, the ship was open to visitors most afternoons to the consternation of the duty watch. On one occasion as we waited for the crowds, everyone hung back when hordes of schoolchildren arrived on the quayside. A master came over the brow first and was seen talking to Lieutenant Tetley, the Officer of the Day. Language was the problem as few of the visitors could speak any English and no one aboard could speak Spanish but Tetley had a bright idea.

"Able Seaman Smith, you can speak fairly fluent French," he said when he had called me forward. "If you explain the various parts of the ship to this gentleman in French he will translate for the benefit of his pupils." Only a limited number of kids could be included in each party so I spent the next hour speaking French until he had acquired enough knowledge of the ship to explain to the children himself. All part of showing the flag! La plume de ma tante had triumphed.

On another occasion we were invited to the local Coca Cola factory and travelled there by coach where we were met by a VIP of the organisation. Fortunately, he could speak English so we followed him round the bottling plant but, when someone asked about the ingredients, all he could say was that they were a secret. We were then taken into a room where waitresses handed out glasses of rum which disappeared down the throats of the majority of matelots before it was explained that the Coca Cola had to be added. This meant a refill of rum before the Coke arrived. Unfortunately there were one or two who declined the Coke when it came round!

On another occasion, we were taken by coach to a club where there was some music but we soon found out that the place was essentially a brothel, frequented by businessmen mainly. One of these explained to me that it was quite normal to patronise such establishments but later he told a group of us that, during the war, Nazi U-boats came into Barranquila to refuel and re-provision. One U-boat, when it left, was not heard of again! Although we nodded at this, we did not fully believe him because we knew that most of the later U-boats were supplied by the 'milchkuhs' or milkcows, the larger supply U-boats. There was a possibility however that the event had happened soon after the US entered the war when Operation Paukenschlag was instrumental in sinking many allied vessels, particularly tankers transporting oil to the US and Britain. Admiral King, the US Commander-in-Chief resolutely refused to adopt the convoy system and the result was the finest 'Happy Days' for the U-boat commanders, until the Admiral was forced to change his mind. The Admiral disliked anything British and he was extremely stubborn so the change took quite a long time to materialise!

Our time in Barranquila over, we prepared for sea once more as the weather was beginning to worsen. It was a large harbour and so most of the wires had been stowed away on the reels before we left the harbour bar. Some of us were still on the fo'c'sle as we met the sea when the bows dropped and a wall of water appeared before us, towering many feet above. Someone shouted "hang on" and we did just that as the bows lifted and spray came over us. Our job done, we made our way aft as quickly as possible, drenched to the skin. Thereafter the seas were not too rough but the initial exit from the harbour was quite worrying.

Our next port was Orangestadt, Aruba, the second of the Dutch West Indies Islands after Curaçao where we arrived four days later, by which time the weather had improved. There were several British people living there so a couple of us were entertained at the home of a couple who originated from the "the Trent area" without finding out precisely where. Anyway, the meal was excellent and a most welcome change from our more normal diet which now often consisted of tinned sausages, triangular in section which tasted like, and probably consisted of, sawdust.

After two days in Orangestadt, Aruba we set off once more for a place where each watch was to be given two days' leave, Trinidad, one of the Windward Islands lying close to the South American mainland. Port of

Spain, the capital, lies to the north of the island and that was where we secured, ostensibly for seven days. There is a large Indian population on the island and, while English is the generally accepted language, various Hindu dialects together with French, patois and Spanish were often heard in the multicultural island. Cricket seems almost a religion there with excellent facilities in Queen's Park Savannah where we watched a few overs before going on to Aggie's where we stayed for our leave. Sad to relate, sleeping in a bed with sheets was the greatest attraction for me rather than visiting the world's largest natural asphalt deposits or any of the other natural features.

The forty-eight-hour leave over, we made our way to the harbour and, arriving in good time to rejoin the ship, found to our absolute consternation, *Porlock Bay* had gone. There was a small army unit in the docks so we reported there but no one knew why the ship had departed early. We had to regard ourselves as being under open arrest in the meantime and it was extremely worrying not knowing if indeed the old ship would return or whether it would be necessary to make our way to the next port in the nearby island of Tobago. After about four hours, the mast of the ship and then the whole vessel was spotted on the horizon, making her way towards us. Eventually, we were able to clamber aboard to find that she had had to go out to meet an RN Auxiliary Oiler to refuel and, most comforting, we were not in 'the rattle'. We sailed immediately for Tobago feeling much relieved.

Tobago was only a few miles north east of Trinidad and we arrived there the same day. We found out that the population in Tobago at one time vastly exceeded that of Trinidad but had fallen back in more recent years. We also found out that there was daily boat service from Port of Spain to Scarborough in Tobago so, provided we could have afforded the fare, we could have rejoined the old ship there.

It was during our stay in Tobago that we saw some of the reports in the Trinidad newspapers. We learnt more about our own Captain who told the *Gazette* reporters that he had previously been to Trinidad in HMS *Rodney*, the ship that so many of our gunnery ratings had served in during the war. He also told the reporters of his experience as a Prisoner of War of the Japanese which he described as, "A tragic episode in the history of his career," and that he had been held in Hiroshima but moved shortly before the first atom bomb almost obliterated the city. It seemed strange that we should have to find out these facts about our own skipper from the West Indies press.

After three days in Tobago, we set off in a north-north-easterly direction for an island which stuck out in the Atlantic away from the other Windwards, Barbados. Of all the islands in the West Indies, Barbados was my favourite for several reasons, not least of which was the fact that my twentieth birthday was celebrated there. I was no longer a teenager but the milestone almost went unnoticed and it was only because, while in a bar ashore, someone mentioned that it was the 7th of September, that the importance of the date suddenly struck home! Of course it meant a few more tots of rum, naturally Barbados rum, with my mates before returning aboard. Another reason for liking the place was that, not only was there a Trafalgar Square in Bridgetown but Nelson's column stood within it, making us feel almost at home! The climate seemed ideal and, on a bus tour of the island, we had a swim-stop at a truly wonderful beach. The island was still under British rule, having been a colony continuously since 1625 and the British influence was most noticeable. Sugar plantations occupied much of the island and, understandably, that product accounted for over ninety per cent of their exports, a good proportion of which found its way to Britain. On the bus trip, someone remarked that it could be an ideal tourist island if only a few hotels could be built – how prophetic! On returning to the ship after the bus tour, there were several birthday cards among the post for me, together with my National Savings Bank Book which I had requested from home as we had recently taken aboard a Chief Writer who was empowered to take deposits for investments and make payments from it. It had been announced that War Gratuities and Post War Credits were shortly to be paid out and it seemed the most sensible thing to do was to invest it in National Savings, at least for the time being.

After reluctantly (for me) leaving Barbados, the ship then sailed south to the mainland of South America and headed for Georgetown, British Guiana. Heavy rain had apparently been falling inland and the river where we were to stay for the next seven days was in full spate. Accordingly, wires were doubled up immediately we secured at the jetty and a continuous watch was kept to ensure that we were not swept along with the flow! Several quite large animals were observed, obviously having been drowned in rapidly rising floods, as they floated by at a quite rapid rate.

My most memorable recollection of Georgetown was a trip to the botanical gardens with all the tropical flora and a large, well stocked lake, containing a group of manatees in addition to some massive fish. These large mammals appeared when our guide, an English lady, called them by splashing a handful of long grass in the water and, cautiously stepping back, we were told that they were strictly herbivorous and no danger to humans. How anyone could associate them with mermaids however was a complete mystery as they appeared so ungainly, nothing like the shapely mermaids we see in kids' picture books!

It was very hot and humid in British Guiana, so much so that we were glad when our visit came to an end and we could get out to sea once more. Not that we had not enjoyed the hospitality of the British community but there seemed more 'air' in the open sea. However, there was a little too much 'air' as we sailed into a hurricane, missing the 'eye' but feeling the effects of winds blowing at 120 m.p.h. What a shame we had not stayed longer in Georgetown but it was necessary to keep our appointment in Santiago, Cuba so we had to weather the storm. *Porlock Bay* did just that and we were much relieved that the 'Bay' class were such good sea boats.

The seas subsided as we sailed on and, on one hot afternoon, sitting in the mess in the afternoon, having had a 'tot' which made me feel quite light headed, a click was heard as the SRE was switched on. A voice came over to us saying, "This is the Captain speaking. A message has just been received from the Admiralty to the effect that, due to the dollar crisis, this ship is to return to the United Kingdom at the end of this cruise. Further details will be given to you in due course."

We looked at one another in stunned silence for a few seconds. Who could it be, playing a practical joke like that? But it really was the Captain's voice and, realising the message was genuine, the mess deck emptied in an orgy of shouting and cheering. Missiles were thrown about from one mess to another in the excitement and pandemonium reigned for the next five minutes or so.

It all seemed unbelievable to hear the news so soon after the itinerary for our next cruise had been put on the notice board outside the Regulating Office. Although the full list of ports which were to be visited escapes me, the cruise was the 'plum' one for the America and West Indies Squadron, sailing back through the Caribbean to Panama and thence through the canal to the Galapagos Islands, Valparaiso, round Cape Horn to the Falkland Islands and back to Bermuda via Rio de Janeiro and Montevideo. Although we all wanted to get home as soon as possible and get our 'release' papers, most of us were in a quandary. The cruise would be the chance of a lifetime to see some of the most interesting places in the world and, for the sake of a few months longer in the Navy, we could be turning down a wonderful opportunity by not volunteering to serve the extra time. For two weeks, we had been agonising over the choice and our recall to the UK solved the problem – the ship would be going home and we would be going with her!

The ship's mail box was filled with all the letters home, telling our parents, friends and loved ones that we would soon be with them adding in my case, "get out my civvies". In fact, some of the ratings had civvies with them as the regulations requiring us to go ashore in the rig of the day had been relaxed but mine only included flannels and my old school blazer as I had never actually been a 'civilian' before joining up.

All our thoughts now were directed to going home with increasing emphasis on our future jobs. However, we had two more ports to visit before we arrived back in Bermuda to refuel, re-stock with provisions and get away. Unfortunately, things would not run too smoothly and we were due some troublesome times which were totally unforeseen.

We duly arrived in Santiago de Cuba at the eastern end of the largest of the Caribbean islands having been challenged once more by the United States authorities at Guantanamo Bay. It was clear from the start that we were most welcome as the local people in the ports were very pro-British. One of the first things we learnt was that, during the war, the people had had a collection to buy a Spitfire for the RAF which had been named 'Marti the Apostle' so the portents sounded good.

While the majority had been invited to a party ashore, the first part of port watch were on duty, cutting out any participation by me. As the lads came back aboard, they all said what a wonderful time they had had at the party with plenty of girls, drink and food. Apparently, the local people had given each man two tickets, one as a pass to get into the dance and the other to get a few free drinks. Unfortunately, whether due to ignorance or perhaps it was deliberate, several used both tickets in exchange for drinks which meant that the 'kitty' had been overspent and our hosts had had to raise more money to settle the bill.

Commander Twiss was advised about this and the following morning he had lower deck cleared to give the whole ship's company a 'rocket'. He did not conceal his anger against those who had perpetrated the swindle, calling all those who went to the party a load of 'spivs'. Several looked extremely sheepish as he continued his tirade but, for me, not knowing any of the details it was difficult to understand. No one knows for certain but it seems that the Captain himself reimbursed the organisers of the party. In any case, everyone was quiet and subdued as the ratings left the quarterdeck and, below decks, recriminations began.

We learnt that Santiago de Cuba was originally the capital of Cuba but had suffered much from earthquakes, fortunately not while we were there. At the time of the First World War, Cuba provided a quarter of the world's supply of sugar, after which production declined only to be increased again during the Second World War. Almost every island we had visited in the Caribbean had relied largely on sugar for exports so it seemed rather surprising that such a large proportion of the world supply came from Cuba. Rather surprisingly also, none of our chaps bought cigars to take home despite their relatively cheap price in the shops ashore!

Two days after our departure from Santiago de Cuba we arrived in Miami, Florida and proceeded along a straight waterway to our berth there. The weather was far from good and, looking round, we could hardly see a tree standing for the city had recently been hit by a hurricane. The hospitality of the local people exceeded that of anywhere we had been previously and a dance had been arranged for the ship's company on the day after our arrival. There were girls in abundance but we soon found out that the majority were G.I. Brides who had conveniently left their husbands at home, all of them by this time, speaking with strong American accents. One motherly lady came over to our group and said to me in her southern drawl… "Well what do think of my Emma?" to which I very stupidly replied, "I have not yet met your Emma," which raised a loud laugh from the lady. What she had actually said was, "What do you think of Miami?" but I had misconstrued her meaning. Fortunately she could see the funny side of the situation.

We were invited to many of the large hotels to use their swimming pools and were taken on a coach ride around the city, passing a stockaded property once owned by Al Capone who apparently died there. Trees were lying all over the place as the local authority was inundated with calls to take them away after the hurricane. It was indeed a sorry sight but the population were slowly returning to normal and generally made light of the situation – "after all it had happened before and would no doubt happen again" – seemed to be their attitude.

While on duty watch on the second evening, news spread that stoker 'Dicky' Bird, the only other chap from Warwickshire, had not returned from the previous night's shore leave. Apparently, he had friends or relatives living in Florida and it was thought that he had gone to visit them. It seemed strange that anyone should go AWOL at this time when we were almost on our way home but then came the news that a body had been found floating off Biscayne Boulevard. The Officer of the Day, Lieutenant Tetley, and PO Taff Penney went over to the local mortuary and there they identified the body as that of Stoker Bird. He had, apparently, much bruising to his face and body and it was thought at first that it was a case of murder. He had left a party of other Stokers to return to ship, having had a few drinks and, at the autopsy, it was said that he was a non-swimmer and, in the darkness had fallen into the water. The verdict was 'accidental death' although there are still some who think otherwise.

His death ashore meant that he would be buried in the local cemetery and, of course, that would involve all the formalities of a funeral firing party. None of us in the guard had ever had to carry out these duties before so we were given a half-hour practice, provided by the G.I. Petty Officer Bill Scurfield. We were to stand at the graveside 'on arms reversed' before going to the firing position – quite a simple manoeuvre but our first effort was far from good. "Have you got that?" enquired Bill, to which I shouted out "No". He then proceeded to demonstrate the move slowly and so we greatly improved our drill at the next attempt.

Fully belted and gaitered and carrying rifles we were taken by coach to the cemetery where we formed up at the graveside. Bill Scurfield came round and gave each member of the guard three blank rounds which were slid into our pristine white belts. We then assumed the 'arms reversed' position and, no sooner had we done so, the heavens opened and the heaviest rain I have ever experienced came down. Of course, with bowed heads, the rain just poured down our necks to completely soak us but we had to stand like statues and just let it happen. The service was short and the coffin lowered into the grave as the rain continued to descend in torrents. We were then brought to the firing position and everyone, having learnt the routine, moved as one man. One round was loaded and Bill, in a voice that was heard by all of us, but not too prominent, gave the order, "Fire". Again, we were all together as we were twice more and so we were then marched away to the coach for the return aboard. The local newspaper photographer had braved the weather and had taken an exposure just as we fired but our faces were all streaked with white which had come from the blanco freshly applied to our caps.

Back aboard, we returned rifles, belts and gaiters before we could go below to get our wet clothes off. With a quick rub down and a fresh pair of underpants, my Number Six suit was put in a bucket to dhobey and we all sat around in the mess looking very dejected. We were still there about ten minutes later when one of the older, continuous service ratings said to me, "Cheer up, young'un. Dicky Bird has now got his release from Naval Service but you're still in!" Well, that was perhaps one way of looking at the situation but it did not make me feel any happier.

My cap and cap tally were ruined and it meant buying a replacement out of my KUA but this sacrifice was insignificant when we thought of Dickie Bird. He was another non-swimmer but many were convinced that he had been murdered and it had been suggested by folks ashore that anti-British members of the Jewish community could have been responsible. On the evening that we heard of his death, a group of us had been ashore and because the street lights had been affected by the recent hurricane. I heard a voice behind me calling, "Hey! Sailor". Looking back, a very large chap had almost caught me up and soon he towered over me. Fortunately, he turned out to be a former US serviceman, a sergeant who had served in Europe and who had married a girl from Leicester. She had not been able to see over the ship the previous day when we were open to visitors and he asked whether it would be possible for her to do so, hopefully the next afternoon.

This was easily arranged and she duly turned up at the brow at the appointed time, a really stunning girl who turned everyone's head as I took her over the ship. She told me that she had been unable to get a babysitter when the ship was officially open to visitors but that her husband's mother was acting in that capacity now. As she left, she asked me to bring one of my mates for dinner at their bungalow – her husband would pick us up and return us afterwards. True to her word, Jimmy High arrived in a brand new convertible and the lads on board looked on with envy as Johnny Stoker and I drove off with him to their home for an excellent meal. Jimmy was the owner of a gas station which we discovered was a petrol filling station. How true were the words of George Bernard Shaw when he said that we were two Nations *divided* by a common language!

Our visit to Miami had been most memorable and at the end of it we prepared to leave just as the wind started to freshen once more. Having singled up, we eventually set off from the dockside where there were overhanging buildings. Soon we were going straight into the jetty and, while an emergency full astern was rung through on the engine room telegraphs, we grabbed the bearing-off spars on the quarterdeck. The wind had really caught the ship but, making a second attempt, we finally steamed down the waterway, glancing at the tall buildings as we went, until we reached the open sea.

We were expecting rough seas and rough they were! On our way from Cuba to Florida, two plates in the ship had been sprung and the Asdic Compartment was the next to be sealed off. Apart from the flooded compartments, *Porlock Bay* had proved herself in the Caribbean hurricane season and, earlier, in the north Atlantic storms, without damage which would have caused concern. Of great concern however was some further news from the Admiralty stating that the majority of the continuous service ratings would *not* be going home. We were to transfer all these unfortunate individuals, including Able Seaman Slack whose honeymoon would be further delayed, to our flagship and, in return, take aboard all her HOs whose demob numbers were coming up in the near future. The news obviously created some gloom and despondency but, having survived the war, they took the news with creditable complacency and accepted the situation with a fatalism that was typical of the regular seamen.

For the rest of us, we made out slop chits to get mainly underwear to take home, thinking that we would have a hard time financially once demobbed – this, in my case, became only too true! The twenty sets of vests and underpants at one and nine-pence each proved a good investment! All this kit raised a new problem which was quite difficult to solve. While on board we had lockers which, with the square cushions, provided the seats we used when eating our meals. Quite often ratings would sleep on the cushions to the annoyance of the locker owners waiting to get items out. Our large kit bags were stored on the racks between the seats and the ship's side together with the smaller, black steaming bags, our new green suitcases with their leather corners and the smaller attaché cases but would these suffice to hold all our possessions?

We headed back to Bermuda, buffeted by heavy seas most of the way until the low lines of the islands came into view. We went through the narrows once more, saluted Admiralty House and proceeded, for the last time, into the harbour. Here, another batch of mail awaited us, amongst which was a letter from my cousin and his wife who were expecting their second child, asking me to be godfather to the offspring, sex unknown at the time. Other letters asked for details of our homecoming, the precise date for which we were unable to give immediately but all said that details were required as soon as possible in order to arrange parties.

13

HOMECOMING

"Home is the sailor, home from the sea."
Robert Louis Stevenson

There were so many things to do before our departure, not least of which was to go ashore to buy 'rabbits' to take home including food for our forthcoming parties. In my case, a christening present for my godchild-to-be was called for and a visit to a jeweller in Front Street, Hamilton was my most important requirement. To pay for all the loot to take home, we dug deep into the funds in our Post Office Savings Bank, so recently supplemented by the payment of war gratuities and post-war credits which had arrived at a most opportune time.

All this time we were totally oblivious to the necessary work being carried out by the dockyard workers to patch up the three holes in our hull and to make our ship seaworthy. Rather surprisingly, we did not have to go into the floating dock again so the work of the dockyard people must have been difficult as much of it had, of necessity, to be carried out underwater. Fortunately they completed their task in time for our departure.

Letters from home all seemed to ask if friends and relatives could be admitted into Devonport dockyard to see our homecoming but we could not tell them the precise date and time of our homecoming, as we did not know it ourselves. The main reason for this was that a hurricane which was sweeping through the Caribbean could swing out into the Atlantic and hit Bermuda. Surely it couldn't happen now; after all, it was umpteen years since the last hurricane hit the islands, which were a mere dot on a map of the Atlantic, so why did it have to threaten us now?

Soon we had orders to batten down and double up all mooring wires, several with hurricane hawsers. In the meantime, the flagship and most of the remaining ships of the Squadron left harbour to ride out the forthcoming storm but, of course, we were unable to go to sea as the holes in the hull had not yet been patched up. All we could do was wait and hope.

Although none of us saw the barometer, the air pressure dropped dramatically and the skies turned black, leading to winds which became more and more intense every minute. Very soon we were experiencing winds of more than 120 miles per hour, whipping up the water in the harbour and generally making life pretty unpleasant on board. We remained in our own part of ship in case required but otherwise we were 'off duty' throughout. Those of us who ventured on deck suddenly saw all the slates on one of the old dockyard buildings go flying into the air and we took shelter from these flying objects which could have been lethal. After what seemed an age but was in fact about two to three hours, the winds dropped but the skies were still very black. We were now in the 'eye' of the hurricane and the 'reassuring' voice of one of the old salts was heard saying, "we will now be hit from the other direction and it will be many times worse than before!"

True enough, we were hit again from the opposite direction and this time, some of us who went on deck had steel helmets on as protection against slates and other flying objects. It seemed most incongruous to see the chaos in steel helmets while wearing only shorts but at least no one lingered for long on deck, and fortunately the hurricane hawsers held the old ship to the bollards on land. As usual, we had the 'cats' between us and the dockside and these were chafing against the ship's side but what is a lick of paint to what might have happened?

On a visit to Hamilton before the hurricane, one or two of us had paid a visit to the library to find out about the natural phenomenon which 'rarely hit the island' and found the report about HMS *Calcutta* under the command of Captain A.B. Cunningham which was in the south part of the harbour at the time under maintenance when, after the 'eye' of the hurricane had passed, an offshore wind of at least 138 m.p.h blew her away from her moorings and she came to rest against the north east breakwater at the entrance to the harbour. She needed her engines at full speed ahead to keep her head into the wind and several men had leapt on to the breakwater to secure the ship. They were successful and eventually when the winds had subsided, *Calcutta* was able to return to the oil wharf where it was found that only superficial damage had been done to the hull. The main damage was, in fact, to the radio aerials which had been swept away.

While the *Calcutta* drama was taking place, HMS *Valerian* was returning to Bermuda after giving assistance in the Bahamas following a hurricane there, when she too was hit by the same extremely high winds. Those on board had been told that Bermuda had not been hit by a hurricane in October for over 100 years and, anyway, the weather reports suggested that the storm would pass about 300 miles north of the islands. She signalled the Commander-in-Chief that she had hoved to about five miles south west of Gibb's Hill Lighthouse and that was the last anyone heard of her. The reefs surrounding the islands had claimed yet another victim.

We therefore breathed multiple sighs of relief when the winds abated and we were able to inspect the remarkably slight damage to *Porlock Bay*. Although our departure would be delayed, we had at least survived what could have been a disastrous storm. Ashore, there were many reports of damage to property and one telegraph linesman had been killed in Hamilton. The corrugated metal roof on the Phoenix Drug Store had just disappeared, never to be seen again but, on our next visit, the capital was returning to almost normal. To misquote George Bernard Shaw in the elocution lesson of *Pygmalion*, "In Hereford, Hertfordshire and Hampshire, hurricanes hardly ever happen," which may well be true but never believe anyone who states that they never happen in Bermuda in October. We had certainly found out that it was not correct!

Stores were taken aboard for our homeward journey and the exchange took place of the ship's company. In return for our continuous service ratings we received several HOs from *Sheffield*, and the sudden realisation became apparent. *We* were now the experienced seamen, the old salts who would have to show their new chaps, who had served in 'big ships' the ropes. There were only a few days to do so before our penultimate day in Bermuda but it was not too difficult and soon they settled in to a new life. Whereas they had been used to having meals prepared for them, they now had to do the job themselves and, fortunately on my mess, no one had said that they couldn't cook!

The evening before our departure saw a mass exodus from *Porlock Bay* and *Sheffield* when everyone not on duty watch proceeded to the Fleet Canteen for a farewell drink. The canteen was packed, the beer flowed but, whereas there was normally singing, the euphoria was tinged with sadness. There was no "I'll see you home again, Kathleen", which had previously been a favourite, and "There's an old mill by the stream, Nellie Dean" was forgotten as ratings sat, unusually well behaved, at the tables, talking about the experiences we had had since our arrival on the A & WI Station. Noel Coward could have used the occasion to entitle one of his shows "Bitter Sweet!"

One by one the ratings left the canteen, some very much the worse for drink to make their way back to either their old ship or to their new one. Unknown at the time was the condition of Able Seaman Jock Rea – he had been drinking but had he been drinking to excess? No one could satisfactorily answer that question as every person had other things to think about but, the following morning, as everyone was still feeling the effects, the ship was searched from top to bottom.

The Officer of the Day, accompanied by the coxswain and preceded by the Bosun's Mate, stormed through the ship, searching in every possible nook and cranny. My job was to open up the magazines and it was only then that the truth emerged. They were looking for Jock, that irrepressible Scottish Nationalist who had so recently shouted "Gott Straff England" and who, having been transferred to *Sheffield*, may be trying to get back to the UK aboard his old ship. He had definitely been in the canteen but his station card was in *Sheffield*'s Regulating Office, awaiting collection and he was nowhere to be seen aboard the flagship.

The search proved fruitless and, after about an hour, was abandoned. We all had plenty to do before our mid-afternoon departure so Jock was temporarily forgotten and we would not hear about him until some time after our arrival in the UK.

The joyous moment had arrived. The engine room telegraphs started ringing, the coxswain was on the wheel, wires were slipped from the shore bollards and the order, "Slow astern port," given. The remaining wire was slipped and then we went forward slowly, with our paying off pendant billowing out in the slight breeze, with a balloon on the end. We had all put in at least one stitch into the paying off pendant in accordance with tradition and we now saw the fruit of that labour, such as it was, in its full glory.

As we passed each ship, the 'still' was piped and the various ships' companies cheered as they lined the sides to say goodbye. Many ribald shouts were heard from the flagship as we slowly made our way to the harbour mouth, shouts from those transferred so recently who must be wondering why they were not going home too, including poor old Able Seaman Slack. Suddenly, someone called my name from across the water –

"Good Luck, Smithy!" It was none other than Bungy Williams who had certainly redeemed himself, in my estimation at least. The voices continued until we swung round in the southern part of the harbour and, gradually increasing speed, proceeded into Grassy Bay. Then it was out through the narrows, but before doing so, we saluted Admiralty House for the last time.

The wind was still fresh as we went ahead into seas which were still a little rough after the hurricane. How would the new ratings take to their new ship? *Porlock Bay* was a first class ship in stormy weather but they were used to a larger ship which would be less lively in a seaway. One of their number was soon in difficulties as he developed toothache and we had no doctor on board, let alone a dentist. In view of my own experiences when five teeth were extracted in as many seconds, my sympathy was with him and so I lent him my old school scarf to wrap around his painful jaw. Later, when the pain was almost unbearable, I even kept a watch for him to obviate the need to go up in the howling gale to stand look-out on the bridge.

Readers will no doubt have realised that Humphrey Ixer and I were now having to revert to being deck seamen rather than enjoying the benefit of being able to take our watch in the 293 Radar Office. This was due to the fact that the old ship had had several Radar Plot Ratings transferred to her from the *Sheffield* and, as they were fully qualified in that field (or should I say office?) they were automatically selected for the 'indoor' job. It seemed so ironic that, in the heat of the West Indies, we had to endure the almost suffocating conditions of the Radar Office but when we headed north-east towards home, through the bad weather of the North Atlantic, we had to take our watch as sea-boats crew, bridge messenger, in the wheelhouse or, worst of all, as bridge look-outs. We considered ourselves as 'born losers' at the time although, in retrospect, we had enjoyed a far better time than those serving during the war on, say, the Russian Convoys. Anyway it is always the seaman's prerogative to have a moan! Additionally, we had to remember that we were going home, hopefully for demob.

After two days an echo appeared on the 293 PPI which slowly developed into a yacht seen by one of the look-outs. The yacht was in trouble as it had been demasted in the hurricane and consequently had lost its radio aerial. We went alongside and asked if the occupants needed assistance but, fortunately for both of us, the yacht's engine was still working and they assured us that they could reach Bermuda. Our hearts, which had sunk when we thought we would have to tow the yacht back into Bermuda, were uplifted again when their answer came across, so, making a signal back to our old base giving the position of the yacht, we were able to wish them well and resume our former course.

Our speed, which was our normal cruising speed, seemed dreadfully slow but, on our return journey, we would not have to call in at the Azores as we did on the outward leg. The seas became rougher and rougher and the weather became much colder as we progressed across the Atlantic so, out came the pullovers and the other items of sea rig which had been packed away for so long. A competition was started, requiring a stake of one shilling-a-go to estimate the time we would pass the breakwater to Plymouth Sound and it seemed that everyone on board had risked their money by the time the 'book' closed.

Eventually there was a shout which brought almost everyone up on deck. Bishop Rock Lighthouse had been sighted! The previous day we had seen trawlers being thrown about in the sea and most of the ratings had gone 'up top' to see them, but Bishop Rock was the first, albeit small, bit of land. Few of us gave much thought to the return home of Admiral Sir Cloudesley Shovell whose fleet, through a navigational error, came to grief off the Scilly Isles. Fortunately, Harrison's chronometer had later overcome the problem of determining longitude and, anyway, we had Lieutenant Tetley to see that we steered a precise course to avoid the Scillies.

With equal accuracy, we passed the breakwater and made for a buoy in the sound. It was a dark night and there was no welcome for us as Able Seaman Bungy Edwards, taken over in the whaler, secured to the buoy. What an anti-climax! It was almost as if we were ashamed of ourselves, slipping in under cover of darkness to lie there until the morning. For me, however, our return had its compensation for my guess as to the time we passed the breakwater was the correct one and I collected the entire amount of ten pounds. It might have been a thousand such was my excitement at getting such a fortune!

Shore leave was granted to a few who particularly wanted to land on English soil for the first time in ages and they were taken by motor cutter to Mill Bay Docks. Most of us were prepared to wait till we went alongside at about midday the following day so, in my case an early night was called for.

"Call the hands, heavo, heavo, heavo," came too early and we were told that, before we could proceed up the Hamoaze, the ship's paintwork had to be touched up to hide the ravages of the Atlantic crossing. On the third of November the water was most uninviting so everyone took care to stay on the stages while swinging over the side. It was a typical November morning which seemed so cold that we almost wished to be back in Bermuda but, as daylight broke, we could see the hoe with a few twinkling lights still showing and began to look forward to the morning's events.

Mid-morning, the paintwork finished to the satisfaction of the buffer, Bungy Edwards did his job again but in reverse and we prepared to cross the Sound past Drake's Island. By this time the paying off pendant was flying proudly from the masthead and the seamen had changed into their Number Threes. The weak autumn sun was beginning to shine as we proceeded up the Hamoaze almost to the adulation it seemed of the other vessels lying alongside. The 'still' was piped incessantly as we made our way passed flagstaff steps towards our berth and, then, we saw the reception party on the quayside, all those who had taken a chance on getting into the dockyard.

We had no guard this time for entering harbour so, as a fo'c'sle man, I took my place in the bows as we approached HMS *Burghead Bay*, a sister 'Bay' class frigate. We seemed to be approaching at too great an angle and the speed was a little fast with the result that we went into *Burghead Bay*'s motor cutter with such a crunch that the ship's boat suddenly became like matchwood. We had arrived home. Wires went out and we were soon tied up alongside *Burghead Bay*. Even a telephone line was fixed up to the old ship in double quick time before those wonderful words were heard, "Finished with main engines." Our pelagic peregrinations were finally over.

There were many friends and relatives on the quayside and I looked around, hoping that my folks had disregarded my advice, but there was no sign of them. Very soon, my name was called to answer the phone so rushing away, knocking everyone out of the way, I grasped the receiver. It was not from home, much to my disappointment, but the call from leading Seaman 'Guts' Freeman, the killik of my mess when I first joined *Porlock Bay*, was most welcome. He had returned to the UK to train as a sailmaker, a trade in which he was now qualified, and he now lived more-or-less permanently in Plymouth. He suggested getting one or two of the lads together for a drink in the 'Unicorn' in Union Street to chat about the Commission. He had not been back to Old Milverton, the village of his boyhood which was only two miles from my home, and was now firmly established with his wife near to the dockyard.

The receiver had only just been replaced when it was announced that Customs Officers would shortly come aboard to check on the 'rabbits'. They took over the Regulating Office and, one by one, we appeared before them with our few bits and pieces which were carefully examined and then the invoices were written out. In my case, the napkin ring bought so recently in Front Street, Hamilton attracted the most duty as they declared it to be sterling silver, hall marked in Birmingham – only twenty miles from my home! The stingy blighters required duty on every single item as, in those days, there was no allowance under which goods could be brought into the country duty-free. We were advised to keep our receipts as they would be required to show to the authorities on Albert Gate before we could go ashore with the goods and we certainly did not wish to pay twice. What a welcome home.

The good news was that we would be able to go ashore that afternoon while those in charge worked out the leave roster for the ship's company. Obviously, everyone wanted to get home immediately but there must be at least a skeleton crew left even if there was no intention of putting to sea.

Walking ashore in Devonport for the first time for ages was most exhilarating despite the general dockyard scene with bits of wire still scattered about and puddles still standing in the black ground. No thought was given to such trivial matters as these as we made our way towards the Albert Gate and thence out to catch the number seven double decker bus to Union Street. Stopping every few hundred yards, we went jerkily towards our first destination and, in my case, this was Octagon Square where I alighted and looked across the road towards the Seamen's Rest; Aggie's.

Looking exactly the same as ever, Aggie's was my first call in order to book a bed for the night (still one and six pence) and to have the greatest luxury since we set off to Bermuda, a bath. The baths were in the basement and so, filling one (almost) to the brim, I climbed into the warm water and just lay back, wallowing in such wonderful comfort. When I awoke, half an hour later, the water was quite cool so, letting out about half the water, I turned on the hot tap again, only to fall asleep once more. By this time, my skin seemed to be shrivelling up so I got out, dried myself down to sit on a stool for a few minutes before putting on my uniform.

The word 'uniform' suddenly made me remember that I had ordered a new Number One suit, complete with gold badge, from a naval tailor ashore and that this must be collected fairly soon. The suit had been ordered by post, midway through the last cruise but before we had heard the joyous news of our homecoming. It was the first proper Number One suit for me as, hitherto, one of my issue, blue, uniforms had sufficed, with the additions of an RC3 badge in gold, of course. My next call therefore was to the tailor where my new suit was awaiting me. Suit, blue, serge, with gold wire badge; everything was perfect even to the extent of the wide bell-bottoms which did seem exceptionally wide, probably thirty-two inches! It seemed ironic that the suit had been made for me just before we would be going through the Release from Service procedures but the bill was paid all the same and, with a brown parcel containing my old suit under my arm, I left the shop. The prize so recently paid to me for guessing the precise time of arrival helped and I was soon on my way to the NAAFI Club.

There was no apparent change in the appearance of the Club; still the same old Nissan Huts, joined together with corridors but the canteen beckoned as the smell of cooking wafted through the buildings. My old friend, Humphrey Ixer was already there so, ordering chicken (such a delicacy) and chips at the counter, I joined him at a table for two. It was as if we had not met for ages instead of a few hours, as we talked about going home and, out of the corner of my eye, I saw the most beautiful Wren imaginable, standing in the queue awaiting her meal. Humphrey must have seen the focus of my attraction because, with a sharp intake of breath he said, "Cor, she really is a smasher. I bet when I go, she'll come and sit with you, you jammy B..." He then left and I continued with my chicken and chips, when I suddenly became aware of someone behind me who asked, in a voice as beautiful as her appearance, "May I join you?" It was the Wren.

"Please do," I replied, but then, seeing the amusing side of Humphrey's remark, I must have swallowed a bone because a bad fit of coughing ensued; so bad that I just had to snatch up my brown paper parcel, apologise for leaving and hastily make my way to the toilets where I was violently sick, losing all my lovely chicken and chips down the lavatory pan.

"How ironic," were my immediate thoughts, "that we should come across the Atlantic with its October / November storms without suffering from mal de mer and now this should happen." My eyes wandered around the toilet cubicle as I waited before going back, only to see the same crude graffiti that had been there before we left for the West Indies. "Does nothing change?" After washing out my mouth, I made my way back to the canteen to find that, not only had the beautiful Wren gone, but so had the remains of my meal. What a waste of three and six pence!

The sickness continued over the next few days, after I had reached home, so it seemed almost certain that the cause was salmonella passed on by undercooked chicken. At least that was my diagnosis, wishing that the public health inspectors of today had been operating in 1947. C'est la vie!

Humphrey had been waiting in the other part of the Club and so we set off down the road to the Corporation Billiards Saloon which was also in Union Street for a game of snooker, a game that I have never been able to play well and tonight was no exception. "Hit it where it shines," was my motto but there is possibly more to the game than that.

After losing badly, we walked further along Union Street to where we had both booked a bed for the night but first, a call in the 'Unicorn' was called for.

"Two pints of Ind Coope please," was my order to the same barmaid as before but, this time, she was heavily pregnant. For the second time in two hours, the expression 'C'est la vie' came to mind!

Across the road was Aggie's and so, after a long and very eventful day, we went across to find an evening service just starting. We joined in, probably singing "Eternal Father strong to save ..." words that we knew by heart but feeling so exhausted we were both almost asleep standing up. Eventually, after making our laborious way up the stone steps, we reached our respective cubicles, a space no more than six foot by nine foot where I collapsed onto the bed. It was sheer bliss to lie there on a proper bed with real sheets and my joy was comparable to the bath that was my first priority ashore.

After a wonderful night's sleep, with no one knocking my hammock as they did on board, the 'waker-upper' knocked hard on my door, calling, "six-thirty," as he did to every other door on that floor. At least that was a welcome change to, "Call the hands, heave, heavo, heavo," and, furthermore, there was no dawn chorus! On with the uniform, down to the line of wash basins for a 'lick and a promise' before crossing the road to a disreputable little café which served bacon butties and tea, sweetened whether you liked it or not. After this glorious repast, back across the road where the double decker, red number seven bus was rapidly filling up with matelots, hardly awake and some suffering from over indulgence the previous night; it was not a pretty sight.

Back in a westerly direction, most of the lads staggered out when we reached the Albert Gate to make their slow way back to their respective ships where, after managing to salute the quarterdeck, most ratings slumped down below to their mess deck. A change into overalls was the rig of the day for most but, for us, the ship's notice board gave news of leave. At last! A two week spell away from the Navy for me so, without changing, I hastily packed my black steering bag with the rabbits and other essential items which, together with my attaché case, formed my luggage. At least when I got home, my uniform would not be seen for fourteen whole days.

Rather surprisingly the only other person travelling up to the Midlands was Chief Engine Room Artificer George Badland, who had joined the ship from the Squadron's Boom Defence Vessel, HMS *Moorpout* and who had a drink problem as a result of his war experiences. Accordingly, the two of us made our way to Plymouth North Road Station, armed with travel warrants and our luggage, where we climbed aboard the 11.15 train. By strange coincidence we found ourselves in the coach next to the refreshment coach which had a good supply of Guinness.

No sooner had the train left the station than George went along to the next coach, returning with a couple of bottles. After each stop along the way, one of us would repeat the process, bringing back a couple of bottles until the table was covered with empties. Newton Abbot, Exeter, Taunton, Bristol and Gloucester were passed before I suddenly thought that I had better go more steadily as my doting parents would be expecting the same young, sober lad who had not long left school when they last saw me. But, perhaps one more for the road at Cheltenham before we arrived at the station where I would change trains, Stratford-upon-Avon. In those days, Stratford-upon-Avon was a main line station at which the express trains stopped before continuing to Birmingham and Wolverhampton where George would stagger out, to be met by no one perhaps but where he would no doubt call at his local before going to what he called 'home'. Poor George, a victim of the war if ever there was one, seemed to have drink as his only consolation. At least, I too had 'consoled' him on the journey to Stratford.

The train slowly pulled into the station and, before it came to a halt, I spotted my father on the platform. George helped me out with my steaming bag while I went back to where my father was standing. As we were shaking hands, George came along, saying, "Don't believe him if he tells you he's behaved himself – he's been as pissed as a fart the whole cruise!" Fortunately, my father could see the funny side as he himself had been in the Royal Navy Air Service during the First World War, and thoroughly enjoyed the situation.

We had to wait for the local train to take my father and me to Warwick and it was only then that I realised that my arrival home was such an important event. Fireworks were going off all around, rockets were lighting the sky and the air positively reeked of bonfires.

"Fire over England" were my thoughts as I asked him the date.

"November the fifth," was his reply. "Why?"

"No reason, no reason at all," was my only response, as I went on to tell him about our arrival in Devonport.

Stopping at all the small stations, the train trundled along until familiar sights were seen in Warwick. It stopped at the station and there was my mother, waiting for us patiently. Mr Taylor, the local taxi driver was waiting in his car outside and we were soon on our way home. It was all so well arranged, but then, trains generally ran on time during and just after the war and it was possible to expect their arrival within a few minutes of the time stated in the time tables. How times changed during the next fifty years!

Fortunately, no parties had been arranged for that night as I was in no condition to attend one, mainly through tiredness although the drink had contributed! We talked about everything but nothing in particular. Handing over my ration card, I learnt that, now the war was over, rationing was even more strict. Even bread was now rationed – something that never happened during the war and, in my ration documents were the 'Bread Units'. Coal was in short supply, meaning that our Edwardian home was always cold as we could only have one open fire. Thus was the country to which I had longed to return. Economically, England was bankrupt and soon after our homecoming, the Chancellor of the Exchequer made his historic speech on the radio to the effect that our currency had been devalued from just over four dollars to the pound to two-seventy-something dollars. It had been bad enough for us to exist on four dollars to the pound in the States but, at the new rate the fellows out there would have to go around with begging bowls! England had burnt herself out during the war and, but for the generosity of the Americans in letting us off our lease-lend debts, our financial standing in the world would have been in a complete abyss. The economists would have described it in other words no doubt but, to me, the situation seemed desperate. To cap it all, the Government had embarked on the Ground Nuts Scheme and this was doomed to complete failure. Why had we ever returned?

14

BECOMING CIVILIANS ONCE MORE

"L'homme est né libre, et partout il est dans les fers."
Jean Jacques Rousseau

My old bed was a luxury that I soon rediscovered. With crisp white sheets and its position a few feet from an open window despite the cold it was all I could wish for. Sleeping until 0830 hours was another joy with a cup of tea to wake me instead of the duty PO's stick on the side of my hammock. It all seemed so unreal.

Slowly getting dressed in flannels and my school blazer, minus the badge, breakfast was then taken, the newspaper was read and then I suggested going into Leamington with my mother for a mid-morning cup of coffee. Accordingly, we set off in the red bus from the bus stop opposite, getting off at Regent Street to walk down the Parade to Bobby's, the largest store in town which also had a café. It was while we were talking and enjoying my first cup of coffee for ages that a friend of my mother's came up to our table and said, "Is this your big lad? Which school does he go to now?"

Feeling an old veteran of many moons in the Navy, it was completely humiliating to be referred to in that way but, before I could say a word, my mother had put her friend right in no uncertain terms – whether they continued as friends is not certain.

It was not until I tried contacting my old school friends that I realised there were none in the locality. Most had stayed on at school after I had joined up and gone to university. They were the sensible ones but others had been called up, one as a 'Bevin Boy' to serve in the coal mines. Alan Bennett, a good cricketer and football player who had trained in the School Air Training Corps and who desperately wanted to join the RAF as Air Crew, had become one of the 'one-in-ten' to be claimed by the Coal Board. As a country lad, living in Bishops Itchington, a village not far from Leamington, he had always had a healthy outdoor life but, after being invalided out of the mines with 'dusticuloscis' he was to die at an early age. Certainly, life in the Royal Navy was better than that.

Two Old Warwickians were however on leave towards the end of my leave. Arthur Fretwell and John Healey were serving in the Army and Royal Air Force respectively; Arthur being a sergeant in the Intelligence Corps and John an aircraftsman. John Healey was the son of Donald Healey whose eponymous racing cars were later to win the Le Man's twenty-four hour race, and he had the use of his mother's car, a Riley – not a Healey, unfortunately! We decided to pay a visit to the old school, driven there by John who was in uniform, as was Arthur, but, for me, my old sports jacket was good enough. Not much had changed and, after a fleeting meeting with some of our former masters during 'break' we had a walk over the playing fields for old times' sake.

On the last day of our leave an important national event took place. This was the marriage between Princess Elizabeth to Philip, Duke of Edinburgh, a serving Lieutenant in the Royal Navy. We were unable to listen to the radio broadcast because we were on our way back to Plymouth North Road and could only read about it in the following day's newspaper.

The leave was over too quickly and we were on our way to the ship when we learnt that she was now in dry dock for inspection of the hull. It seemed strange to go over the brow with no water around the ship and the horrible thought struck each of us as we did so – would we have to swing over on stages to do yet more painting? Everything else seemed quite normal as we collected our station cards and went below to a fairly empty mess deck. Our first question was, "How much longer will we have to wait for demob?" but, of course, no one knew. C.P.O. Rhodes, the coxswain, was on leave together with most of the others who had missed the first one and so we would just have to wait for our 'call'. Surprisingly, Commander Twiss had left the ship as had the First Lieutenant, leaving Lieutenant Hill, who had not long been with the ship, as Officer in Command.

It was then that we heard the news of Able Seaman Jock Rea for whom we searched so thoroughly on the morning of our last day in Bermuda. Word had come through, probably from the fellows in HMS *Padstow Bay*, who had now returned home that, as we left harbour that momentous day, Jock's body had been found, probably churned up by our screws as we left. He had been transferred to *Sheffield* two days before and had been in the fleet canteen for a farewell drink which, in fact, was a drink or two too many. He had been seen staggering back to the dockyard and then he just seemed to disappear. Was he trying to get back aboard *Porlock Bay*? We will never know.

Apparently, he had been given a full Naval funeral, his body in a coffin carried by a gun carriage and taken to the Glade cemetery which we had passed so often on our shore leaves or to play cricket. There he had been laid to rest and, as they did so, a volley was fired by a funeral firing party from HMS *Sheffield*. He had never learnt to swim; he was a rebel but he did not deserve to die in such a fashion.

Fifty years later, when taking a holiday in Bermuda, I laid a wreath on his grave, marked with the simple war graves commission headstone. The inscription, however, stated that his ship was HMS *Sheffield* in which he had served less than two days.

On the first Saturday after our return aboard several of us decided to go to a football match in Plymouth. For me, it was another 'first' as my education in soccer was sadly lacking, so off to the Plymouth Argyle ground we went to see the match against Newcastle United. The ground was quite full so we stood more-or-less in one corner where an obvious expert was alternately shouting encouragement, and making disparaging remarks, at the local team, one of whom was a player called Tadman. All through the match, Tadman was the butt of most of his anger.

"He's completely useless! Why put him in the team? Look at that – missed again!" Until suddenly, Tadman scored the winning goal, whereupon the 'expert' said, "As I've told you, Tadman can do it if he tries!" That was my initiation into soccer and one which left me thinking that I would not bother to go to another match. I would in any case, far rather take part in a sport than be a spectator.

Soon *Porlock Bay* was to be moved out of dry dock into a basin with the assistance of a tug. There were still plenty of warships around despite a large number being sent 'up river' beyond the Tamar railway bridge where they were put 'in cotton wool' until a decision was taken as to their future.

We were secured alongside a minesweeper in the basin and, at times, with very much reduced ship's companies, we had to 'share' an Officer of the Day. On one occasion when we were going on a run ashore, Petty Officer 'Buck' Ryan very correctly lined us up for inspection and, saluting a bewhiskered two ringer with both First and Second World War ribbons on his chest, reported, "Liberty-men correct for inspection Sir".

"Ok, carry on," was the response, without even looking at us. There were no 'pusser' formalities on a minesweeper apparently!

Without much warning, orders came for about a dozen of us to be transferred into barracks. Although we were half expecting it, the news seemed rather sudden and, what was more, the dockyard train would be passing by shortly and so we hurriedly grabbed our large kitbag, our steaming bags, our large green suitcases, our hammocks and our attaché cases to place them all by the track, taking two journeys to do so. Soon the little steam engine appeared and we loaded our kit before sitting down on the wooden seats of the small carriages. Taking what would probably be a last look at *Porlock Bay*, the dockyard train trundled along northwards to the gate into barracks where we alighted, putting our luggage on the ground while one of us went to fetch a handcart. This done, we were admitted through the gate and made our way to DFDO again.

We were allotted to one of the large barrack buildings, heated only by three coke stoves which were burning permanently, and reported at one of the mess tables. Every morning, we reported at the Drill Shed, lining up while a Petty Officer called out demob groups well below ours and stopping before Group sixty-eight. While the lucky ones fell in at the far end of the shed, we were dismissed to carry out menial tasks about the barracks. Day after day, the same routine occurred, until we almost gave up hope of getting our demob, when, one day, a letter arrived for me telling me that the Christening of my new Godson would take place on 30th December in Canterbury. Would we be released in time for me to attend?

We had left our old ship so hurriedly and while a large number of our old colleagues were on leave. Humphrey Ixer joined me in a last return visit to her. We left the Barracks Gate and proceeded to the Albert Gate, to find *Porlock Bay* still in the same position as we had left her. There was a new Quartermaster and Bosun's Mate on the quarterdeck as we went aboard, saluting of course as we did so, and, seeing our cap tallies stating HMS *Porlock Bay*, we were allowed to go below decks with no trouble. It was a Sunday afternoon and the few ratings there were lounging about seemingly with nothing much to do. They were all newcomers and not a single person from just three weeks before was left on the lower seamen's mess deck. Seeing our cap tallies, there was an immediate shout, "Can we buy one off you?" They were all from the training establishment and apparently there were no tallies left, leaving them with nothing with which to identify themselves other than HMS.

We learnt that the G.I. was still on leave and that the coxswain, CPO Ginger Rhodes was trying to buy himself out of the Navy with his substantial War Gratuities and Post-War Credits. We had no opportunity to say "cheerio" to anyone from 'the old days' and left feeling rather disappointed. What a crying shame if Ginger was leaving before his time was up as the Navy certainly required persons of his calibre but we could fully understand his reasons for wanting to do so.

It almost seemed that they were playing a cat and mouse game with us, each day stopping before our group was called. Christmas was approaching and we would certainly not be home for the festive season. It seemed that they had deliberately delayed our release so that we could remain in barracks while others could go on seasonal leave. Three Christmases and not a single one at home – it didn't seem fair. In fact, on Christmas night my 'duty' was as sentry on the officers' pig bins to ensure that no tin cans were thrown in with the waste food to be boiled up for pig swill.

Two days after Boxing Day we lined up at one end of the Drill Shed while the groups were called. Amazingly, Group sixty-eight was called and a stampede ensued towards the far end. No Olympic sprinter could have overtaken us as we made sure that we did not miss out this time.

Demob routine had really begun but, should I apply for leave for the Christening? Reluctantly, my decision was taken. Nothing should stand in the way of my release. First of all, our kit had to be returned, starting with two suits, blue, seamen for the use of! Fortunately, I was able to so as I now had my recently acquired Number One suit. Secondly, those two wretched white, canvas suits were gladly thrown onto the pile; two completely useless items of kit. Finally, one hammock, two bed covers and hammock bed together with a set of clews went their way back into Naval stores, probably to be sold to Government Surplus dealers at some date in the future.

Then, stand-easy, when we could have a cup of tea and go to the 'heads' before continuing the routine. Next, however, the medicals but, before we saw any of the Surgeon Lieutenants, we had to provide a 'sample'. So soon after going to the heads! Each one of us was given a beaker but, without exception, no one could manage to pass a single drop. Taps were turned on in an attempt to induce a few drops but all we could do was to stand around and wait. The more we tried the longer it seemed to take until at last it was possible to provide a few drops!

There were lectures and, finally, before our last night in that unhealthy barrack block where only the perpetual draught saved us from asphyxiation, we were able to have a last drink in the canteen. Next morning, we went into a lecture room to be called, one by one, to collect our demob paper, a simple sheet entitled 'Order for Release from Naval Service,' and to be thanked by a Lieutenant for our services.

From there we made arrangements for our kit bags to be delivered to our home address, making sure that our names were preceded with the title MR! Finally, there was a coach waiting to take us to Plymouth North Road station to catch the train to Portsmouth. Just as the coach was about to pass through the main gate, one of the ratings spotted a Regulating Petty Officer and hurled an apple core at him, missing him by inches! My heart was in my mouth as the coach moved forward into the road and we were not recalled. Perhaps the Petty Officer could see the funny side of it. Or was it because he knew that we all had our Release Papers and, although we were still in uniform we were now, technically, civilians?

Transferring to the train, we soon found a coach with plenty of empty seats whereupon someone immediately produced a pack of cards, suggesting a game of pontoon. Not being a real card player, the idea did not appeal to me much but not wanting to be the odd one out, I agreed. In the Navy, playing cards for money was strictly forbidden but we were now civilians and no longer bound by KRs and AIs. Very soon, I became 'banker' and the money started rolling in as others in the coach joined in. The 'bank' remained in my possession almost as long as it took to reach Portsmouth! Past Exeter St Davids and all the other stations until, outside, it became dark but on we played until I had gained about ten pounds. Another real fortune on top of the ten pounds that I had already won, estimating our time of arrival past the Plymouth Sound breakwater. In my miserly way it seemed fortunate that there was no restaurant car on the train as it would have been necessary to treat everyone to a drink!

Eventually, the train pulled into the main station at Portsmouth where one Petty Officer was waiting to take about a hundred of us through the street towards the barracks for our last night. Insisting that we were civilians we readily fell in outside for our last march. How reminiscent of that first day in the Navy, when we had arrived at Skegness station to be greeted by a PO shouting "Get fell in ahtside, free fick," in his cockney twang, but this was different – the PO sounded almost like Sergeant Wilson in "Dads Army", asking, rather than ordering, us to fall in.

Through the gate we marched into a barrack block which was so much better than any at Devonport. What was more, we had bunk beds with real sheets on them! A meal was waiting for us which, admittedly we had to collect, but it was almost like going into a hotel. Not a single person wanted a run ashore that evening as everyone seemed exhausted, contented to just lie back on his bunk, thinking about their past Naval life perhaps, which was now at an end. With all the day's activities, however, sleep did not come too easily; after all, there was so much to do the following day. Eventually the sleep of absolute contentment came.

We were still called early the following morning when we washed, dressed and sat down to breakfast of bacon, sausage and egg. What luxury there was in Portsmouth compared with Devonport or was this repast put on solely because it was our last day? Possibly it was because we were now civilians and the Navy wanted to impress us but, whatever the reason, the euphoria knew no bounds and we were soon boarding a coach to Cosham where the Civilian Clothing Centre was situated.

The demob suits were distributed from what appeared to be the shell of a former bombed-out cinema and we went round collecting the various items without having much choice. A blue pin stripe suit, two shirts, a pair of shoes, cuff-links and studs, front and back were all thrust into my arms, together with a tie and a pair of braces. Then, a raincoat and, before I had said I didn't want one, a trilby hat was thrust on my head, which, with my arms full, it was not possible to remove. All collected, we continued to a counter where very considerate assistants packed the various items into brown cardboard boxes, tied them securely with string and bade us good luck.

Back into the coach for the short journey to the station for the train to take us to Victoria, where we would ultimately disperse for the final part of the journey home. Fortunately, the train was not full so with a compartment to ourselves, one or two could not contain themselves any longer and undid the string tying up their brown boxes. In the rush, Arthur Stelfox had been given what appeared to be a purple suit at the CCC, which rather disappointed him. We reminded him that there was no opportunity to change it now, a reminder which he accepted philosophically. In our excitement we realised that we had not exchanged home addresses and, at once, scraps of paper and pens were produced to scribble down the necessary information, but only in respect of those in the compartment. We were forgetting others on the train including Able Seamen Willoughby and Sven Zaar who were going to work in the same hotel that they had worked in during our leave and who apparently had no home to go to.

All change and goodbye at Victoria Station before, in my case, a trip on the underground to Paddington for the last leg. The date was 31st December; New Year's Eve, but demob was of greater importance now and, as I settled down in a corner seat by the train window, familiar landmarks came into view – Burton Dassett Hills with the windmill remains and its Beacon Tower before the train pulled into Leamington Spa station. When we received our travel warrants at Devonport, a Petty Officer had suggested asking for one to, say, the north of Scotland in order that we could stop off at home before taking a holiday and, in fact, one of our number had his warrant made out to the Isle of Man where we had done our radar training. However, in my case I was quite happy to get off at Leamington Station, leaving the two-mile journey to Warwick unused on my warrant!

The short bus trip brought me home from the station and, to my utter amazement, my large orange kit bag was already standing in the hall having been delivered that day. With my new Number Ones complete with the ribbon of the 1939/45 War Service medal and gold badge, my suggestion to go to a pub to see the New Year in was readily accepted. It was to be the one and only time that I had been seen in uniform at home as it had always been dark both when arriving and departing. After today, my uniform would be folded up and packed away for good.

The radio in the pub rang out the chimes at midnight. A New Year and a new era had begun.

15

SETTLING DOWN AS CIVILIANS

"Our revels now are ended. These our actors,
As I foretold you, were all spirits and
Are melted into air, into thin air:
And, like the baseless fabric of this vision,
The cloud-capp'd towers, the gorgeous palaces,
The solemn temples, the great globe itself,
Yea, all which it inherit, shall dissolve
And, like this insubstantial pageant faded,
Leave not a rack behind. We are such stuff
As dreams are made on, and our little life
Is rounded with a sleep."
The Tempest, by William Shakespeare

These words seemed strangely appropriate as we began our two months' demob leave plus five days' Special Overseas Leave. Our close mates had almost melted from our thoughts, as had our memories of those interesting places we had visited. We could not afford to sleep for long however as it was essential to get our future mapped out, and no time could be wasted. In my case, a trip to Birmingham was taken to visit the Principal of the College of Art and Crafts, to try to start on their architectural course which, hopefully, would be subsidised by an ex-service grant. The bad news soon became apparent as soon as I had been accepted – it was not possible to commence studies as the college year was already three months old and the next 'intake' would be in September, nine months hence. Furthermore, the grant had to be taken up within six months of leaving the services except under special circumstances.

In the meantime, a temporary job had to be found and this was in the Finance Department of a branch of the Civil Service where, to my consternation, almost all the top brass were conscientious objectors or people who had, for some reason or other, been excused military service. Courses in accountancy by correspondence were arranged but my salary gave me a gross income of under four pounds per week with the prospect of more as the various exams were passed.

What was real was that food rationing was tighter now than it had been during the war. With only temporary ration cards issued to us in Devonport for the two months of leave it was necessary to visit the local food office which was situated in Salisbury Hall, Leamington to get a ration book, an identity card (QEPO44/3) and clothing coupons. With regard to the latter, demob suits had been given to us but, with such a pittance on which to live, many of us sold the coupons as we just could not afford new wardrobes. Some of mine were sold to an elderly lady who wanted new curtains and, as any fabric required clothing coupons, they were necessary before the material could be supplied.

The pay during our two months' leave was not paid before we left Devonport but, by taking the Order for Release to the Post Office, we were paid in two instalments, having our papers stamped on the back to ensure that no one was paid twice. After that, we were on our own!

Before starting work, I met another of my school friends, Ken Webley, who was down from Cambridge where he was in his final year. We arranged to meet in the Bath Hotel, Leamington for a quiet drink and were sitting discussing life in general when the manager came up behind me to ask if I was over eighteen. My response was to get out of the breast pocket of my old sports coat my Order for Release from Naval Service which was handed to the manager without a word while continuing to talk to my friend. The manager made some sort of apology but, feeling furious at his question, I drained my half pint and, telling my friend to do the same, said, "Let us get out of this lousy place and find somewhere more conducive to private conversation." With the manager protesting that he had made a mistake, we left to find a more suitable hostelry. Fairly soon afterwards, the historic Bath Hotel was demolished to make way for a small supermarket although it is unlikely that it was due to our altercation there! My dignity, such as it was, had been injured for the second time since returning from Bermuda and so the answer appeared to be to grow a moustache in an attempt to add a few years to my age.

At about the same time, an announcement appeared in the local press to the effect that a branch of the Royal Naval Old Comrades Association (later to be known as the Royal Naval Association) was to be formed in Leamington and so, going to the Carpenter's Arms, Leamington Spa where the landlord was Joe Tilley, himself a former seaman, I joined. After a short time, however, I found that the cost of drinking was draining my resources too much and my membership lapsed.

That first summer was a particularly good one and, becoming involved with a crowd of ex-RAF Air Crew who, similarly were finding it difficult to settle down to civilian life, I chose to drink with them after playing tennis with them at the weekends. In due course, the others found girls who they married and the crowd broke up.

Next, it was announced that a Fencing Club was to be formed in Leamington and so, as instruction was to be given, another sport was taken up. The initial cost of equipment was met by the War Gratuities and Post-War Credits that had been added to my Post Office savings bank while in the Navy and so my determination was to do well to justify the expense. After two years, I won the Warwickshire Epée Championship but, more importantly, I fell madly in love with one of the girl fencers in the Club. Here again, my shortage of funds, lack of time due to study and absence of transport meant losing her, making it the nadir of my life. Why had I volunteered for the Navy instead of going to university where, with a degree, my life would have been so different? My training had been in seamanship and gunnery which was not much use in the centre of England where peace reigned but, had I qualified soon after leaving school in architecture instead, my salary would have been reasonable.

The branch of the Civil Service was closing and so yet another change in career was called for. A vacancy in the Town Planning Department for a trainee beckoned which offered a chance to enter another profession. It also meant starting on a salary of just under four pounds per week! Again! Unfortunately, the Department was headed by the meanest man in Warwickshire – not my words but the words of the person's own wife, who had to take a job on the bacon counter of a local grocers in view of his extreme parsimony.

My time in the Royal Navy had not only been wasted time, it had been costly in terms of my career prospects and I began to really regret my years in the Service. The conflict in Korea was now beginning with several ex-servicemen being recalled under the 'Z' training scheme, when an envelope arrived for me containing a printed letter, requiring me to give them details of my present work, any training being carried out and other questions relating to my employment. This I ignored, feeling so bitter that I had been finagled into the Navy that I was determined they would not get me back. After three weeks a second envelope arrived, recorded delivery, requiring me to provide the information immediately and pointing out that I was on the Reserve. Obviously the command had to be obeyed and fortunately nothing further was heard. Fifty years later, the order not countermanded, we must presumably still regard ourselves as being Reservists; those still remaining, of course, in the land of the living.

The immediate post-war government had meanwhile introduced the National Health Service which was supposed to look after everyone, irrespective of their means, from the cradle to the grave. At the time, my worry was not only that my contributions were taking some of my pitifully small income but could the Service be fully sustainable in future years when the youngsters now became pensioners? The answers emerged very soon when prescription charges were brought in by the Government in spite of the protestations of the Minister of Health. Nowadays when, after so many more charges have been brought in, yet still the hospitals and our pensions are increasingly in doubt, it is clear that the service was *not* sustainable. In 1948 it was said that there would be no need for the various charities to continue in view of the 'cradle to grave' welfare conditions but, fifty-five years later there are a vastly *greater* number, most of them sending out regular begging letters. How can the population of this country be so gullible as to trust the politicians? Anyway, although earning only four pounds per week, I had to pay tax and National Health Contributions in addition to superannuation payments of six per cent of my gross salary.

16

THE HANDOVER: *PORLOCK BAY* BECOMES *MATTI KURKI*

Although we were not aware of the fact, HMS *Porlock Bay* had apparently been 'mothballed' to join dozens of similar warships now lying to the north of the Tamar (railway) bridge. She did not merit regular mention and so she merely remained in our memories until a report in the Daily Newspapers gave the information that she was to be sold to Finland. It was pleasing to know that she could still fulfil a useful role, albeit in another Navy and so I wrote to the Dockyard Superintendent asking if it was possible to see the 'Handing Over' Ceremony. The reply told me that, not only would I be able to watch the ceremony, I would be able to do so from an allotted position on 'X' gun deck, overlooking the quarterdeck, where it would all take place.

Then came the bad news. The ceremony would be held just before Easter when I had entered for the International Fencing Tournament to be held by Birmingham Fencing Club in the Town Hall, Leamington Spa. Why did the dates have to clash? My club had entered me in both epée and sabre team events and I was also to take part in the individual Foil, Sabre and Epée events. As it turned out, I scraped into the semi-finals of the Sabre Championships, my least favourite weapon, but at least my absence from the handing over ceremony was partly justified. *Porlock Bay* had sailed away without so much as a 'goodbye' from any of her old ship's complement.

FNS Matti Kurki *at firing practice*

Several years were to pass before a booklet arrived for me from Finland giving details of the handing over. Beforehand, the ship had to be made ready for sea – Shipshape and Bristol Fashion of course. This involved sea trials with both Finnish seamen and Royal Naval personnel and ammunition as, in reserve, her magazines were empty. True to fashion, the Admiralty left no stone unturned to make sure that the ceremony went off without a hitch, giving a full programme for 'Handover Day, 19th April 1962.

FNS Matti Kurki *arriving in Finland*

The Handover: *Porlock Bay* Becomes *Matti Kurki*

The programme arranged for the Senior Office Reserve Ships to provide a guard in HMS *Tyne*, a depot ship, and for the Royal Marines Band of the Commander-in-Chief, Plymouth, to play at the ceremony. The Superintending Naval Store Officer was requested to provide transport for the Finnish people arriving at Plymouth North Road Station, including His Excellency Herra Leo Tnominen, the Ambassador, and his wife, and Captain Salmine, the Naval Attaché and his wife. All the guests were driven to Admiralty House, for a dinner to be given by the Commander-in-Chief, Plymouth, Admiral Sir Charles Madden, Bt., K.C.B. on the evening before 'H' day, and orders given to the RN Officers to be dressed in full evening dress with decorations; civilians to wear white tie with decorations.

On the day itself, the instructions were even more elaborate. The ceremony was to take place at Number Thirteen wharf, Devonport, when Admiral Maden would formally hand over the ship to the Finnish Navy. His Excellency, the Finnish Ambassador would receive the ship on behalf of the Finnish Government. The Admiralty would be represented by Mr J.M. Mackay, the Deputy Secretary, and the Foreign Office by Mr A.D. Wilson, C.M.G., the Under Secretary. All this formality for just one small ship, albeit *our* ship, HMS *Porlock Bay*!

At 1115 hours in the forenoon of 'H' Day the Royal Marines Band fell in on board HMS *Tyne* together with the Royal Naval Guard while the Finnish Officers, Guard and Ship's Company fell in on board our old ship. At 1123 hours, the Admiral Superintendent, Rear Admiral G.D.A. Gregory, D.S.O., and his wife arrived on board HMS *Tyne* together with Mrs Tnominent, Lady Madden, Mrs Wilson and Mrs Salminen. Seven minutes later, the Commander-in-Chief was received on board HMS *Tyne* by Captain B. Pengelly, D.S.C., followed by His Excellency the Finnish Ambassador attended by the Finnish Naval Attaché and the Royal Naval Liaison Officer, Lieutenant Commander R. Booth.

There then followed the formal ceremony before the distinguished visitors and invited guests proceeded to the Wardroom of the *Matti Kurki*, which our beloved old ship had now become. The white ensign had been lowered for the last time, the guards and band marched off and it was all at an end. After the invited guests had walked around the ship, they were invited to lunch in HMS Tyne as guests of Captain Pengelly, D.S.C., the Senior Officer Reserve Ships, Plymouth before being driven to Plymouth North Road Station for the return to London. The whole episode over the two days had been carried out in a fitting tribute to the ship that had been our 'home' so long ago but she was going to a good home herself instead of going, as so many of the 'Bay' Class had gone, to the shipbreakers. Should I have attended or was it more appropriate to participate in the Fencing Tournament? There would surely have been a lump in my throat to see the old ship change hands; instead there were bruises on my body as a result of hits against me during the tournament.

KL *Matti Kurki* sailed away that evening to Suomenlinna Island, the Finnish Naval Academy near to Helsinki, the capital. She became the training ship of the Finnish Navy, a role in which she would visit several ports in the USA and Canada, in addition to several ports in Europe, the Mediterranean and Scandinavia between 1962 and 1974. She served her purpose excellently, sailing through the rough seas of the North Atlantic in a similar way to *Porlock Bay* and hundreds of young Finns benefited from their time serving in her.

Then, in 1976, I decided to go on a cruise around the Baltic which was due to call at Helsinki. My letter to the Finnish Embassy, asking if *Matti Kurki* would be in Finland on the date of my future visit, was answered promptly by the Naval Attaché who said that my letter had been passed to the Commodore of the Training Squadron for a full reply. This duly arrived soon afterwards, inviting me to go aboard the old ship in Suomenlinna Island when I arrived in Helsinki. They would be expecting me on the date mentioned in my letter, a date which would be altered without my knowledge until after I joined the cruise liner, SS *Calypso*, formerly the Shaw Saville ship *Southern Cross*.

Immediately on receiving this letter, I gave an order to a company specialising in ship's badges to make two wall plaques bearing the *Porlock Bay* badge, enclosing with my order, a letterhead showing an eagle arising from rocks, our old design. Apart from an acknowledgement I heard nothing further until the morning that I was due to depart when a parcel arrived from the company. There was just time to open the package before setting off and, to my absolute horror, they had shown an incorrect badge in which an oak tree with oversized acorns appeared. There was no way that these badges could be presented to whoever met me and so, scribbling a brief note to the company, I caught the London train, leaving the wall plaques at home.

On my return two weeks later a letter was awaiting me among all the other post stating that they had obtained the design from Chatham Dockyard where all the details of ship's badges were kept. They admitted however that they had seen 'our' badge which was certainly different and had, in fact, returned my letterhead with a note to the effect that it was not required as "they had all the details."

Meantime, I travelled by rail to Tilbury where, after waiting for two hours on the quayside, passengers were finally allowed on board. The ship proceeded out to sea on its passage to Rotterdam where some disturbing news became known. We would not be going through the Kiel Canal – some said the cost was too great, others that the ship was too wide to get through – but, we would be sailing north of Denmark, through the Kattegat into the Baltic. This was disastrous because our revised itinerary would take the ship to Helsinki two days before I had told the Finnish Authorities to expect me and there was no way to get a message through to them giving them the new timings.

The weather, hot from the beginning of the cruise, was getting still hotter as we left Rotterdam for the Baltic. Unbelievably, every record for the highest temperature was broken as we progressed, via Leningrad (now St Petersburg), to Helsinki, and was to continue to do so throughout the cruise. There was no exception when the ship passed Suomenlinna Island to berth at the main docks near to the centre of Helsinki early in the morning. Making special arrangements to go ashore as early as possible, I left the ship before anyone else, missing my breakfast in doing so, to walk and run to the market area in front of the beautiful Cathedral with its classical lines. There were small ferryboats lying nearby and, after buying my ticket from a kiosk without knowing a single word of the Finnish language, I boarded the one marked Suomenlinna. The small boat retraced the route taken by *Calypso* but in the opposite direction while the Cathedral ashore became smaller as we chugged towards our destination. Arriving at the jetty, there was a rush to get ashore by the, mainly, dockyard workers, leaving me to look around, searching for the old ship. Very soon, the well-remembered masthead appeared, the same one that I had had to paint years before, so how could I forget it?

Thoughts suddenly hit me as I made my way to the old ship.

"They will not be expecting me as we should not be in Helsinki for another two days. What should I do?" Wearing my blazer with the Royal Naval Crown badge, there seemed only one thing to do; go aboard. As soon as I crossed the brow, the quartermaster stepped forward and saluted.

"Good morning, Sir," he said, in perfect English. "We were expecting you and I will ring the Captain to tell him you have arrived."

While he contacted the Captain who happened to be in the building ashore, I had a look at the quarterdeck to see what changes had been made.

There were changes to the Quartermaster's lobby and, of course, *Porlock Bay* had now become *Matti Kurki* on the name plate but otherwise everything seemed the same.

Very soon, the Captain, Komm Kapt Visa arrived to shake hands and say, "Good morning, Mr Smith. Welcome to your old ship." He spoke in perfect English without any hint of a foreign accent which made me wonder, how many English people know even a single word of Finnish? We went up to the Captain's Day Cabin where Komm Kapt Visa ordered coffee which we drank while talking about the activities of the ship since she left Devonport in 1962. Apparently she had been back to Britain on one or two occasions on training cruises, visiting Falmouth and Leith inter alia in the process. He had been most impressed with her seagoing qualities, speaking lovingly of "the old lady".

Komm Kapt Visa, Commander of FNS Matti Kurki, *1976, Helsinki (later Vice-Admiral Visa)*

The Handover: *Porlock Bay* Becomes *Matti Kurki*

Somewhat embarrassed, I explained that it had been my intention to bring with me the wall plaques of the *Porlock Bay* badge and promised to send these to him when the badges showing the revised design were received. He thanked me and gave me a *Matti Kurki* paperweight and several items relating to the ship which I have treasured ever since. In his cabin was the original metal *Porlock Bay* badge mounted on wood which had been

Komm Kapt Visa with the Author, Roger Smith, on the quarterdeck of FNS Matti Kurki, *Suomenlinna Island, Helsinki, 1976*

presented to the first Captain, Mats Wikberg, when he took over command in 1962. This, of course, showed the eagle arising from rocks which we knew as our emblem and which was always placed on a stand, surrounded by a lifebelt, when we were alongside.

Komm Kapt Visa told me that it was decided to purchase *Porlock Bay* in 1960 when the old Sailing Ship *Suomen Toutsen* was due for replacement. *Porlock Bay* was considered suitable as the new training ship as she fulfilled the new criteria. She was still truly Shipshape and Bristol Fashion and so was purchased to be handed over as described earlier. In all, *Matti Kurki* made a total of sixteen long voyages beyond the Finnish archipelago but her future was now in doubt. Shortly, a decision would have to be taken as to whether she should be handed over to the dockyard for major refurbishment or whether she should be scrapped.

Under Sergeant Fred Sunden, the Author's guide in Suomenlinna Island

The Handover: *Porlock Bay* Becomes *Matti Kurki*

At that point, Komm Kapt Visa showed me over the ship, down to the old lower seaman's mess deck and up to the bridge, indeed almost everywhere. Noticing my camera, he invited me to take as many photographs as I wanted, including one of himself. That done, he called the Quartermaster to take one of the two of us, which he, the QM, obligingly did.

By this time, a rating appeared and I was introduced to Under Sergeant Fred Sundén who was asked to take me on a tour of Suomenlinna Island. Fred, who also spoke perfect English, explained that he was a National Serviceman, not a regular, and that, before being called up for Naval Service, he had qualified as a Chemical Engineer. His wife was a doctor and their home was in Finland's second city, Turku. He said that the Finnish language was one of the most difficult to learn but many of the people spoke Swedish as he did when I complemented him on his command of the English language. We saw an old Finnish submarine and several old pieces of artillery before he took me to the Naval canteen for a meal. Twenty-five years later when I met Fred again he reminded me that, as he was on duty, he could not have a drink with me. However, Kapt Visa had said that he was to take me anywhere and do everything I wanted and so, if I wanted him to have a drink, he just had to oblige. Accordingly, I ordered him to have a drink with me and he readily accepted! Suitably refreshed, I was taken back to the ferry, promising to send Fred one of the plaques and he, in turn, promised to send me details of the decision on *Matti Kurki* when it was published, probably sometime in the following month.

Having said goodbye, I left on the ferry to return to the mainland to visit the main Cathedral and the Uspenski Cathedral before rejoining *Calypso* in time for the evening departure. It was with extreme sadness as the ship steamed past Suomenlinna Island that I took what was likely to be my last look at *Matti Kurki*. Perhaps it was sixth sense but I felt sure I would not see her again.

True enough, a letter arrived from Finland, giving the dreaded news. "*Matti Kurki* hugs app," was the headline of the Helsinki paper which Fred had enclosed for me. Apparently, it meant that the old ship was to go to the ship-breakers. It was only a pipe dream to imagine that she could be preserved and so I resigned myself to the thought that she would soon be converted to razor blades.

For my part, I sent away again for the *Porlock Bay* wall plaques which the company insisted was the incorrect design but which they would make to my specification. These were eventually received and forwarded to

Komm Kapt Visa and Fred Sundén with my compliments. The true story of the badge did not unfold until several years later when the HMS *Porlock Bay* Association members visited Devonport's South Yard during a reunion in Plymouth. Readers may be interested in Appendix One of this book in which a report on the ships badges, official and unofficial, is given.

As *Calypso* left Helsinki to sail past Suomenlinna where the mast for the old ship could be seen, I little expected that, twenty-nine years later our Association members would be visiting the area for a meeting with members of the *Matti Kurki* Association.

FNS Matti Kurki, *Suomenlinna Island, Helsinki, 1976.*
Possibly the last photograph of the ship before she was scrapped

17

THE HMS *PORLOCK BAY* ASSOCIATION

"Should auld acquaintance be forgot
And never brought to mind?
Should auld acquaintance be forgot
And auld lang syne?"
***Auld Lang Syne,* by Robert (Rabbie) Burns**

Civilian life continued, with Christmas cards passing between the few former shipmates and perhaps the odd letter. For my part, living within half a mile of the alleged centre of England, the sea seemed far away, a fact that, at first, I was pleased to accept. After about five years, however, my yearning for the sea came to the fore and a cruise seemed attractive, particularly as the cost for a two week holiday afloat was exactly forty pounds, a sum which included everything except shore excursions. The cruise was with the Orient Line and the ship was the *Orsova* in which my cabin, shared with two others, was on the lowest passenger deck. Compared with *Porlock Bay*, the accommodation and food seemed veritably luxurious and so, a cruise each year became my norm.

The other fellows from *Porlock Bay* had, by this time all got married and several had children but my money did not stretch to that level, except for cruising and, having been 'ditched' a second time, I determined to remain a bachelor, at least for the next few years. Study for the exams of the Royal Town Planning Institute kept me tied down anyway, together with a call from the West Midland Section of the Amateur Fencing Association to

HMS Porlock Bay *Reunion, Plymouth, Sept 1995*
l to r Albert Moorman, Norman Terrell, Fred Amos

join the Regional team. The call came by post one Saturday morning, telling me that I had been selected to fight against Wales that afternoon. We were not on the phone at the time and the letter had been sent out in view of the decimation of the regular team due to Asian Flu. My kit, still soaking from fencing the previous evening, was packed into a bag and I raced to Warwick station to catch the Stratford train where I was to meet the other members of the team, who were mainly from Birmingham, and continue to Cardiff for the match. The rest of the team were hanging out of the carriage windows as their train pulled into Stratford Station and I never felt more popular in my life, because, had I not turned up, some other member, not an epée specialist, would have had to take part in the team. Briefly, the match was a very tight one; West Midlands winning the ladies team event and the sabre but losing at foil so everything hinged on epée. The thought went through my head that I should not really be there but, as I *was* there, go in and have a go! The result was that our team's number one lost two bouts and won one, the number two lost all three but, winning all three, my efforts brought the overall team score to 17-19. A win for the West Midlands, which would take them to the Winton Cup finals at Lilleshall, the National Sports Centre, the following month! Thereafter, my training was taken more seriously, but why had we not had an instructor on *Porlock Bay* when we had, for a time at least, all the equipment necessary?

Humphrey and Gladys Ixer, Exmouth Reunion 2003

    Many years later, as my fencing days were coming to an end, I began to think more about my old shipmates, when quite unexpectedly, a local coach firm announced that they would be running an excursion to Southend which was close enough to Leigh-on-Sea where Humphrey Ixer lived. Joined by a couple of ex-colleague widowers, I set off and met the chap who had gone through all the training and had joined *Porlock Bay* with me. Lunch was taken, followed by a walk along the one-mile-long pier, after which we had tea. My suggestion that we should try to get together as many of the lads to a reunion was met with enthusiasm.

At about the same time, an elderly lady from Derby whom I had met on a cruise invited me over for the day and, looking at the map, I noticed that Allestree was quite close by. Accordingly, I phoned to see whether Arthur Stelfox would be likely to be at home and as the reply was in the affirmative, I arranged to call before going to see my elderly friend. Drawing up at their house, the door opened and Arthur's wife, Rose, ran out to kiss me on the cheek before asking if I was Roger. My reply that I was the milkman, calling for the money, resulted in a slight embarrassment before I admitted that I was indeed the person she had been expecting. Sadly, Rose who was to suffer ill health for a number of years, died a few years later. A truly lovely lady.

*The first HMS Porlock Bay reunion 1992 (this was a 'mini' reunion)
l to r Gladys Ixer, Humphrey Ixer, Mike Sheppard, Arthur Stelfox*

The following year, I arranged a mini-reunion at the Manor House Hotel, Leamington, the site of the first lawn tennis club in the world, inviting Arthur Stelfox, Mike Sheppard and Humphrey Ixer and his wife Gladys. We had such an excellent time together, looking around Leamington and going over to Stratford that we decided to form an Association to which we would invite as many of our old shipmates as possible. To this end, we contacted all those whose addresses were known to us and I placed an advertisement in *Navy News*. The latter produced better results that I had anticipated, the first two to respond being two of the most valued members. They were Bernard Griffiths, formerly a leading telegraphist and Philip Coulson, a Chief Engine Room Artificer, both of whom have, sadly, since 'crossed the bar.'

HMS Porlock Bay *reunion 1993 at Ship Hotel, Porlock Weir*
l to r Ken Faulkner, Brian Lightfoot, Bernard Griffith (first hon sec)

The first meeting was arranged for September, to be held appropriately at the 'Ship' in Porlock Weir. We stayed in the 'Anchor' but the inaugural meeting was held in the 'out of hours' bar of the 'Ship', where it was enthusiastically agreed to form an Association. Who was to be the Secretary? Ivor Hambling, whose home was now in Ontario, Canada, suggested that we should appoint Bernard Griffiths to the post in his absence and what an excellent Secretary / Treasurer he turned out to be. As for Chairman, I was appointed to the post and have remained so ever since. A most important item on the agenda was the venue for the next reunion and, because of its central position, and a flourishing Naval Club, the members chose Leamington Spa, which meant little travelling for me. We met in the Regent Hotel, which was the largest hotel in Europe when it was built in the early nineteenth century and in which many important people had stayed, including Princess Victoria and her mother, the Duchess of Kent together with many other notable persons.

HMS Porlock Bay *reunion 1994, Jephson Gardens, Royal Leamington Spa*

On Saturday evening, we had asked for an early dinner in order to go on later to the Naval Club in Adelaide Road and this arrangement had been agreed with the management. However, it was not to the liking of the temperamental chef who came into the dining area to make his views known. Perhaps thinking that the customer should always be right, one or two of our members took exception to his attitude and answered back; after all we were no longer in the Navy now, and after a few minutes the owner of the hotel appeared to calm things down. Mrs Cridlan, the owner, came over to my table to apologise later, possibly as another group with which I was associated, met every Wednesday in the Hotel but a small incident like that would certainly not have any effect upon my patronage. During the meal, I made reference to the fact that two chaps from the Hotel had been awarded the Victoria Cross in the First World War – Cridlan Barratt, and the doorman 'Napper' Tandy who was the most decorated private soldier, having been awarded, in addition to the Victoria Cross, the Conspicuous Gallantry Medal and the Military Medal. Apparently, he captured a prisoner by the name of Adolf Hitler who, it is rumoured, asked after his erstwhile captor when he became dictator of Nazi Germany.

The meal over, we all proceeded to the Naval Club, which by this time was heaving with people attending the very popular dance but, because of the difficulty of getting a drink, we returned to the Regent Hotel for a quieter evening. The beautiful chandeliers in the Hotel were swinging all evening as we discussed 'old times' over a pint or two in the otherwise empty lounge.

One of the main topics discussed was the sad death of our President who had joined the ship in Bermuda as a recently promoted Commander and who ended his career as Admiral Sir Frank Twiss, Second Sea Lord and who later became Black Rod in the Palace of Westminster. At the previous reunion in Porlock Weir, I had been charged with writing to the Admiral to invite him to become our President but, before I did so, I attended a Garden Party at Charlecote Park in aid of the Army Benevolent Fund. There, I was in conversation with Captain Hugh Lee, D.S.C., R.N., who asked about my somewhat lowly career in the Navy and, and in particular the name of the ship's captain. Hugh Lee had been awarded the D.S.C. early in the war when serving in HMS *Fortune* and he was responsible for the sinking of U-Boat 27. Not only that, he married Pauline, the Admiral's daughter, who is also a direct descendent of the Earl of Northesk, the third in command in Trafalgar. When I said, "Commander Twiss," he retorted, "Do you mean old Frank?"

to which I answered in the affirmative and mentioned that the lads had asked me to write to him to invite him to be our President. Apparently, both of them had been at the Royal Naval College, Dartmouth at the same time and had remained friends ever since.

"He lives in Wiltshire now, so write to him as soon as possible because I am certain he will be delighted to hear from you," were his words. Unfortunately, with all the happenings at the Garden Party, I did not ask his address and so had to go to the County Library in Warwick to look up *Who's Who* and to discover that our old Captain now lived in the village of Bratton on the edge of Salisbury Plain. This was a surprise for me as my cousin and his wife had moved to the same village after retiring as Principal of an Estate Agency in Canterbury, in order to be nearer to their son.

My letter was answered immediately and with such enthusiasm that had hardly been expected. In addition he sent me an account of his life in the RN, including the story of his joining *Porlock Bay* and his trepidation at taking over from Lieutenant Davenport who, he fully realised, was a most popular and respected Commanding Officer. Little did we realise that our new Captain was so apprehensive about joining the ship. The account had been typed as indeed had his letter in which he told me that his eyesight was failing, probably through ill treatment as a Prisoner of War of the Japanese. Later, on receiving my donation to St Dunstan's, the Secretary acknowledged my letter, telling me that Admiral Twiss had been a patient for quite a long time and, while there, had been taught to type.

Our new President's Report had originally been written solely for the benefit of his grandchildren but was incorporated into a book which was published later, entitled *Social Change in the Royal Navy, 1924 to 1970*. Who better to write about social change than Admiral Twiss who, as Second Sea Lord, was responsible for the personnel of the Navy and as such he had made so many much-needed changes to a Service that had hitherto changed little from the days of Lord Nelson. One particular change about which he was somewhat apprehensive was the discontinuance of the rum ration to ratings. In the modern Navy, the practice of a daily tot was an anachronism but, would the lower deck agree to giving up one of the few perks that was still available to them? It certainly made sense to put an end to the ration in view of the fact that many ratings had to operate sophisticated technological instruments. My own experience told me that, particularly in hot climates, the rum made me quite drowsy, especially if sippers or gulpers had been drunk in addition to the normal tot. Rather amazingly, the lower deck

HMS Porlock Bay *reunion 1994, Regent Hotel, Royal Leamington Spa*

accepted the withdrawal of the 'tot' and it was issued for the last time in 1970, accompanied by compensation in the form of 'The Sailor's Fund', primed with a lump sum of £2.75m. Admiral Twiss told the story in his book about a question put to him at the time.

"This scheme of yours, is there going to be a mutiny?" which was asked in all seriousness. The diplomacy with which he dealt with the tricky situation emphasises the remarkable tact that he had when dealing with Government Ministers on the one hand and the lower deck on the other. A truly genuine man and it came as no surprise to me when he was appointed Black Rod at the Palace of Westminster.

When the Old Warwickian Association held their annual dinner in the dining room of the House of Commons some years previously, we were taken on a tour of both Houses and I happened to ask our guide if he saw much of Admiral Twiss.

"Oh yes," he replied, "he lives in a flat within the Palace of Westminster. A most charming gentleman."

At the state opening of Parliament it was always a 'must' to watch on television our former Captain, clad in knee breaches and his full regalia, walk from the Lords to the Commons where the door was slammed in his face as part of the tradition. Three blows on the door with the staff was then followed by his request for Members to accompany him to the Lord's Chamber. His task was always carried out with such precision and professionalism.

Just before the Leamington reunion, my cousin wrote to me and, in his letter, he said that Admiral Twiss had attended a village event, adding that he appeared to be a very sick man, leaning heavily on Lady Twiss as he went around. It was therefore not a great surprise when, soon afterwards, the *Daily Telegraph* carried an announcement of his death and an obituary which gave details of his service life, some known to us, but plenty which was not known including brief details of his time in captivity as a Prisoner of War of the Japanese.

Soon afterwards there was another announcement to the effect that a Memorial Service for the life of Admiral Sir Frank Twiss would be held at the Admiralty Church of St Martins in the Fields. The Secretary of the *Porlock Bay* Association and I arranged to attend and we duly made our separate ways to London on Wednesday, 23rd March 1994. There, on the steps of the church, I met a chap with whom I entered into conversation about general matters before realising that he had known our former Captain for a long time.

"Yes", he said, "I am his cousin."

After a while, Bernard Griffiths, our Secretary, arrived and we entered the church for the service. There was not a uniform in sight but we sensed that many of the congregation that day were Naval Officers and that a large proportion were of Flag Rank. In fact, I would estimate that Admirals outnumbered Able Seamen by a ratio of about twenty to one that day!

The service was conducted by the Vicar, Canon Geoffrey Brown and was one of the most memorable that I have attended. The first Lesson from Ecclesiastes was read by Captain Anthony Chilton, RN, the stepson of Admiral Twiss, and this was followed by Psalm 107 which contains the appropriate words:

> They that go down to the sea in ships,
> that do business in great waters;
> these see the works of the Lord,
> and his wonders in the deep.

The Son of Admiral Twiss, Hugh Twiss, then gave a reading from Albert Schweitzer entitled *Memoirs of Childhood and Youth* and, after the Anthem by Purcell, "Rejoice in the Lord always," an address was given by Admiral Sir Desmond Dreyer who came from an old Naval family and who had been a contemporary of 'our Captain'. A final Anthem, "I was Glad," by Parry concluded the service and, as we left the Church, we met members of the Twiss family including Captain Chilton who, when I mentioned that I was the Chairman of the HMS *Porlock Bay* Association, immediately spoke to his mother, Lady Rosemary Twiss. She appeared so pleased that Bernard and I had attended the memorial service, and we were engaged in a long conversation with her, keeping Admirals and other high ranking officers waiting, while we talked. It seemed as if we were all of the same family and, in a sense, we were.

Some time later when visiting my cousin and his wife in Bratton, he took me to the small church, detached from the village, where we placed some flowers on the grave of Admiral Sir Frank Twiss, K.C.B., K.C.V.O., D.S.C., the headstone of which was a plain war graves commission slab bearing his title, name and distinctions. The simplicity of the grave lying in the Churchyard among the graves of other villagers left me in even greater admiration for the man who had had such a vast impact on the Royal Navy and yet who now lies in the village churchyard with only a simple headstone to commemorate his achievements; a truly great man.

For the 1995 Reunion of the *Porlock Bay* Association we chose to make a sentimental return to Plymouth where we stayed in a hotel just off the Hoe. During our stay there we arranged to go by taxis to the South Yard, Devonport Dockyard, where we were met by a former Petty Officer, 'Jan' Goddard for a tour of the historic site. Few of us had been into that part of the Dockyard before and, in fact, the Yard had not then been fully opened to the public and we were able to see the covered shipway and also the mound from which King William IV watched his fleet. Another surprising item in part of an old rope walk was the existence of a gallows, still in working order where, upon pulling a lever, the trap opened very noisily allowing the victim to drop below where surgeons waited for the condemned man's body.

Bournemouth reunion

In one of the old buildings we saw, inter alia, the uniform of Admiral Sir Frank Twiss and several artefacts and pieces of memorabilia from the Second World War. It was there that the question of the official badge of HMS *Porlock Bay* was raised.

"Simple," said Jan Goddard as he disappeared for a few minutes, returning with a Xerox copy of the official design. This showed an oak tree with large acorns – the design on the badge ordered from the Naval tailors! Jan told us that it was not unknown for a Captain to choose a more appropriate badge and this was obviously what Lieutenant Davenport had done, selecting the arms of the Lord of the Manor of Porlock as the base. Letterheads had been printed using the 'unofficial' design as had the ship's badge which, kept normally in the wardroom, was used on a stand surrounded by a lifebelt to stand next to the brow whenever we were alongside. Not a single person, other than Lieutenant Davenport, was apparently aware that this was not the 'official' badge.

On a windswept Hoe, the majority of our members with their wives presented themselves for a group photograph. Although we were not to know it at the time, this would be the last appearance of Jack Robinson, the former Asdic Operator, and Lorna, his wife, because, having settled in Spain, Jack developed a brain tumour and died shortly afterwards. Jack had tried civilian life immediately following demob but decided after a while to join the Army, rising to the rank of Regimental Sergeant Major before finally leaving the Services.

The main item to generate discussion at our Annual General Meeting was always the matter of the venue for the next reunion. However, someone suggested that, as it was fifty years since we were in Bermuda, we should hold the 1996 reunion in Porlock and this was resolved very quickly. The majority of our party booked into the Ship Inn and, arriving early in the pouring rain, my wife was left in the car while I braved the elements to call on the rector of St Dubritius Church in order to see him about the morning service on the Sunday. The Reverend Barry Priory invited me into his study where I learnt that he had not long been ordained after many years as an accountant. Even more surprising was that he had worked with a company by the name of IDC in Stratford-upon-Avon, no more than a mile away from my place of employment with the District Council. The previous year at Devonport, our Association had ordered some wall plaques depicting the ship's badge and it

HMS Porlock Bay *reunion, Porlock dinner at the Ship Inn*

was arranged that one of these would be placed in the church alongside the larger badge placed there exactly fifty years before when the ship had made that brief call on her namesake town. It was also arranged that the Naval Hymn would replace the hymn selected for the service. After discussing a variety of subjects, the sudden thought that my wife had been left alone for more than an hour struck me. There was no need to worry – she was asleep in the car.

HMS Porlock Bay *reunion in Porlock. Group taken at the museum after presenting a ship's wall plaque*

The Porlock Reunion was one of the most memorable as we had a reception at the small town museum where a second wall plaque was presented to the curator and our members were asked about our experiences abroad. After morning service, we were invited to have coffee and biscuits in the church when the children from Sunday School joined in to show the drawings they had made of the ship. For some strange reason, the children had, without exception, decided that *Porlock Bay* was a submarine!

A somewhat disappointing feature of our visit to Porlock was the fact that no one that we met in the small township had been there fifty years before and we were therefore not able to express our thanks personally to the ladies who had sent out the comfort parcels which had proved so useful, particularly when we had operated around Newfoundland.

As the 'Porlock' reunion was reasonably near to Kingskerswell, it was possible for John Bailey to join us with his wife Sheila. John had been taken ill suddenly on holiday the previous year and, although he was able to enjoy the meal, be was obviously a sick man. The following year, several of us were able to visit him at his home on the edge of Dartmoor when our reunion took us to the Trecarn Hotel at Babbacombe but his health had deteriorated further and he crossed the bar not long afterwards.

On another occasion when our reunion took us again to the Trecarn Hotel we joined forces with members of the Castle Class Corvette Association, and were able to enjoy the wonderful entertainment provided there. As part of an impromptu 'sods opera' one of their members sang the words of 'Mack the Knife' to a recorded accompaniment. He would have graced any professional stage and, naturally, he received thunderous applause before handing back the microphone. He then resumed his seat in the ballroom where he had a massive heart attack and died, surrounded by his mates who, only a few moments earlier, had acclaimed his vocal talents. At least he had gone out on such a high note – probably in the way he would have wished. The church service in that same ballroom the following morning conducted by Peter Haywood, the Southwest England Representative of the Seamen's Christian Friend Society, was even more poignant in view of the fact that one of our members had so recently crossed the bar. It is however an inevitable fact of life that, as the youngest approach the age of eighty and the oldest become ever more frail, we will be required to accept these losses from time to time.

After a few beers we often discuss the ways of the world and, not unnaturally, we consider if the efforts of the British servicemen had been worthwhile. Certainly, in the case of the Second World War, we felt justified in volunteering in order to fight against Nazism and everything that had been associated with such a dreadful regime, not forgetting the barbaric and treacherous Japanese people. But, had the world learnt the lessons of that conflict and had the world become a better place in which to live? With our varied experiences in later life most of us have come to the conclusion that politicians in the various governments of this country have let the people down. That a wonderful haven for immigrants, both legal and illegal, has been provided in this country cannot be denied but was that the real reason for the fact that so many of our countrymen had died fighting for freedom? There is no freedom of speech any longer and in fact the Advocate-General of the European Union is reported as saying:

> "Criticism of the European Union is akin to
> blasphemy and could be restricted without violating
> freedom of speech."

Such pronouncements are themselves a contradiction surely and thoughts immediately go to the frightening novel by George Orwell entitled *1984*, particularly in view of the fact that 'Orwell' was only a pseudonym for the author, Eric Blair (was there any connection?) Could it be that he was intending to be prophetic as a warning to following generations? What a shame that the warning was not heeded and we now are required to be scrupulously politically correct in everything we utter otherwise we could upset sections of the community and the sensibilities of other countries and land up in court.

Perhaps it is appropriate to quote from Shakespeare's *Henry V* when, in the "Royal throne of Kings" speech, he ends:

> "England, bound in with the triumphant sea is now
> bound in with shame, with inky blots and rotten
> parchment bonds, that England that was wont to
> conquer others hath made a shameful conquest
> of itself."

Was Shakespeare also being prophetic as the Government today (2004) is on the verge of signing the new European Union constitution – purely as a tidying up exercise, of course!

Perhaps the most popular place for our reunions has been the Trecarn, managed by Brian Pitman and his dedicated staff. We have held our annual reunion on no fewer than four occasions in Babbacombe and have enjoyed excellent meals there together with members of other ships' associations. Unfortunately, the ladies are not quite so enthusiastic about Babbacombe as it is, for them, too far away from the shops in Torquay! However, some first class 'outings' have been held; visiting Paignton Zoo; going by steam railway to Kingswear and thence by pleasure boat up the Dart from

Dartmouth; and taking a guided tour of the Britannia Royal Naval College, Dartmouth; all of which have been thoroughly enjoyed by all our members.

It is inevitable that our numbers will decline over the years as they cross the bar or find it difficult to travel to our reunions. It is perhaps invidious to mention anyone but we have certainly missed two of our stalwarts. Bernard Griffiths, our first Secretary who, we found out later, had written about another of his ships, HMS *Duff* in his book, *MacNamaras' Band*, and the always cheerful Philip Coulson, the former Chief Engine Room Artificer who always came to the reunions with his sister, 'Bonnie' Ford and their dog, together with their brother George whenever he happened to be in England on holiday from Canada where he now resides.

HMS Porlock Bay *reunion 2004, Savoy Hotel, Bournemouth*
l to r: *Lt John Burman, RNVR, Audrey Lightfoot, Mary Smith, Gladys Ixer, Albert Moorman, Lt Commander Harris O'Taylor, USN, who had been at Pearl Harbour, 8 December 1941*

The reduced numbers have meant that we are no longer able to afford to charter a coach for our outings although, for our 2003 reunion in Exmouth, we were able to take a pleasure steamer trip up the Exe estuary as it was only a short walk to the embarkation jetty. Some of us also made our way by car to the nearby churchyard where we were able to see the tomb of Lady Nelson which had only recently been restored, mainly by members of the local Royal Naval Association. Lady Nelson had of course lived in Exmouth in a home on the 'Beacon' which is now aptly named 'Nelson House'. It was while I was taking a photograph of the plaque outside that the present owners arrived home and invited me in to see some stained glass in the hallway depicting the Nelson occupancy of the House. Apparently, the name of Emma, Lady Hamilton, is never mentioned in the House!

HMS Porlock Bay *reunion Sept 2003, Exmouth.*
Group taken during trip up the Exe estuary

A few months before our 2003 reunion, Ken Faulkner, our Secretary forwarded to me a letter from Finland which indicated that members of the ship's company of KL *Matti Kurki* had formed an Association and that they wished to come over to England to meet our members. As we all served in the same ship, we readily agreed and made arrangements to meet in Portsmouth on 23rd April, a most appropriate day as it was St George's Day. The *Matti Kurki* people are generally much younger than our members and so the ship, which was born in Charles Hill's Yard, Bristol, will now be remembered by a greater number of her old crew for much longer.

The first meeting with the Finns was a resounding success but, for my wife and me, the journey to Portsmouth was a nightmare. We arrived at Leamington Station where, glancing at the monitor giving times of arrival, I saw that our train to Portsmouth was 'on time'. Going on to the platform,

First meeting with Finns – K L Matti Kurki, *April 23 2003, Royal Sailors' Home Club, Portsmouth*
l to r: Arthur Stelfox, David Sewell, Audrey Lightfoot, Tuula Suöström, Ralph Suöström, Mary Smith, Ilkka Ignatius

we waited, and waited until a crowd began to form around a station official who told us that a bridge to the south of Leamington had been struck by a lorry and that no trains would be allowed along that track until the safety officers had inspected the bridge. Transport to Oxford in the form of coaches would be provided but we had to wait over an hour for them to arrive. On disembarking at Oxford Station, with no one to advise us as to the best route, we caught a train to Reading and made enquiries there. On being told that we should catch the next train to Guildford and enquire there, my wife went out to find a taxi which we boarded, only to discover that the driver did not know the way to Portsmouth.

The Finnish contingent at the Royal Sailors' Home Club, Portsmouth, 2003
l to r: *Martti Leino, Ralph Suöström, Ilkka Ignatius*

After being told which route to take, the driver, prompted by the possibility of a large tip if he could get us there on time, set off at a cracking pace. On arrival in Portsmouth, I was able to direct him to Queen Street where the Royal Sailor's Home Club is situated and we eventually reached the Club with ten minutes to go before the meal was due to be taken. Taking a quick wash in our bedroom, we sat down for dinner at precisely 2000 hours, the appointed time. Virgin Railways did, I am pleased to say, reimburse me with the £110 fare taken in the taxi.

The following morning, members of the two associations walked the short distance to the Historic Dockyard where Arthur Stelfox paid for everyone to go in to see *Warrior*, the *Mary Rose* and, of course *Victory*, the ship which was of such great interest to our visitors. It is a sad reflection on our schools today, that the Finns have a far greater knowledge of Trafalgar and our maritime history than the general public here. We took our visitors for a boat trip around the harbour and umpteen photographs were taken by them, copies of which were later sent to us in the form of a compact disc. The Finnish people are far more up-to-date in their knowledge of electronic equipment than we are, possibly due to the existence of that excellent firm, Nokia, and we were to find out later that the son of the Chairman of the *Matti Kurki* Association is an executive with that company.

At the Gala Dinner that evening presentations of our ship's badge were made to each of the men, Ilkka Ignatius, Martti Leino, and Ralph Suöström and, in return they presented me with a Naval Reservists Cap on which was embroidered, on one side, FNS *Matti Kurki*, and on the other, *Porlock Bay*. Speeches of welcome were made and we drank several toasts in Pusser's Rum, a favourite with our new friends.

The Finnish contingent and their wives, Sinikka, Tuula and Inka, had indicated their wish to go to London and so I had booked accommodation at the Victory Club in Seymour Street. It was necessary to accompany our friends because although Finland is a member of the European Community, the country is not a member of NATO. It was no hardship for Mary and me to travel up to Victoria Coach Station on the Flights coach where we took two taxis to the Victory Club.

In London, we took them first to St Paul's Cathedral where we showed them Nelson's tomb in the crypt and then, while the wives went their separate ways and Ralph went to the Finnish Church, Ilkka, Martti and I went to see HMS *Belfast*, the Second World War cruiser now lying near Tower Bridge. As a member of the Friends of the Imperial War Museum, I produced my card and told the cashier at the pay desk that I had representatives of the Finnish Navy with me, whereupon we were given red carpet treatment. Ilkka, now in the Reserve, was still a Chief Warrant Officer (Gunnery) and he was most impressed with all he saw, particularly the six-inch guns in their triple turrets. Dragging ourselves away from the old ship, we went to a bar on the quayside to sample English beer.

18

RETURN TO BERMUDA

"Look on my works, ye mighty, and despair!
Nothing beside remains:"
Ozymandias of Egypt, **by P. B. Shelley**

Exactly fifty years after HMS *Porlock Bay* departed in such style from Bermuda, my wife and I decided to have our annual holiday in those idyllic islands. Most of the ship's company had been only too anxious to get home and this was perhaps only natural as we had realised by now that a career in the Royal Navy was no longer attractive. We could only envisage a life in a new profession in civilian clothes, well divorced from the regimental existence of naval routine. Time, however, being a great healer was also a great catalyst for bringing together folk with an erstwhile wonderful place in our memories.

Accordingly, my wife and I examined the brochures, particularly those from British Airways whose shares had been bought when the floatation issues were put on the market and, due to their ownership, we were able to take advantage of the discount offered. Accommodation prices varied from the large hotels such as the 'Princess', down to self-catering properties but we chose a small hotel, the 'Rosedon' in Hamilton, situated not far from the centre of the city. This proved to be an excellent choice as we were able to walk to the various eating places each evening or to the ferries and to the bus station during the day without any difficulty despite the hot climate.

The DC10 in which we flew from Number Four Terminal, Heathrow Airport, was comfortable enough but we had to sit in the centre block of four seats well to the rear of the aircraft. This was despite arriving at the airport almost four hours before departure and being first in the queue at the check-in desk. The company had informed us that seats could not be pre-booked but, on asking for window seats the reply had been, "they had all gone!" So much for being a shareholder in the company but we were not alone as the mother of the pilot of the aircraft was also sitting near to us in the centre section so we felt a little less discriminated against. The lady was, however, staying at the 'Princess' which was situated little more than a stone's throw from our hotel.

After about seven and a half hours the aircraft began its descent and soon the old dockyard came into view on the starboard side as we made our way towards the former US airfield which now formed the main, and only, international airport of the islands. An immaculate landing was followed by baggage collection and the simplest of formalities before passengers were met in the fading light of evening by a group of taxis and mini-buses and conveyed to their respective holiday accommodation.

HMS Malabar *with the Naval Dockyard, Bermuda*

Six of us were duly deposited at the 'Rosedon' where a swizzle party was in full swing so, before registering or even going to our rooms, we sampled the wonderful punch offered by the management, while getting to know the other guests, both newly arrived and those who had been there for some time. Our fellow newcomers included a couple from Charlesbury, Oxon who knew friends of my late mother, giving us something in common for a start. The gentleman happened to be a former Fleet Air Arm Pilot who had been one of the 'few' to take part in the Battle of Britain and his wife had served as an Officer in the WAAF, stationed for a time at the flying boat base on Darrels Island, Bermuda.

As people started drifting away from the party, we were escorted to our room by Antoine where our baggage had already been deposited by the staff, probably Antoine himself. The air was still very warm but fortunately there was an overhead fan to make sleeping reasonable although, after a full day's travelling, followed by a party, we needed no rocking! Our reverie was in fact only broken by a gentle tapping on our door by a large coloured man who asked where we would like to take our breakfast – in our room, on the balcony or around the pool? Opting for the balcony, Beau, the coloured head waiter, arranged table and chairs and brought an excellent tray of food for us. He stayed long enough to tell us about the hotel which was owned by the former Dockyard Superintendent, Commander Kitson R.N. (Retd) and his wife who left most of the everyday running of the place to Muriel Robertson, a lady who was as charming and efficient as she was smartly dressed. Little wonder that the 'Rosedon' won the first prize awarded by the Bermuda Tourism Board.

The view from our balcony that first morning was indescribably beautiful with an inviting swimming pool below around which were other bedrooms, each with a balcony on which guests were enjoying their first meal of the day. As we watched, the local birds or Kiskadees swooped down to get a drink from the pool which they did without alighting as they made their onomatopoeic call before flying off again. Around us, small lizards darted about at a great rate, taking very little notice of the people or of the food on the trays and of course there was the inevitable sound of the tiny tree frogs as they moved unseen among the trees. This was the 'heaven' which, fifty years previously, we were unable to enjoy in the confined space of the old mess deck. Would the lads have been anxious to return home if they had experienced the conditions and surroundings which we were now enjoying? No wonder Commander Kitson and his wife had decided to settle here in retirement.

It was tempting to stay where we were for the duration of our holiday but my main aim was to revisit all my old haunts while, at the same time, introduce my wife to the sights, sounds and tastes of the islands. Accordingly, we set off on our first day towards the centre of Hamilton, passing the hotel that, years ago, had been the Sailor's Home where for a few cents we would book a bed for the night.

Onwards to the shopping area, past the policeman directing traffic from his 'birdcage' which had become such a feature for tourists with their cameras, stopping at the Tourist Information Office where we were able to buy tickets giving us unlimited travel, not only on the buses but also on the ferries which plied to various points in the Great Sound from the same jetty where we used to board or disembark from the MFVs. In terms of transport, we found that the railway which used to run along Front Street had disappeared, sold in fact to a company in what used to be British Guiana, but the buses which replaced it covered greater areas, albeit with less comfort. On a journey to St George's the traveller had quite a bone-shaking experience as the bus made its way along roads which were mere tracks before the Second World War – there was a maximum speed limit of twenty miles per hour for everyone, car owners, moped riders and the buses themselves, but who wanted to go fast through such beautiful surroundings anyway? The cars on the islands were all privately owned – only one per household – and it was completely impossible to hire one although the mopeds could be used by tourists as could the bicycles. While we would have liked to have had our own transport we could not help thinking that the policy makers had made a good decision as there were never any traffic jams and few accidents.

Front Street did not seem to have changed at all, with many of the familiar stores still trading. However, they were now often overlooked by the huge passenger ships, bringing hordes of American tourists, berthed on the other side of the road. Looking out into the Great Sound, the various islands stood out in the sparkling blue water as they had fifty years ago but there appeared a greater feeling of habitation on them. All the dwellings had those unique stepped roofs.

As we had only bed and breakfast accommodation at 'Rosedon' we had to make a 'recce' of the food shops and eating places as a priority measure, finding a supermarket almost opposite the cathedral which had a delicatessen in the course of our exploration. The supermarket itself was the very one that had sold the foodstuffs that I had bought to send home years previously but the ready-prepared food, sold by weight in plastic containers, was of greater value to me now. For our evening meal we called at a pub called the 'Hogpenny' on our first day and found the food so excellent that we returned there several further times. The manageress, a young girl, who had originated from Suffolk and whose father had been a petty officer D.E.M.S. gunner during the war, made us feel so welcome that we resolved to go right through the menu during our several visits there. In addition, the bar sold Bass, chilled to just the correct temperature for the sub-tropical conditions enjoyed by Bermuda.

On our first day in Hamilton, a visit to a florist in Reid Street was made to order a wreath to place on the grave of my messmate, Jock Rea, who had been so tragically drowned the night before we set sail for home. This was duly collected the following morning and taken, by bus, along the spine road through familiar sounding places such as Warwick and Southampton until we reached Ireland Island South, having passed through Somerset and Boaz Islands on our way. Here we alighted to walk the final few yards to the Royal Naval Cemetery, known to all as The Glade where so many serving men over the years since the early 1800s lie buried. Nearer the road, the graves were all fairly old, including those of three former Vice Admirals who had died in Bermuda, but we were searching for the more recent graves marked by the, now, standard War Graves Commission headstone. These we found some distance into the Glade and the wreath was carefully placed against the headstone which, we noticed immediately, gave HMS *Sheffield* as Jock's ship. While this was perhaps quite true it seemed so ironic that Jock had been drafted to *Sheffield* only days before his death after being a member of the ship's company of *Porlock Bay* for so long. Looking around at the hundreds of graves, we formed the impression that, although the grass in the cemetery had been cut at regular intervals, there was not one grave that had been lovingly tended for a long time. Ours was the only wreath to be seen, a fact that made us feel sad for all the others who had died on active service but at the same time glad that we had made the effort to visit the last resting place of an old shipmate.

Bidding farewell to the cemetery with its largely untold stories of Naval Service, we walked on towards Ireland Island North, past the spot where the Naval Canteen once stood and eventually arrived at the old dockyard gate, still displaying its Royal Coat of Arms. Unlike the old days when, just inside the gate, there was always a member of the Naval Regulating Branch only too eager to examine passes etc., the place was completely deserted. The notice "keep out" was obviously not being enforced and so we walked through the ghost-like dockyard, past the spot where the floating dock lay in which *Porlock Bay* had been scrubbed and her lower hull repainted. Everywhere was so silent now and stopping only to take a photograph of some of the ship's badges on a wall, we made our way to the old sail loft and to the clocktower building where we at last found signs of life.

The clocktower building outwardly had not changed – it still had the two towers with a clockface on each, one telling the time and the other giving the state of the tide. Inside however it was quite different as the building had been transformed into a shopping centre with the former offices and stores now used as individual shops. My only memory of the inside of the building was when my front teeth were quickly removed and dropped into what sounded like a bucket, but it was still possible to imagine the general bustle of the place when the squadron was in harbour. The land outside which, in our day, was covered with wires and other paraphernalia was now extremely tidy with palm trees planted where, once, cable drums occupied the space. Some bollards and capstans had been retained but these had been painted black and white. The small building near to the spot where the guard for the King's birthday parade formed up and which lost its roof in the hurricane just before we left, had been completely removed. The camber sticking out into the dockyard seemed to be in great demand by the small boats which were being repaired there and my mind turned to the days when ships were built there, possibly including the sloop, HMS *Pickle*, which brought the news of the great victory at Trafalgar back to Falmouth and thence by Lieutenant Lapenotière to London. Unfortunately, there was not sufficient time to investigate such matters at the Island's Record Office but, suffice to say, *Pickle* was built in Bermuda from the island's cedar.

On another occasion we caught the bus at the depot near to the City Hall and travelled to St George's, the one-time capital of the islands, passing the airport on the way. While we had briefly visited St George's during our Naval days, there was much to see in the town that I personally had missed earlier and a new tourist attraction, in the form of a replica of an old ship, the *Deliverance*, on Ordnance Island which had been a British Army arsenal was standing, high and dry.

Nearby was a ducking stool which is apparently still used to show visitors how 'scolds' and petty offenders were punished and this, together with the town's stocks are much photographed. However, a colourful figure appeared ringing his bell and making announcements to everyone around. He was the Town Crier dressed in his robes who was only too willing to pose with visitors for further photographs, explaining as he did so that he originally came from Yorkshire. We had not taken much notice of the buildings of the erstwhile capital earlier but now, obviously due to my vocation as a planner, I was in my element as I visited all those open to the public. The Bridge House, Tucker House and the Town Hall received much of my attention together with the White Horse Tavern, of course, where we had a cool beer. The Tavern was, we were told, originally the home of John Davenport who hid his wealth in arrowroot kegs in the basement. Could John Davenport have been an ancestor of our first captain, Lieutenant Dudley Davenport by any chance?

Perhaps the most important building in St George's was St Peter's Church dating from 1713, and replacing an earlier building. It is in fact the oldest Anglican Church in continuous use in the Western Hemisphere and the churchyard is of particular interest to researchers. Among the graves are those of the post-war Governor and his A.D.C. who were murdered and now lie buried in plots adjoining the church.

Every building appeared to have been recently painted in a variety of bright, but not garish, colours. Names of streets such as One Gun Alley, Shinbone Alley, Featherbed Alley and Old Maid's Lane give further colour to the wonderful old town with the result that, now armed with a Hasselblad camera in place of my old kodak box, I went almost berserk taking transparencies which I can now project to remind me of the place. It seemed remarkable that even now there are no high buildings to visually disrupt the wonderful street scenes which fortunately have been conserved in much the same way as they have stood for two centuries. Buildings such as Tucker's House (now a museum), Bridge House and King's Square with its pillory and stocks are wonderful examples of the excellent work carried out by the Authorities to maintain buildings in their original state as far as possible.

During our stay in Bermuda, I felt that I must have a look at Admiralty House, the building which was the home to the C-in-C of the America and West Indies Squadron and one which we had to salute each time we went out or returned from the sea. A plan of Bermuda was purchased and we caught the bus which took us to a point near to the House, but try as we would, we could only find foundations and a building that had been converted into a community centre. On making further enquiries, we discovered that the once imposing building had been deliberately burnt down, a fact that I found particularly distressing. The Admiral's small private harbour, from which he would sail across to the dockyard, was still there as was a reminder of the good old days in the form of a tennis court but it seemed sheer vandalism to destroy the main building by fire.

As the site of Admiralty House was within walking distance of Spanish Point, we made the extra few yards to where the first floating dock lies, rusting away in the wonderfully blue waters. She broke loose from her tow as she was being taken away from the dockyard and, having stranded herself on the sharp rocks, they just left the remains to rot away.

Before leaving home, I had written to the curator of the Admiralty Museum to say that the HMS *Porlock Bay* Association wished to present them with our 'unofficial' badge and had received a charming reply. Accordingly, we caught the ferry (no longer an MFV) to the dockyard and made our way through the old buildings to where the various artefacts were stored. The curator was a most pleasant girl (everyone appears young to me anyway) and she showed us some of the items but, when I asked her about the immediate post-war squadron, her records were virtually blank. They were only aware of the flagship, HMS *Sheffield* but of the *Kenya*, *Sparrow*, *Snipe*, *Porlock Bay* and *Padstow Bay* there was nothing. She said that there were several badges in the former munitions buildings but, of the old squadron only the badge of *Sparrow* was to be found. To partially put the records straight I presented the HMS *Porlock Bay* badge to her while my wife took a photograph if only to prove that we had in fact carried out the task.

There appears to be quite a hole in the island's history with regard to the squadron of which we were part and even in the excellent book entitled *The Andrew and the Onions* there is scant reference to our presence there just after the war.

Having bidden farewell to the curator, we made a visit to the Munitions store, the old guns placed to guard Admiralty Island and the rum store, now a restaurant, passing the old building in which some of us were accommodated years ago but which is now without a roof. At least some attempt had been made to preserve some of the historic buildings although the former dockyard superintendent's house was, at the time, encased in rusty scaffolding and the weaponry together with the old anchors had been merely left to rot.

Back in Hamilton, the shops in Front Street looked as smart as they did in the 1940s with names such as Goslings still selling wines and spirits, Trimingham's and Smiths, which were the two main stores, selling their fashionable goods mainly now to the hordes of tourists from the American

Continent. Not one building was lacking a coat of paint and these included all the residential properties which, we understood, were required to be painted white each year. The cathedral was maintained in excellent order and we were pleased to see the white ensign proudly displayed there. We followed our route taken by the guard for the King's birthday parade, again noting the smart condition of the flags on the war memorial to which we gave more than a smart 'eyes-right' as we passed. We stopped to take photographs of the memorial as a reminder that the local population still have regard to the days when their island was such an important strategic point in the battle of the Atlantic.

It was not my intention to produce a travelogue of Bermuda as all these details can surely be found in the various guide books but we felt justified in being rather nostalgic at the sight of so many of the old familiar places that came back to mind as soon as I saw them again after fifty years.

On our return, our next reunion was held once more at the Trecarn Hotel, Babbacombe and the manager kindly made arrangements for my transparencies to be shown to our members.

19

LIAISON WITH THE FINNISH VETERANS

"Anyone who has been to sea knows that for all sailors, no matter what the nationality, the greatest enemy is the sea. And the joy of being a sailor is they share a brotherhood of the sea that knows no boundaries."
Admiral Sir Alan West RN
First Sea Lord

The HMS *Porlock Bay* Association continued to flourish over the years with members being 'found' all over the world but, at the same time, sadly others have 'crossed the bar' to deplete our numbers. Our Association has always tried to avoid members merely fading away by visiting sick ex-colleagues whenever possible and by being represented when one of our members has 'crossed the bar,' whatever his rank or his position in his later civilian occupation.

Our first secretary, Bernard Griffiths, who was instrumental in doing so much for the Association had a serious stroke soon after returning from a reunion and despite all the care he received, he died in Leominster Hospital in November 1998. While he lay seriously ill, Jim Cretney, who was a former General Practitioner in Leicester, travelled over to see him but he realised that nothing more could be done to keep Bernard alive. True to his wonderful public spirit, Bernard had instructed that his body should be left for medical research which meant that he did not have a funeral but, a few weeks later, a memorial service was held in the Priory Church, Leominster.

The service was attended by fourteen of our members and many tributes were paid to Bernard by his grandson Justin and also on behalf of the Association. Afterwards, in talking to Bernard's widow, Olive, I learned of another side of his unassuming manner because although we were all aware of most of each other's achievements, he had never mentioned that he had written a book about a previous ship in which he had served. The ship was HMS *Duff*, one of the 'Captains' class, most of which had been named after prominent ship's captains who served at Trafalgar. These ships were to play such an important part in the Battle of the Atlantic and the Normandy landings. Captain Duff, after whom the ship was named, had been in command of HMS *Mars*, a seventy-four-gun ship which suffered heavily in the battle losing twenty-nine men, including the Captain who was decapitated by round shot.

Bernard's book, entitled *MacNamaras' Band*, outlined his experiences in the ship, commanded by a fellow Canadian, Lieutenant Frederick Brock, R.C.N.V.R., who always had a record played of 'MacNamaras' Band' whenever the ship entered or left harbour. Bernard, who had been born in Canada, wrote of his Captain:

> "… few ship's companies could have had that spirit so firmly implanted in us. His leadership and his moral strength, unexpressed but constantly with us, made us proud to serve in the Duff…"

HMS *Duff* was often in action against E-Boats and human torpedoes but unfortunately it was a mine that ended her active life. After striking the mine she was taken in tow and actually reached port but she had been so badly damaged that she was considered beyond repair and was later scrapped.

Bernard was a regular attendee at HMS *Duff* reunions and, for our association, he produced a regular newssheet for members. However, he did not live to know the effect that his foresight in putting *Porlock Bay* on the Internet would have. Apart from 'finding' at least two new members, his action was instrumental in making links with Finland, the country which had bought our old ship.

While we were fully aware that the ship had been renamed KL *Matti Kurki* as the main training ship and, in fact, I had visited her in Suomenlinna Island in 1975, we did not know that her ship's company had formed an association similar to our own. The first indication we had was when Olive Griffiths received a letter from Ralph Suöström suggesting a meeting. Olive forwarded the letter to our current Secretary, Ken Faulkner who, in turn, sent me a copy. It crossed my mind that we would probably be unique because we knew of no other association that had 'twinned' with an association of the ship's company of the same ship belonging to another country.

As described in Chapter Seventeen our first joint meeting took place in Portsmouth at the, then, Portsmouth Royal Sailors' Home Club. At the first meal that we had together we learnt much about our new-found friends and their way of life. Previously, we had been in contact with the Finns by correspondence and many telephone calls but now we had the chance to meet them and their wives in the flesh. Ilkka Ignatius seemed even larger than his photograph suggested and we had no language difficulty as they could all speak English, particularly Sinikka, Ilkka's wife, who was able to help out with some of the more difficult turns of phrase which she was able to translate for him.

It seemed as if we had known our new-found friends for ages and we resolved to keep the liaison between our two associations going. With this in mind it was provisionally arranged that a group from the *Porlock Bay* Association would travel to Helsinki the following year to meet up with their members and to visit the naval establishments in or around the city. The thought was certainly attractive to me but would it be possible to persuade a group to accompany me? The answer would not be known until the Annual General Meeting in September, but, in the meantime several letters passed between this country and Helsinki, together with many telephone calls.

Fortunately, the response at the meeting was favourable. Our reunion was held at the Grand Hotel, Exmouth where all the necessary arrangements were made to view the photographs recorded on a compact disc, taken by our Scandinavian friends. Whether it was the photographs or not, the vote taken at the AGM was firmly in favour of going to Helsinki in 2004 with no less than fourteen of our members indicating their wish to make the trip.

On our return home a telephone call was duly made to Helsinki to convey our decision to visit the *Matti Kurki* people, possibly in August of the following year. Many arrangements would have to be made both in Helsinki and in England for our means of travel and our accommodation in Helsinki. To this end we resolved to make our own individual bookings with the majority opting to fly from Manchester direct to Helsinki while my wife and I decided to go from Birmingham Airport, involving a stopover in Copenhagen. By this time, our numbers had been reduced to ten which was a far more manageable party for our hosts to handle and it seemed that the Finns were quite relieved to be receiving smaller numbers.

My travel arrangements were made with a company in London specialising in Scandinavian travel, namely Norvista. Their representative was a Finnish person, Paula Haapenan, who was able to advise on the best accommodation in Helsinki from the point of view of proximity to the places of interest. Instead of our original choice of hotel, she suggested that the Radisson Plaza SAS would be the most appropriate and this was good advice as we were to find out when we eventually arrived. The most important thing Paula did for us was to arrange the Banquet in our hotel which was to be held in a separate dining room, enabling us to remain there as long as we wished without annoying other hotel guests. The menu was also agreed between the Finns and ourselves together with table settings and other matters concerning the 'big night'.

From the telephone calls it soon transpired that we were to be entertained in far greater style than we had done for them in Portsmouth the previous year and so it was agreed that we would take charge of the Banquet while our hosts would make all the arrangements for the various other events. It was also necessary to put in hand the presents which were to made at the Banquet and in this respect, an order was given to an advertiser in *Navy News* to supply six engraved glass tankards bearing the two names of our ship and an outline of the vessel. The artist providing these items turned out to be a former naval rating who had served in HMS *Ambuscade* and who took great pride in his work, operating from a small workshop in Wellingborough, Northants.

Ilkka in the meantime was very busy making arrangements for visits to the Naval Academy, a harbour trip, tours of the Presidential Palace, the British Embassy and the Army / Navy base. As was only to be expected, changes would have to be made but the outline plan was generally adhered to. All the time, refinements to the plans were being made until in a telephone call, Ilkka told me that three Naval Crosses had been authorised for presentation to our group – one was for me but who should receive the other two? It meant an instant decision as the citations were to be prepared as soon as possible so my immediate thought was that the two remaining crosses should go to the Secretary and the Treasurer of the HMS *Porlock Bay* Association; Ken Faulkner and Michael Sheppard. Ilkka asked me to keep quiet about the presentation although it would be possible for me to alert the two members concerned.

Eventually the time came to set off for Helsinki, but how were we to take the pint tankards together with the other presents and the white ensign and other flags to adorn the banqueting room? This was achieved by cutting down on personal clothing and, by wrapping the tankards in bubble wrap, they would go in the suitcase. All was now set. The taxi to Birmingham Airport arrived on time and we were off!

The SAS aircraft left on time for a comfortable flight to Copenhagen, flying over large sections of the Dutch and Danish coasts. It meant a two-hour wait in the terminal building but this was the outward journey and we did not object even if there was any point in objecting. Refreshments were available but it became obvious that, whereas Denmark was a member of the European Union, she had not adopted the Euro as the currency and so it was possible to pay for food in our Euros although the change was given in Danish Krone. The wait over, we proceeded to the appropriate gate for the second leg of our journey, admiring all the time the design of the airport building. With the minimum of fuss we were soon aloft again, flying east north east through the skies over the Baltic until the low-lying coast of Finland appeared below. For the major part the land seemed uninhabited with large expanses covered by lakes and this continued until the 'seat belts on' order was displayed as we began the descent to the capital. Another fine landing and we were soon taxiing towards the wonderful Helsinki Airport. Wonderful because it embodies all the good aspects of traffic integration, allowing passengers to transfer from the airport to bus transport or private car with maximum ease. Additionally, the aesthetic quality of the building was so pleasing that I had no hesitation in awarding it 'top airport' status.

Such a pleasant arrival was made even more pleasant by the fact that, waiting at the barrier, stood Ilkka and his wife Sinikka with their car standing nearby in the covered car park. The sun was brilliant; far better weather than the last television forecast for Britain and we were soon on our way to the Radisson Plaza Hotel. Ilkka proudly announced that the airport had received universal acclaim when I said that the integrated transport system was most impressive, far superior to Heathrow's Terminal One.

Arriving at the hotel, Ilkka and his wife left us to drive back to their home in Espoo about thirty miles away but we were not alone as the other eight members of our party were already there, including Alan Barnard who had travelled on his own from Hampshire via Heathrow, together with four of our hosts to answer our questions.

Knowing that we would probably be hungry, the Finns took us to an area of the city where there were crowds of people in a long, linear open space and showed us a restaurant where we could have a meal while they went back to their respective homes to prepare for the morrow. Difficulty number one came when the menus were put before us, in Finnish, but when the waitresses came back to take our order, all was well because they could all speak perfect English.

We were all fairly tired after the journey and it was necessary to unpack so the celebrations were postponed until the morning, although we remained in the large foyer of the hotel talking and discussing various aspects of our somewhat hectic itinerary until quite late. After that sleep came quite easily.

The alarm went off at the crack of dawn when we saw the street outside being swept – and it was only 0600 hours. Breakfast was taken buffet fashion, plenty of it despite our routine at home which cut out all cooked food but we excused ourselves with the explanation that it would be necessary if we were to enjoy the active morning that the itinerary suggested.

The detailed itinerary for our first morning in Helsinki required us to report at the harbour at 0930 hours and, just to make sure we were there on time, Ralph and Martti appeared, punctually, at our hotel at 0900 hours to walk the half mile or so with us. Here, we were met by the Deputy Harbour Master, Captain Kaj Sarpavena and taken to the excellently turned out Harbour Launch. We never did find out why his title was 'Deputy' Harbour Master when he was definitely the boss – perhaps his position was similar to the 'Deputy' Surveyor of the New Forest in England.

The launch took us past a Saga cruise liner and the extremely powerful icebreakers maintained in Helsinki to keep the waterways to the city open during the winter months. Pictures were produced of the icing-up of the area indicating the necessity of having such powerful vessels to break up the ice. As we proceeded past an island preserved as a natural zoological garden we opened a bottle of Pusser's rum brought by Brian Lightfoot which was poured into the plastic glasses miraculously produced by the D.H.M., and drank a toast to a successful visit. Later, a ship's decanter full of Pusser's Rum was presented to Captain Sarpavena, the decanter having been brought by Arthur Stelfox for such an occasion. It was suggested that the Captain may wish to share the contents with his Harbour Board although a counter suggestion was made that he would probably prefer to take it home for his personal enjoyment.

The launch proceeded on to an island in the archipelago where we were met by Commander Ove Enquist. Kuivassaari Island had been a strongly fortified island but was now uninhabited except for a caretaker. However, weaponry of all sorts had been retained and a radar aerial was still operating there, linked to the harbour office on the mainland. The main purpose of our visit was to see a gun turret with two twelve-inch guns dating from 1904. These were of Russian manufacture and despite their age, they were still potentially active and had, in fact, been fired only a few years before. We entered the turret along a system of corridors where once dozens of coastal defence troops lived underground to maintain the guns, and eventually came to the lower chamber containing the ammunition hoists. The more active members then climbed a vertical ladder until we were in the turret proper to see the well-polished breeches of the guns themselves.

Retracing our steps, we then were taken to the gunnery control compartment, the equivalent of a ship's T.S., and saw some of the old instruments and the communications within the turrets. Following this we emerged into the strong sunlight once more to stand on top of the turret for a photo call. The turret was only just above ground level and would have been difficult to see with the naked eye from any warship approaching Helsinki but its use was never tested against an enemy force.

Because the island was largely deserted, the land had become a nature reserve from which it was forbidden to take or pick any of the wild flowers. The flora was most interesting to see in the short time we were there but we were allowed to pick and eat the wild strawberries which abounded there. Time was indeed short, enabling us just a cursory glance at the remaining weaponry before we had to return to the small jetty where the launch was waiting to take us to Suomenlinna Island and the Navy Academy, 'Merisotakoula'.

In glorious sunshine, we were taken back towards Helsinki to stop off at Suomenlinna which was in fact the cradle of civilisation in Finland. For me, particularly, it was a sentimental journey as we passed the spot where *Matti Kurki* had lain when I visited her in 1975, almost thirty years previously. The berth where she had been was now empty but it had been maintained in good order and it occurred to me how difficult it must have been to manoeuvre a 300-foot-long vessel into such a small space. There was no time to ponder on this as we had to pass through the archway of the Naval Academy where the Director, Captain Kai Varsio was waiting to greet us. An extremely tall man, the Director agreed to more photographs in the Courtyard of the Academy before taking us into the building where an interesting ceremony took place.

Ilkka had warned me earlier that there would be a wreath-laying to carry out at the Academy and, for this purpose, it had been necessary for me to buy a beret as he was similarly dressed. While all the members of our party and our hosts climbed a staircase, Ilkka motioned to me to stay with him while he collected the flowers and we stood at the foot of the stairs at attention. Suddenly a ship's bell rang out eight bells and we started up the red carpeted staircase to stand at the top in front of a board containing the names of those Finnish seamen who had been killed in battle. Standing on either side of the board were two immaculately dressed seamen while Ilkka spoke, in his own language, to say that the flowers were laid in memory of all seamen killed in battle and then it was my turn to say the same, in English, before the flowers were laid. We then replaced our berets, saluted and joined the others who had taken several photographs of the event.

The combined Porlock Bay/Matti Kurki party at the Naval Academy, Helsinki. The director of the Academy is the tall person, third from right

The ceremony over, we all trooped into the refectory with the Director where lunch was served. Mary and I were seated on either side of the Director and the others found a place around the table for the welcome meal. At the end, it was up to me to thank the Director for his hospitality and to say a few words about our visit. Pointing out that Finland had selected our ship from the hundreds of escort vessels available at the end of the war, I

Ilkka Ignatius and Roger Smith laying wreath at War Memorial – Naval Academy, Helsinki

complimented their Navy for buying the *best* and that, after becoming their main training ship, *Matti Kurki*, had served for fourteen years until the sad decision was taken to scrap the old ship. They had looked after a much loved ship for which we had a particular affection and which had outlasted all the other 'Bay' Class frigates.

In reply, Captain Varsio welcomed us to the Academy, saying that he would give details of the Finnish Navy at session later in the afternoon. In the meantime we were taken to the Staff Wardroom of the Naval Academy to see the various artefacts from the old ship which had been saved when she was scrapped. There on the far wall was the ship's wheel which brought such a nostalgic feeling among all of us who had handled it in all weathers in the West Indies. The imitation fireplace complete with electric fire was opposite and, wonder of wonders, above it was the metal *Porlock Bay* badge which was always displayed alongside the brow in harbour. The seating had all been taken from the old ship and was now put to good use by the Academy staff officers. We spent quite a while there, looking at the other badges which adorned the walls, together with several naval photographs before leaving the wardroom and seeing the 'official' ship's badge which our hosts told us had been found in the Petty Officer's Mess.

This depicted an Oak tree with out-of-proportion acorns which our first Captain, Lieutenant Davenport, had decided he did not like so he had changed it for the badge which we all recognised.

Captain Kai Varsio, the Director of the Academy, then took us to a mini-cinema where a film, taken in 1967, was shown of *Matti Kurki* in rough seas which were seen washing over the quarterdeck. Scenes of a more placid existence in America and Canada were also seen followed by the return to Finland. Captain Varsio then explained the organisations of the Finnish Navy and its role, with the Army, in the defence of the country. The armed forces apparently consist largely of conscripts who are obliged, unless they are physically disabled or are Jehovah's Witnesses, to serve one year full time. Probably this accounts for the fact that vandalism is almost unknown in Finland, proving to us at least, the value of requiring all young people to accept the discipline of the Services. Surprisingly there was almost no liaison with the country's Air Force in the Defence organisation as that branch was an autonomous unit.

Ilkka Ignatius with beret, Author – Memorial to Seamen killed in battle, Suomenlinna – Helsinki Naval Academy

Roger Smith and Ilkka Ignatius in wardroom of Naval Academy, Helsinki

After the talk on the ships of the Finnish Navy, we bade farewell to the Director, retraced our steps past the creek where *Matti Kurki* lay before being scrapped and spent a while in a bar outside the Academy where ice cold beer was most acceptable in the afternoon heat as we waited for the public ferry back to the mainland. Having put a couple of Euros into a slot machine on the jetty we got our tickets although these were not inspected or collected on board. As we stepped on to the ferry however, I felt a hand on my shoulder and, thinking that the ticket collector required me to show that I had paid, looked round to find the Director in civilian clothes, returning to his home.

The journey only took about twenty minutes before we landed near to the market where we spent some time among the stalls, not with any intention of buying but generally taking in an impression of the place. After that, a walk of just under a mile to our hotel to relax and prepare for the next day, the most important day of our tour.

Punctually at 0900 hours we were escorted by Ralph and Martti with their wives to the Presidential Palace where a certain amount of reconstruction work was in progress requiring us to enter by a side door. We had been told that the President, Mrs Hallonen had expressed her regret that she would be away from Helsinki attending a Military Tattoo many miles away otherwise she would have met us and accompanied us on a tour of the Palace. In her place, her secretary, speaking perfect English, escorted us around, showing us the various rooms and explaining the various phases of the building, started by the Russians and extended when Finland became a separate state in 1917. With no restrictions on photography, our party, including the Finns, went to town snapping away, particularly in the President's Room where, one by one, they sat in the President's chair for a snap to display in the family album!

This room at the front of the building overlooking the market and the waterfront had a balcony but this was 'out of bounds' for us. The sound of drills outside together with the bustle of traffic made it somewhat noisy but presumably the pneumatic drills would only be there in the absence of the President. In an adjoining room, we saw the pictures of all the Presidents'

Back row: Alan Barnard, Ilkka Ignatius, Tuula Suöström
Middle row: Mike Sheppard, Ken Faulkner, Brian Lightfoot,
Ralph Suöström, Martti Leino
Front row: Mary Sheppard, Arthur Stelfox, Audrey Lightfoot, Inka Leino,
Mary Smith & Roger Smith in the Presidential Palace, Helsinki, 2004

Ilkka Ignatius, Drawing Room, President's Palace, Helsinki, 2004

Consorts including the one man who was the husband of the present incumbent of the post. The two main Assembly Rooms had recently been redecorated so they appeared in pristine condition as if just awaiting our visit.

Our tour over, we split up with some going across the road to the reddish building which was the Uspenski Cathedral before another visit to the market to buy flowers for the lady members of the Finnish party who would be attending the evening's banquet in our hotel. While some took the opportunity to see the city from the top of a sightseeing double decker bus, Mary and I remained in the hotel to help with the decorating of the dining room. From a balcony overlooking the room, a Finnish Naval battle ensign and a large White Ensign borrowed from the British Embassy were hung and my smaller white ensign and St George's and Union flags decorated the room itself. Ilkka explained that his wife had visited the British Embassy to make arrangements for our Reception there but, as the Ambassador was also attending the Military activities in the north of the country, we had been invited to the Residence of the British Defence Attaché instead on the following evening. However, she had managed to 'borrow' the large white Ensign which now hung proudly from the balcony of the Dining Room, making a very colourful sight.

LIAISON WITH THE FINNISH VETERANS

Martti Leino, President's Palace, Helsinki

The combined dinner at the Radisson Plaza Hotel, Helsinki

The combined dinner at the Radisson Plaza Hotel, Helsinki

A quick shower and change was called for before the entire party came down to the dining room in which Ilkka had put name-cards in each place at the table. I learned that a surprise guest would be attending – the under-sergeant who showed me around Suomenlinna Island twenty-nine years previously. Fred Sundén was a Chemical Engineer who had been attending a Conference and just happened to be in Helsinki that evening before returning to his doctor wife. Also attending the dinner would be Captain Vitikka, a former Captain of *Matti Kurki* who, as Finnish Naval Attaché in London, had been invested by the Queen with the insignia of Commander of the Royal Victoria Order.

The 'locals' arrived in due course and these included a Reserve Lieutenant Commander who, in civilian life was a dentist together with a Warrant Officer and his wife. Before sitting down for the banquet however, another VIP in the form of Admiral Klenberg arrived, having driven about 300 kilometres for the occasion. Ilkka, with his meticulous planning, had arranged an Investiture at which Admiral Klenberg decorated three of the

Porlock Bay matelots with a Finnish Naval Cross, a silver cross with a blue enamel centre together with a blue ribbon. The three involved were the Secretary of our Association, Ken Faulkner, the Treasurer, Mike Sheppard and myself as Chairman and the crosses were accompanied by a Citation.

Admiral Klenberg made a short speech to which I responded before our two local friends, Martti Leino and Ralph Suöström were decorated by Captain Vitikka with long service medals. The Investiture over we were able to take our places for the meal at which fillet steak was served in the form of a cube approximately three inches square to the liking of most but a few could not eat the pink, uncooked centre! After the meal, Ilkka asked me to read out a letter from the Chief of the Finnish Defence Staff, Admiral Juhani Kaskeala to the "Veterans of the HMS *Porlock Bay* and FNS *Matti Kurki*". Apparently, Admiral Kaskeala had sailed in the old ship on two occasions between 1967 and 1973, recalling that "it is with great affection I remember our fine frigate. I wish you all the best and I highly appreciate your activity in organising a bi-national union."

The combined dinner at the Radisson Plaza Hotel, Helsinki

The combined dinner at the Radisson Plaza Hotel, Helsinki

It then fell to me to say a few words to the assembled company. My theme was the unique aspects of our old ship, starting with the fact that *Porlock Bay* had been laid down as a 'Loch' Class frigate with the name *Loch Seaforth* but this was changed to *Loch Muick* before she became *Porlock Bay*, all before she took to the water. Several 'Bay' class frigates had been given a 'Loch' name but ours was the only one to have two 'Loch' names before her eventual name.

Secondly, how many ship's companies had formed associations in two countries? Several ships had been sold to foreign nations but how many, having instigated an HMS association, had been sold and a second association been formed for the same ship? This question would subsequently be asked in the *Navy News* and other publications although it was doubtful if there were any similar situations and, in fact, the reports were not published.

Thirdly, how many frigates' Captains had later risen to be Admirals? *Porlock Bay*'s two Captains, Lieutenant Davenport and Commander Twiss had both achieved Flag Rank and no less than three Finnish Captains had similarly become Admirals. We therefore concluded that our old ship was unique and threw out a challenge to any association who could beat our record!

Following these words, presents were given to the Finnish men in the form of glass pint tankards inscribed with the two names of the ship together with a silhouette of her. In addition, Ilkka was also presented with a recently issued silver crown which had a coloured white ensign incorporated into the design. Captain Vitikka was also given a silver coin, the currency of the Bahamas which, on the reverse, had our Queen's portrait to remind him of his voyage to the West Indies and also of his time in England in Naval Attaché. The ladies were not forgotten as my wife had bought bunches of anemones in the market earlier in the afternoon and these were presented in addition to a Silver Jubilee book to Sinikka, Ilkka's wife.

Captain Vitikka spoke about his time as Captain of *Matti Kurki* with particular reference to a combined exercise with the Royal Navy when Prince Michael was transferred at sea between his ship and another of the Royal Navy. Apparently, in the middle of the exercise, with the Prince half way across, the ships came closer together with the result that the Prince was dunked in the sea. Captain Vitikka was suffering from breathing difficulties and so, soon after the meal, he had to leave us to take his medication and he said au revoir to everyone.

The combined dinner at the Radisson Plaza Hotel, Helsinki

The combined dinner at the Radisson Plaza Hotel, Helsinki

The party by this time was breaking up in order that the Finns could fill their new tankards and we could sample the local beer also. There was still time for further chat and for several more photographs which made a good record of the event until, eventually, it was time for the locals to go home and for us to retire to our rooms. It had indeed been a wonderful occasion but we had to get some sleep before another busy day.

With military precision our hosts arrived at our hotel in the morning to take us to the Naval Base at Upinniemi, about thirty miles away by car. Here we were met by Lieutenant Patrick Säilä and were taken around the camp by bus, seeing on our way one of the propellers of the old ship which was mounted on a stand outside the Naval Club, among the trees. More photographs were taken before we were taken further to the shoreline where both anchors had been preserved and, noticing that they had been made in Sunderland, further photographs were taken.

From the anchors we proceeded to the Sea Chapel, a modern building with an appropriate separate campanile. The base chaplain then took us into the chapel where, hanging from the ceiling, was a model of Finland's first Training Ship and elsewhere, memorabilia of ships together with photographs were displayed. The chaplain explained that approximately ninety-five per cent of the country's population were Lutherans, the majority of whom had been confirmed in that religion. The right hand side of the chapel had windows along its entire length, giving wonderful views of the shoreline and giving rise to the question as to how it was possible to retain the attention of the congregation with the competing attraction of the wonderful scenery!

We were then taken to a dock area where several units of the Finnish Navy were lying. No photographs were allowed here but we were able to see the camouflaged patrol vessels and other ships of the Navy before continuing our bus journey to the canteen for lunch with Lieutenant Säilä who then had to leave us to change into combat uniform to take a class in the afternoon. We thanked him and bade farewell before going to the Finnish equivalent of the NAAFI where, true to form, we bought several items of clothing etc, to remind us of the visit. Opposite the 'NAAFI' was the

Ilkka Ignatius with his wife, Sinikka

The combined dinner at the Radisson Plaza Hotel, Helsinki

equivalent of the quarterdeck where a mast stood, similar to most RN Shore Bases and where we rejoined the bus for the short journey to the main gate. Here we got into our hosts' cars for the return trip to Helsinki although, this time, Ilkka and his wife left on their own as their home was approximately half way to the capital at Espoo.

In Helsinki the *Porlock Bay* crowd decided to see as much of the city as possible despite a tiring morning and the prospect of an even more tiring evening. We took a topless bus ride past the 1951 Olympic Stadium and the Opera House among other sights when suddenly the bus was stuck in a traffic jam near to the harbour. A race through the city on foot had to be taken, therefore and we arrived back at our hotel for a quick shower before going to the residence of the British Defence Attaché, Lieutenant Colonel Rick Andrews.

Our reception at the residence was most enjoyable; Lieutenant Colonel Rick Andrews and his charming wife made us most welcome and the Finns in particular formed lasting friendships there, so much so that Rick Andrews and his wife have spent a holiday on Ilkka's island in the archipelago where he has a house. The British Defence Attaché met us wearing his light fawn uniform, unique to the Army Air Corps but apart from that, the evening was very informal perhaps assisted by the drinks which were available. It was a most convivial evening for everyone including the dogs which were let loose after the food had been cleared away to be fussed by the Finns and the British alike.

Our farewells made, we congregated outside the residence to thank our *Matti Kurki* hosts for making our visit so memorable before returning to our hotel for our final night. We promised to make arrangements for a reciprocal visit the following year in our own homeport, Devonport, and bade farewell yet again.

Naturally, we had to make arrangements early for the following year's visit when everyone, Finns and British, were found accommodation at the Royal Fleet Club, Devonport. Our association just managed to finish our Annual General Meeting at the Club before the shout went up, "they've arrived," as several taxis pulled up outside and a much larger party from Finland piled into the entrance. The party now included the Harbour Master and his partner, together with the dentist Lieutenant Commander and his wife, and Timo, a senior Warrant Officer and his wife in addition to the original six who had comprised the party two years previously.

After a meal and a few drinks in the Club, we decided that, in view of their long journey, we would retire early as a full day's programme had been

Lt Säilä (Finnish Navy), Brian Lightfoot, Roger Smith, Ken Faulkner, Alan Barnard, Mike Sheppard, Arthur Stelfox with HMS Porlock Bay *anchors, Naval Base, Upinniemi, Finland, August 2004*

Finnish-British party in front of PB screws

arranged for the morrow. Accordingly, we were fully rested and breakfasted when a coach arrived to take the full party across the Hamoaze on the Torpoint Ferry and, thence, to the main training establishment for the Royal Navy, HMS *Raleigh*. Here we transferred to a RN coach to visit the submarine school and, from there we went to a display by the latest recruits who were training on a fitness course. After so many years our people who had trained at the Trevol Rifle Range were expecting to see the same course but it was completely different and despite our questions as to what had happened to the Rifle Range, no one on the instructional staff seemed to know about it. After sixty years it was only to be expected that the present day staff know little about 'the old days' because none of them had been born when we went out on the assault course and possibly their own fathers were too young to remember any details, even assuming that they had served in the RN. A sure indication of becoming old!

We were taken to the seamanship training school where the new recruits are taught how to make the necessary knots or bends. Following this we were taken to the catering school where we were entertained to lunch in the wardroom, the food having been prepared by the students.

Having thanked our hosts, we then went to the dockyard on the other side of the Hamoaze to visit a nuclear submarine HMS *Courageous* and spent almost two hours aboard while our wives, who did not fancy going down a vertical ladder, stayed in a building alongside. From here we went to the museum where the uniform of our old captain, later Admiral Sir Frank Twiss, is displayed with other interesting artefacts. However, the execution chamber in another long building intrigued our guests considerably, particularly when our guide pulled the lever to spring the trap doors through which the condemned men would drop to land on a surgeon's table below. It was a salutary experience to see the hangman's noose still intact, possibly the only one left in the country.

It had been a full, action-packed, day but the most important aspect was still to take place, namely the dinner for which a room had been suitably decorated with the Finnish battle ensign and the white ensign in addition to the full Nelsonian signal, 'England expects that every man will do his duty', sewn painstakingly by Mary. After the meal, I read out messages from the Commander-in-Chief of the Finnish Defence Staff, Admiral Kaskeala, the Commander-in-Chief Fleet, Admiral Band and another from the Home Secretary, all of whom expressed their wish for the success of our 'reunion'.

The 'survivors' at HMS Raleigh

> **KL Matti Kurki / HMS Porlock Bay**
> **3rd REUNION**
>
> 10.-13.9.2005 Davenport, UK
> This original is dedicated to Sir Roger Smith.
> *With compliments, Martti Leino*

The Author appears to have been knighted!

The bar afterwards was our next venue for a most convivial evening but we had to think about the full programme arranged for the next day when we were due to visit the Royal Naval College, Dartmouth. Accordingly, we turned in at a reasonable hour and were fully prepared when the coach arrived to take us to HMS *Britannia* the following morning. Our visitors were most impressed with the Quarterdeck and the Gun Room where we had coffee and biscuits provided by independent caterers. The shop proved a great attraction to both our visitors and ourselves and much business was done there. Before we left, the Commodore of the Establishment was requested to receive a wall plaque from the Helsinki Naval Academy.

The end of their visit came all too soon and as the Finns' taxis arrived early the next day, we also had to be up at the crack of dawn to see them 'off the premises'.

The Finnish delegation announced that, in 2006, they would be travelling to Sweden the following year and, accordingly would be unable to host a reunion. In Sweden, arrangements had been made to meet the king, himself a former seafarer, and there was also another reason, unknown to us at the time, for celebrating the 2007 reunion. The reason was that it would be the forty-fifth anniversary of the arrival in Finland of our old ship and it was proposed to amalgamate with the Turku section of the *Matti Kurki* Association in order to have a larger reunion.

To this end, nine members of the HMS *Porlock Bay* Association made arrangements to fly to Helsinki on 23rd April, eight of us from Manchester Airport and Alan Barnard from Heathrow. Fortunately, we all arrived within five minutes of one another and a nine-seater 'people carrier' was soon chartered to take us into Helsinki centre where we had accommodation once more at the Radisson Plaza Hotel. Once there we had little time to settle in before we had to order two taxis to take us to the British Embassy where a party had been arranged for St George's Day.

Arriving there, we were met by an old friend, the Defence Attaché Lt Col Rick Andrews, and escorted to the Embassy Bar. A most convivial evening followed during which I was introduced by Rick to a most charming lady with whom I spoke for quite a while before realising that she was indeed the Ambassador who had only been in that position for about a month. My impressions of a most formal gentleman, dressed perhaps in knee

Ilkka Ignatius with Roger Smith with the Finnish Naval Academy badges

Roger Smith (Chairman of HMS Porlock Bay Association) addressing members of both associations at a dinner held in the Royal Fleet Club, DevonportI

breeches, as the Ambassador were at once dashed although I must say that Mrs Valerie Caton was not only suitably qualified for the job, she was a charming conversationalist. Details which emerged later showed that she had been a language student at school and at University; a fact that made me wonder why I had not continued with languages and progressed to University instead of wanting to go to sea. I could well have made more of my life if I had been more sensible sixty-five years earlier.

During the St George's Day party, I surprised the assembled company by reading out a letter from Buckingham Palace in which Her Majesty the Queen sent good wishes to us in response to a message of loyal greetings sent to her on behalf of the *Porlock Bay* Association.

Several photographs were taken at the party before it was decided that we should all have a good night's rest at the hotel as our itinerary for the following day looked, from the schedule given to us, to be fairly exhausting. Two taxis returned us to the hotel where, alarms set for an early start, we all slept soundly.

The following morning we packed and had a good breakfast before walking across the square to the railway station in good time to catch the 9:03 train to Turku. The journey was taken in comfort and, with about fifteen minutes before arrival in Turku, our old friend Ilkka produced his mobile phone to ensure that the naval coach would be waiting for us at Turku station. Several others from Helsinki had joined us for this journey including a former Captain of *Matti Kurki* who had later become the Director of the Naval Academy in Suomenlinna Island.

With typical Finnish efficiency, the coach was waiting and, with the Turku contingent aboard, we soon filled it. We first visited the naval base where the majority of the conscripts for the navy are trained and we were welcomed by the Commandant and had coffee before seeing some of the ships, mainly patrol vessels and indeed going aboard two of them, escorted by two young lieutenants.

Back to the original building for a buffet lunch with the Commandant and then a talk by a Captain on the organisations of the Finnish Navy in their language and then in English, followed by questions. My own were questions on conscription, women in the forces, and whether they had an Air Arm which were all honestly answered.

From here we were taken to the Maritime Museum to be greeted by the young Curator and taken round by him. Of greatest interest for the *Porlock Bay* crowd was the 'hedgehog' taken from the old ship when she was scrapped. With all the modern anti-submarine weapons now in existence it is doubtful if there is another 'hedgehog' remaining in the world. The Curator was interested in the book, this book, that I was writing and requested a copy as soon as possible. Outside the museum looking remarkably smart was the sail training ship that Matti Kurki had replaced, together with other vessels now redundant but maintained in good order.

Once more we boarded the coach to take us to the Mines Museum, cut out of the rock and containing examples of dozens of sea mines so fortunately preserved by the former officer in charge of the 'hedgehog' in *Matti Kurki*, and a good friend of Ilkka Ignatius.

Time was now pressing and we had to hurry to catch the Viking Line ferry *Isabella* for a twenty-four hour voyage to Stockholm and back. No sooner had we settled in our cabins than we had to go to the dining room where several tables had been reserved for our party and a massive buffet dinner was taken with all the drinks included in the cost of the voyage. The total cost for the cabin, the meals and the voyage itself was only ninety-seven euros which seemed remarkably cheap. There was only one unfortunate incident to mar the otherwise wonderful trip and that was when a possible Kurdish stowaway demanded money from me and threatened to cut my throat if I did not hand over the cash! I didn't and lived to tell the tale.

After breakfast the following morning all members of the Matti *Kurki/Porlock Bay* party assembled in the Conference Room where tots of rum were handed round and speeches by the mainly Turku contingent were given. Following these, we were able to see a film pieced together by our old friend Ilkka of the *Matti Kurki* including shots of rough seas breaking over the quarterdeck. The film was in the form of a compact disc and before the day was out a copy had been handed to me. Our party had several presents (no longer called 'rabbits') to give to our hosts and these were graciously received. At the same time, Ken Faulkner and I received the medal of the Turku Maritime Guild together with a citation.

After lunch, we had time to ourselves as we passed through the Archipelago on our way back to Turku. With the free wine in the dining room several of the passengers had imbibed too much although they were generally fairly well behaved. However, as we were disembarking, one fellow, anxious to get ashore, tripped over a case and fell, taking Mary with him, fortunately without injuring her.

Our voyage over, we were taken by taxi to the Hamburger Börs Hotel in the centre of the city where we all stayed for one night and the *Porlock Bay* party a further night. All our bedrooms overlooked the bustling city square with its market stalls selling a variety of fruit and vegetables together with leather goods. It was interesting to note on awakening early on the second morning that, at 0530 hours, mechanical road sweepers were cleaning the square and the market stalls were beginning to open. There is never any litter to be seen on the streets of Finland making a wonderful change from conditions in England where so many of the population have no apparent regard for the environment. The difference is mainly due, in my opinion, to the fact that young people in Finland have to undertake a period of National Service in which they learn to respect other people's property and to generally lead a tidy existence.

One further example of the Finnish courtesy occurred when I mentioned that, in taking off my blazer for security inspection at Manchester Airport, my medication must have tumbled out of a pocket. Our old friend, Fred Sundén immediately rang his doctor wife and in only a few minutes, a prescription for Losartan (blood pressure) tablets had been faxed over through to the hotel and I was able to go to a nearby chemist to have a supply dispensed.

Turku is an old city which at one time was the Capital of the country and because of this, their cathedral is the equivalent of Westminster Abbey. We were taken there by Ilkka and his wife Sinikka before they bade farewell to us to return, by train, to Espoo where they live. They seemed delighted that we suggested a 2008 reunion, this time in Chatham in order to see the dockyard, now a museum. By choosing Chatham, we thought that they will have then seen the three main dockyards in the country and will be able to see where HMS *Victory* was built and where Nelson joined his first ship.

Having been given directions regarding the direct coach service to Helsinki Airport we were on our own for a further night before the homeward journey. However, several decided to travel to Helsinki by that excellent railway service while others opted for a later coach to the airport. Individually therefore we made our way to the airport, fortunately with everyone arriving in time for the flight home.

The Finnair aircraft was again very comfortable and we landed at about 1800 hours at Manchester to be driven in a bus to a small door at the airport. Here I looked around for a lift but was told by a female official that the lift was not for passengers and that we would have to climb four half-flights of stairs. Remarking that this was a sure sign that we were back in England the official said, "don't blame me; blame the management." With both my knees affected by arthritis these were hardly very welcoming words.

Our journey over, we now have to consider our own, *Porlock Bay*, reunion at the Portsmouth Maritime Club where we will no doubt discuss arrangements for entertaining our Finnish guests in Chatham.

There will also be several other matters demanding our attention at the reunion including complaints regarding the treatment of ex-service personnel in this country.

For the majority of the HOs in *Porlock Bay*, service in the Royal Navy had been far from heroic but at least we had been part of a great tradition which is still being enacted by the 'regulars'. Accordingly, it is sad to record that the administration of the navy, based at HMS *Centurion* and presumably staffed by civil servants, saw fit to refuse one of our members his War Service Medal. In a letter to me, the writer quoted from a brochure issued early in the 1939/45 period in which it was stated that young men could volunteer for the RN under the 'Y' Scheme at the age of seventeen but, "No one would be called up for service until they had reached the age of eighteen". That proviso was certainly changed and in our day, *everyone* volunteering under the 'Y' Scheme was called up at seventeen, including all the radar ratings of HMS *Porlock Bay*. On receiving the letter from HMS *Centurion* a letter was sent for publication in Navy News and a large response was expected to confirm our assertion that we joined up before eighteen but the navy's official newspaper merely ignored our letter. In addition, Navy News has declined to publish details of our liaison with the Finnish Navy despite the fact that our international meetings with veterans of *Matti Kurki* are unique in naval circles. This book then is my only means of putting the record straight!

With the experience gained during my service and in civilian life afterwards it is appropriate to consider the question, "was it all worth it?" Life in the navy enabled us to see so many places which we would otherwise not have been able to afford to visit and the comradeship was so important that we still meet up at regular reunions after more than sixty years. On the other hand, our training in seamanship, radar and gunnery has proved of little use in civilian life and, having to start again in a civilian occupation in which so many of the top jobs were held by conscientious objectors and other 'excused' persons was decidedly irksome. We survived but at what cost? Years after leaving the navy and then in my mid-twenties, I was still raking in a salary equal to four pounds per *week* as a trainee compared to the present day's minimum wage of over five pounds per *hour*. On balance therefore, many of us considered that to volunteer for the services at a young age was a personal financial disaster. Would I volunteer (assuming at my age that they would accept me!) to fight for a multi-cultural society dominated by Europe if such a necessity arose? My answer would be a resounding NO.

After twenty years of retirement it is still possible to live in a fairly small local world of my own with my wife and we are remarkably happy despite the several medical problems which haunt us. We have many good friends of long standing whose views on the political situation are similar to ours but we have no means of influencing the politicians. On one visit to the House of Commons a questioner enquired of the guide, "Which side are the Government on?" to which he replied, "Ours, I hope," but, from my experience, I would not be so sure in 2007.

Porlock Bay may have been just one of a bunch of wartime frigates but no other ship has served in two Navies *and* formed an association in each country comprising the respective ship's companies. In addition, the Finnish Postal Authority have produced no less than four postage stamps featuring the old ship which must be a record for an escort vessel.

Three Finnish postage stamps depicting our old ship

Therefore, we feel justified in saying that we, *Porlock Bay* veterans and *Matti Kurki* veterans, are unique, Shipshape and Bristol Fashion. It seems so unfortunate that our old ship had been taken to the breaker's yard so many years before the Associations had met for the first time but at least I had seen the 'old lady' just before she passed away.

The builder's plaque presented to the ship by Messrs Charles Hill

20

EPILOGUE

*"If it be true that good wine needs no bush,
'tis true that a good play needs no epilogue;"*
As You Like It, by William Shakespeare

In view of the above quotation, I am hesitant to write an epilogue but, after all, this book is not a good play and so, here goes.

After over sixty years we can perhaps be forgiven for reminiscing about our old ship and her ship's companies. Our two Associations meet annually to talk of old times and even to 'swing the lamp' but with great affection for the ship that was once our 'home'.

In my own case, joining the Royal Navy straight from school with its cloistered, repressive atmosphere was like jumping out of the proverbial frying pan into the fire as we were subjected to an antiquated form of discipline which had changed little since Nelson's days, all of which was set down in King's Regulations and Admiralty Instructions for everyone to see. We were regarded as little less than criminals except that prisoners in gaol are paid considerably more today than we were as 'free' men in the Navy, and it is encouraging to observe the changes that were made largely as a result of our second Captain becoming the Second Sea Lord, whose primary purpose was to oversee all the personnel matters. Admiral Sir Frank Twiss was concerned with the seamen in the Royal Navy, so much so that he wrote a book on the social changes in the navy from the day he joined 'Britannia' Royal Navy College to the day he ceased to be a serving officer. One significant quotation was that anyone who had endured Dartmouth could withstand being a prisoner of war of the Japanese although any preference would be for the former.

Today's Navy consists of a significantly large proportion of women and, while female company on board may be desirable, their presence at times may not always be conducive to full efficiency. However, in the exigencies of the service this has become a necessity although in a full-scale war this arrangement would have many opponents. The length of overseas duties has, however, been reduced to everyone's advantage as two-and-a-half years was far too long for any seaman to contemplate being away from home and his loved ones. The pay of prisoners in gaol has already been referred to and another analogy of service life compared to being in gaol is that a prisoner is normally allowed visits by his friends and relatives whereas the seaman was, in our day, rarely able to enjoy such a luxury while overseas.

The two previous points regarding service life are however only of minor significance to the ex-serviceman. The state of the country and the changes since the Second World War are far more important. Britain has changed from being a largely white, Christian country to a so-called multicultural society ruled by Europe. Our politicians have, once again, betrayed us to the extent that it is doubtful if our green and pleasant land will remain that way much longer. Thousands more new homes will be required and we are told that these will be located in the south-east while at the same time there is a mad rush to leave the country by the indigenous population to live in France, Spain, Italy and other Mediterranean areas. The whole lifeblood of the country is changing and Britain is receiving drug pedlars, gun runners, murderers and other criminals in exchange for many of the indigenous population. The majority of the newcomers have no allegiance to the crown with at least one section of our community putting their religion before country. At the same time the European parliament is bringing out an incessant stream of legislation and requiring this country to pay ever increasing fees to remain in the European Union.

The relatively few ex-service people left wonder now whether the Second World War has resulted in more freedom when we are forced with a direct tax burden supplemented by an apparently unlimited number of stealth taxes. The *Porlock Bay* personnel were mainly volunteers fired with enthusiasm to put an end to the regimes of Hitler and Tojo which were ghastly enough but was our 'ally', Joseph Stalin any better? Our politicians have much to answer for in recommending that we stay in the Common

Market which was the subject of a referendum in 1974 but they failed to tell us that the Common Market would lead to a European Parliament with its own overpowering bureaucracy. Is this really what our servicemen really fought and many died for?

To use a now well-used expression, our politicians have regularly been 'economic with the truth' but, in my opinion many are little short of being described as liars.

However, to avoid ending on a discordant note, our two associations thrive despite this country being described by the *Daily Telegraph* as "the most spied on nation in the world". We still have our memories of the ship and the ship's companies to talk about at reunions and meetings and always pride ourselves on the fact that HMS *Porlock Bay*/FNS *Matti Kurki* is completely unique for the following reasons:

1 She had three names before she entered the water.
2 Five of her captains later achieved flag rank which must be a record for a mere escort vessel.
3 No other ship has formed an Association in two countries.
4 No other escort vessel has had four postage stamps featuring the ship.

We feel that, for these reasons, we can be excused for being smug and we pride ourselves in the thought that we served in such an excellent Shipshape and Bristol Fashion Ship.

APPENDIX ONE

THE BADGES OF HMS *PORLOCK BAY*

Everyone who served in HMS *Porlock Bay* was aware of the ship's badge. It appeared on letterheads on the Christmas Cards and, every time we went ashore, we saw the badge encircled by a lifebelt which was placed on a stand near to the brow (gangway). It depicted an eagle arising from rocks and included the motto "virtute et veritate".

Shortly before the old ship, which in the meantime had become the *Matti Kurki* in the Finnish Navy, was scrapped, the Chairman of the HMS *Porlock Bay* Association made arrangements through the Finnish Embassy to visit her in Suomenlinna Island, which lies a few miles off Helsinki. It was decided to take a small wall plaque of the badge to present to the Captain and this was duly ordered. Imagine the horror when the postman delivered the badge on the morning of his departure and it depicted an oak tree with greatly oversized acorns! This was returned at once and the manufacturers told to make another in accordance with the design on the ship's letterhead. They protested that the oak tree badge was the official one but that they would prepare another one to the design required.

Several years later at a reunion in Plymouth, the Association made a visit to the Devonport Dockyard museum where our guide was asked about the badge. He produced the official description (blazon) from his records which was as follows:

275

"an Oak Tree fructed proper. The oak tree alludes to the oak jug manufactured in the town of Porlock. This jug is peculiar to the town. The Quarterly gold and red field is taken from the Fitzroger Arms. Sir Simon Fitzroger helped to build Porlock Church in the 13th Century."

Apparently, our first Captain, Lieutenant Dudley Davenport, later to become Rear Admiral Davenport, decided to adopt an unofficial badge based on the Arms of Robert Wynter Blathwayt whose crest depicted an eagle arising, sable, winged or, charged on breast with two bendlets or, on a rock, proper. His motto was Virtute et Veritate. The reason for the Captain's choice of badge was almost certainly that the Blathwayts of Dyrham Park were Lords of the Manors of Dyrham, Langridge and Porlock.

In the Devonport Dockyard museum, David Tilley carried out exhaustive research into the badge, examining several old documents including the 1937 edition of the "Landed Gentry" and he made the badge which the Association presented to the Rector of Porlock for safe keeping in the Parish Church. The shape of the badge is in the form of a shield, which is normally reserved for a destroyer but David Tilley was persuaded, with the assistance of a photograph of the badge in Porlock Church, to base the design on a shield.

The entire ship's company were surprised to find that the badge which we always regarded as the official one was in fact one chosen by Lieutenant Dudley Davenport and that it was not the badge designed by the Ships' Badges Committee. As everyone can see from our letterhead, we will always consider the eagle to be our proper emblem but, in deference to officialdom, we have incorporated the 'official' badge together with that of the Royal Naval Association. We trust that by so doing, we do not upset the people of Porlock although it would appear from our enquiries, that few, if any, know that the oak tree to which the locally manufactured oak jug alludes, is a symbol of the town. However, the reference to Sir Simon Fitzroger who helped to build Porlock Church in the 13th Century should be a matter which can more easily be checked.

APPENDIX TWO

VITAL STATISTICS OF OUR SHIP

HMS *Porlock Bay* was built at Bristol by Charles Hill & Sons in their Albion Shipyard. She was originally intended to be a Loch Class frigate and was named firstly, HMS *Loch Seaforth* and then HMS *Loch Muick* before it was decided to complete her as a Bay Class frigate.

She was commissioned by her first captain, Lieutenant Dudley Davenport R.N. (later Rear Admiral Davenport) who had seen much service during the war, mainly in destroyers and who was a survivor of HMS *Blanche* and HMS *Mashona*. The ship's hull had been laid down on 22nd November 1944 and launched by Mrs Rayne on 14th June 1945. Her Pendant number was K 650.

The Vital Statistics of the ship are as follows:

Displacement:	1,600 tons (2,530 tons full load)
Length:	307 ft overall
Beam:	38.5 ft
Draught:	12.75 ft
Guns:	4 x 4 inch in two double MK XVI mountings.
	6 x 40mm Bofors in two double and two single mountings.
	2 x 20mm Oerlikon.
Anti-Submarine weapons:	1 x Hedgehog multiple spigot mortar.
	Four depth charge throwers plus stern rails.
Complement:	157 Officers and Ratings.
Speed:	19.5 knots (maximum).
Machinery:	2 x Admiralty three drum boilers operating at 2,251 lb per square inch.
	Four cylinder triple expansion engines giving a total of 5,500 i.h.p.
Oil Fuel Capacity:	720 tons.

HMS *Porlock Bay*, Shipshape and Bristol Fashion at all times, only served one full commission in the America and West Indies squadron. Her second captain, who joined her after his release from a Japanese Prisoner of War camp having survived the sinking of HMS *Exeter*, was Commander Frank Twiss, D.S.C., R.N. He later became Admiral Sir Frank Twiss K.C.B., D.S.C., R.N. Second Sea Lord and, after his retirement from the Royal Navy, became the Gentleman Usher of the Black Rod at the Palace of Westminster.

HMS *Porlock Bay* was a Devonport ship and a 'Happy Ship'. She was kept in reserve on her return to the UK before being sold to Finland in April 1962. She became the Finnish *Matti Kurki*, serving as a training ship until she was sold for scrap in September 1975. Thus was the end of a fine ship.

Her crew formed the HMS *Porlock Bay* Association in 1992, with Admiral Frank Twiss as President until his death in 1994. Reunions take place annually at various venues, two of which have been in Porlock Weir and Porlock. Members are anxious to keep in touch with our namesake town where, in St Dubricius Church and the local Dovery Manor Museum, there are wall plaques commemorating our links with Porlock.

Records show that 'our' HMS *Porlock Bay* was the first ship of that name and it is certain that no future ship will bear the name.

APPENDIX THREE

GLOSSARY OF NAVAL TERMS

A rough translation of terms used in the text. Joining the lower deck means learning a whole new language and these terms are those regularly heard in a frigate.

ABU – Auto Barrage Unit
Aggie's – Short for Agnes Weston's – a sailor's hostel
Andrew, the – The Royal Navy
Asdic – Submarine detection equipment now known as sonar

Banyan – A picnic party
Barons – Wealthy people
Baron strangling – Enjoying the hospitality of wealthy people
Barrack Stanchions – Ratings permanently based at a shore station
Bearing-off spar – Wooden spars to push away from jetty etc.
Binnacle – Casing for magnetic compass
Blake (screw) stopper – Used to secure the anchor cable
Bluebell – Metal polish
Bofors – Secondary armament, 40mm guns, mainly anti-aircraft
Bosun's mate (BM) – Rating assisting the Quartermaster, piping orders etc.
Brow – Gangway to landlubbers!
Bubbly bosun – The rating collecting the rum for the mess
Bung – Cheese
Buffer – Chief Bosun's Mate, responsible for keeping the ship clean, etc.
Bulkhead – Vertical partitions separating compartments of a ship

Shipshape and Bristol Fashion

Camber – slipway
Can man – NAAFI canteen manager
Canteen boat – Derogative term for the junior ship of the Squadron
Captain of the Heads – The cleaner of the toilets
Cap tally – Ribbon for naval cap with ship's name or plain HMS
Carley Float – Life raft
Catamaran– Wooden raft to keep ship away from jetty
Chokey – Cells
Clacker – Pastry
Coston gun – Rifle for sending a line to the shore or another ship
Cox'n – Torpedo coxswain – the senior lower deck rating

Dead lights – Placed over scuttles to darken ship
DCT – Director Control Tower. Structure from which armament is directed
DFDO – Detail For Drafting Office
Dhobi session – Washing one's clothes

ERA (c) – Engine Room Artificer (Chief)

Falls – Ropes used to lower ship's boats
Fenders – Rope 'sacks' for protecting ship' sides
Figgy Duff – Any steamed pudding
Fixed Ammunition – Shell and cartridge combined
Fore and Aft Rig – Uniform worn by daymen and Petty Officers
Foxer – Apparatus for countering the acoustic torpedoes

Gash – Rubbish, waste, sometimes 'spare'
GI – Gunnery Instructor, formerly known as Gunner's Mate
Goffer (Gopher) – Any soft drink
Grippoes – See 'Barons'
Guard rails – Wire rope to stop ratings falling overboard!
Gulpers – A gratuitous gulp from a fellow rating's tot
Guns – The Gunnery Officer
Guzz – Plymouth
Gyro Repeat – The compass by which the ship is normally steered

Hard tack – Ship's biscuits
Heads – Ship's toilet

'errings-in – Tin of herrings in tomato sauce
HO – Hostilities only rating
Housewife (Hussif) – Sewing kit

IFF – Identification, friend or foe (Radar)

Jack Dusty – Stores rating
Jagoes Mansions – Devonport barracks
Jimmy – The First Lieutenant

Killick – Leading seaman who has small anchor, (a killick) on his sleeve
KRs and AIs – King's regulations and Admiralty Instructions
KUA – Kit upkeep allowance (six d per day)
Kye – Ship's cocoa

Lanchester – A sub-carbine (light machine gun)
LCH – Landing Craft Headquarters
Liberty Boat (catching the) – Going ashore, not necessarily by boat!
Lower Deck Lawyer – A know-all about KRs and AIs
Low power LTO – Leading torpedo rating responsible for secondary lighting, etc.

Make and Mend – Time to oneself for dhobying, sewing etc.
MC – Motor Cutter
Mess traps – Eating utensils
MFV – Motor Fishing Vessel – used by liberty men

Neaters – Neat rum issue (rather than 'Two and One' issued to ratings below rank of Petty Officer)
North Easter – Reduction in pay
Nutty – Any chocolate (with or without nuts!)

OA – Ordnance Artificer
Oerlikon – 20mm automatic weapon
Officer's Flunky – Officer's servant, batman
'Ogwash, 'Oggin – The sea
Onions – Name given by Bermudan residents to themselves

PO (CPO) – Petty Officer (Chief Petty Officer)
Pongo – A soldier
Pot Mess – Stew
PPI – Plan Position Indicator
Pusser – Official, i.e. Pusser suit, strictly correct
Pusser's Dirk – Issue seaman's knife
Pusser's hard – Yellow soap

Quartermaster (QM) – Takes the wheel at sea, mans the brow or gangway in harbour

Rabbits – Presents to take home
Radar – (Radio Detection and Ranging) for Navigation and Gunnery Control
RC3 – Radar Control Rating, third class
RDF – Radio Director Finder (forerunner of Radar)
Rose Cottage – the VD Mess
RTO – Rail Transport Officer

SBA – Sick Berth Attendant
Sea rig – Any clothing worn at sea
Scribes – The ship's writer or clerical rating
Scuttles – Round openings in ship's sides (portholes for landlubbers!)
Seven-and-five – A rating serving seven years in regular Navy, five in reserve
Sippers – Gratuitous sip from fellow rating's tot
Six suit – Best white uniform (No. 6's)
Slops – Clothing stores
Slop Chit – Requisition for clothing
Smoke, the – London
Sod's Opera – Impromptu ship's concert
Square rig – Seaman's uniform
SRE – Sound reproduction equipment
Stripey – Long service (and good conduct) rating
Swede, to crash one's – To go to sleep

Tanky – Ship's butcher and general food stores rating
Telegraphs – Means of informing engine room of speed required
Three Badger – rating with three good conduct badges (long service)
Tickler – Tobacco, hand-rolled cigarettes
Tiddley Suit – A tailor-made uniform (i.e. not 'Pusser')
Tiddy 'oggies – Cornish pasties
Tiller Flat – Aft-most compartment for general storage of large items, etc. Sometimes used as temporary cells
Tombola – Bingo
Tot – The rum ration
TS – Transmitting Station (gunnery control)

Uckers – Ludo
Up-homers – People ashore who invite rating to their home
Up Spirits – Distribution of rum ration

Very Pistol – Signal pistol

Whaler – Ship's boat, pulled by five (ash) oars
Yeo – Yeoman of Signals

APPENDIX 4

LETTERS TO THE ASSOCIATION

BUCKINGHAM PALACE

Roger Smith Esq.,
Chairman,
H.M.S. PORLOCK BAY Association.

The Queen was pleased to receive your kind message of loyal greetings sent on behalf of the Members of the H.M.S. PORLOCK BAY Association on the occasion of the visit by nine of the members to Helsinki on St. George's Day, 23rd April.

Her Majesty much appreciates your thoughtfulness in writing and sends her warm good wishes to all concerned.

PRIVATE SECRETARY

23rd April, 2007.

Letter from the Queen

APPENDICES

CHIEF OF DEFENCE
FINLAND

Helsinki, 9 July 2004

Dear Veterans of HMS Portock Bay and FNS Matti Kurki

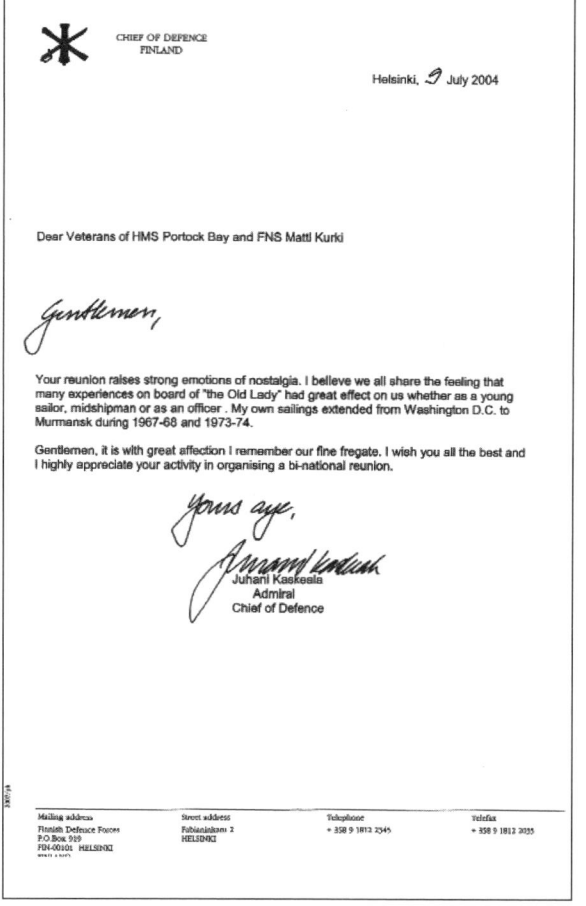

Gentlemen,

Your reunion raises strong emotions of nostalgia. I believe we all share the feeling that many experiences on board of "the Old Lady" had great effect on us whether as a young sailor, midshipman or as an officer. My own sailings extended from Washington D.C. to Murmansk during 1967-68 and 1973-74.

Gentlemen, it is with great affection I remember our fine frigate. I wish you all the best and I highly appreciate your activity in organising a bi-national reunion.

Yours aye,

Juhani Kaskeala
Admiral
Chief of Defence

Mailing address	Street address	Telephone	Telefax
Finnish Defence Forces P.O. Box 919 FIN-00101 HELSINKI	Fabianinkatu 2 HELSINKI	+ 358 9 1812 2545	+ 358 9 1812 2035

Letter from the Chief of Defence Staff (Finland)

285

By Admiral Sir Jonathon Band, Knight Commander of the Order of the Bath, Admiral of Her Majesty's Fleet and Commander in Chief of Her Majesty's Ships and vessels employed and to be employed in the Fleet

VETERANS OF HMS PORLOCK BAY AND FNS MATTI KURKI

It gives me great pleasure to welcome those of you who have travelled from Finland to be present at this reunion. I admire you all for the dedication you have shown in keeping alive the memories of your common heritage; from what I have heard, be it as HMS PORLOCK BAY or as FNS MATTI KURKI, you had a fine ship that served you well.

Of course, in this 'Year of the Sea' and on the bicentennial anniversary of the Battle of Trafalgar and the death of Lord Nelson, maritime history is very much in the thoughts of the Royal Navy. However, it is those who have experienced and value history - such as you - that do so much to keep that history alive for both your countries. For this, my thanks, and I wish you all the very best for your reunion in 2005.

Admiral Sir Jonathon Band KCB
26 July 2005

Letter to Veterans of HMS Porlock Bay and FNS Matti Kurki from Admiral Sir Jonathon Bond KCB

APPENDICES

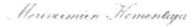

WELCOMING ADDRESS TO THE VETERANS OF TRAINING SHIP MATTI KURKI/ FRIGATE PORLOCK BAY

Honourable veterans of training ship Matti Kurki Frigate Porlock Bay,

It is with great pride and delight that I greet you! I think it is a wonderful thing that this valuable decades-old tradition is still alive and well. To us Finnish naval officers, the importance of the Matti Kurki as a training ship in the 60s and 70s was considerable. The ship arrived in Finland in April 1962. Our previous training ship, the sailing ship Suomen Joutsen had been decommissioned from naval use for good in 1955, so the need for a new training ship was great.

The fourteen training voyages made by the Matti Kurki created a good foundation for the training and know-how of our Finnish naval officers. Our current Navy has been further developed on this solid foundation. The Matti Kurki served the Finnish Navy for all in all 13 years and was finally decommissioned in 1975.

For me personally, this meeting of veterans of the Matti Kurki and the fact that the honourable traditions of the vessel are still maintained is very important. After all, during my career as a naval officer, I myself served on the ship in question as a gunnery officer in 1973-74.

Our current training ship, the minelayer Pohjanmaa, has served since 1979. It carries on the training ship tradition of our naval forces that was laid out by the Matti Kurki.

Due to our limited resources, the Finnish Navy cannot afford to make the wrong choices – this is something our history has also taught us. As I said at the beginning, the importance of the Matti Kurki in our naval officer training was considerable. The lessons and experiences gained on the Matti Kurki were used to form the grounds according to which our next training ship, the minelayer Pohjanmaa, was procured along with our other most important fighting ships in the 70s and 80s. These included especially the Turunmaa-class corvettes and Helsinki-class fast patrol boats.

Within the Finnish Navy, traditions and an awareness of the value of maritime history is of great importance. We have developed, and continue to develop our Navy in order to meet the new challenges of the 21st Century as well as the future. In order for us to know how and in which direction to develop our Navy, we have to be familiar with the history through which we have arrived at this point.

Honourable veterans of training ship Matti Kurki Frigate Porlock Bay!

Your work is of great significance for the development of our Navy. The valuable tradition that you represent and maintain gives us naval officers who are still in service a sound foundation on which to build our future.

With these words, I would like to wish you all a good and rewarding meeting here in Turku.

Commander in Chief of the Finnish Navy

Vice Admiral Hans Holmström

Welcoming speech to the veterans of the Training Ship Matti Kurki *and Frigate* Porlock Bay

APPENDIX 5

ROUTES TAKEN BY FNS *MATTI KURKI*

Routes taken by FNS Matti Kurki

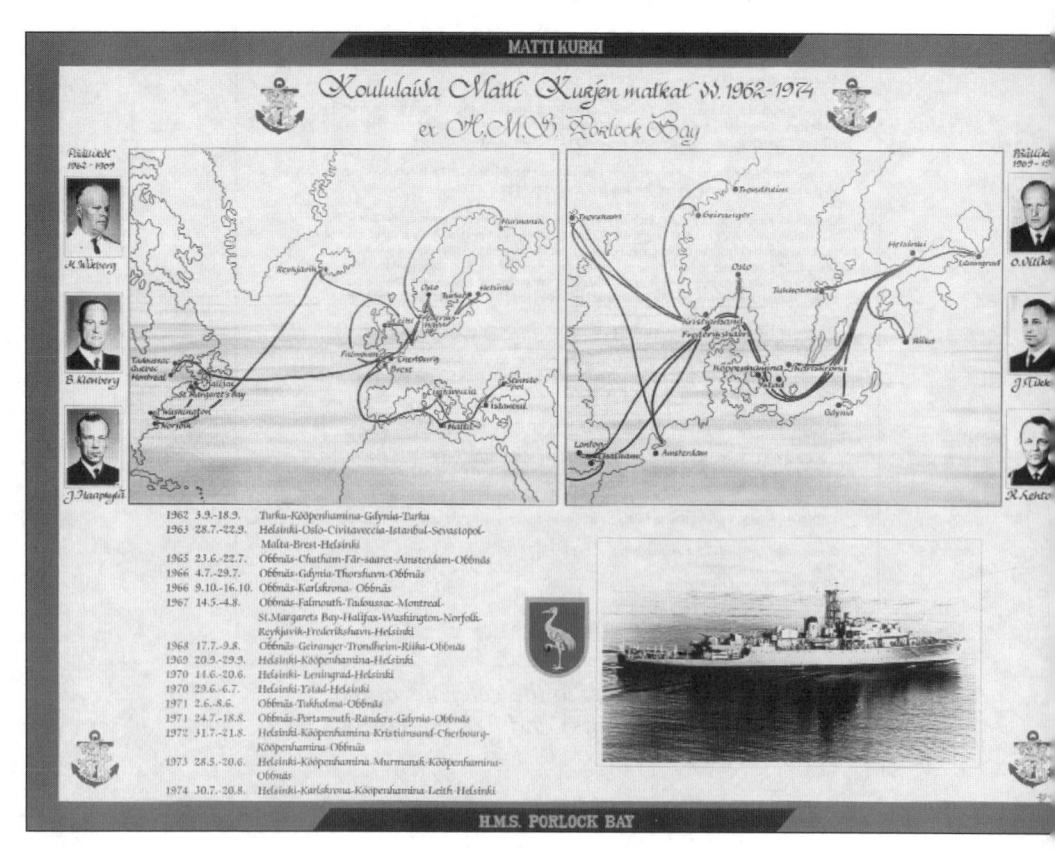

ABOUT THE AUTHOR

Roger Smith was born at Number Sixty-two, The Parade, Leamington Spa, a site which is now occupied by Woolworths. His parents moved to a house in Warwick where he now lives and has, in fact, been there since 1929.

He was educated at Warwick School, leaving at the age of seventeen to join the Navy under the 'Y' Scheme and trained as a Radar Control Rating, serving later in HMS *Porlock Bay*.

On leaving the Navy he studied Accountancy but left that profession to become a trainee Town Planner. He duly qualified and subsequently was elected a Fellow of the Royal Town Planning Institute, retiring as Principal Planning Officer to Stratford-on-Avon District Council.

He now lives in retirement in Warwick where he busies himself with the HMS *Porlock Bay* Association, of which he is Chairman, and with the liaison with the FNS *Matti Kurki* Association of Finland. He is also an active member of the Old Warwickian Association, taking photographs, inter alia, for the *Portcullis* Magazine as well as his unique Ship's Association. In addition, he is at present the Vice Chairman of the Royal Leamington Spa branch of *Probus* and next year he has been invited to become Chairman of the Warwickshire County Council Retired Members' Association. A committee member of the Warwick branch of the Royal Warwickshire Regimental Association completes his retirement duties, although he still has to make time for gardening.